ARISTOPHANEA

Aristophanea

Studies on the Text of Aristophanes

N. G. WILSON

OXFORD
UNIVERSITY PRESS

Great Clarendon Street, Oxford OX2 6DP

Oxford University Press is a department of the University of Oxford.
It furthers the University's objective of excellence in research, scholarship,
and education by publishing worldwide in

Oxford New York

Auckland Cape Town Dar es Salaam Hong Kong Karachi
Kuala Lumpur Madrid Melbourne Mexico City Nairobi
New Delhi Shanghai Taipei Toronto

With offices in

Argentina Austria Brazil Chile Czech Republic France Greece
Guatemala Hungary Italy Japan Poland Portugal Singapore
South Korea Switzerland Thailand Turkey Ukraine Vietnam

Oxford is a registered trade mark of Oxford University Press
in the UK and in certain other countries

Published in the United States
by Oxford University Press Inc., New York

© N. G. Wilson 2007

The moral rights of the author have been asserted
Database right Oxford University Press (maker)

First published 2007

All rights reserved. No part of this publication may be reproduced,
stored in a retrieval system, or transmitted, in any form or by any means,
without the prior permission in writing of Oxford University Press,
or as expressly permitted by law, or under terms agreed with the appropriate
reprographics rights organization. Enquiries concerning reproduction
outside the scope of the above should be sent to the Rights Department,
Oxford University Press, at the address above

You must not circulate this book in any other binding or cover
and you must impose this same condition on any acquirer

British Library Cataloguing in Publication Data

Data available

Library of Congress Cataloging in Publication Data

Data available

Typeset by RefineCatch Limited, Bungay, Suffolk
Printed in Great Britain
on acid-free paper by
Biddles Ltd., King's Lynn, Norfolk

ISBN 978–0–19–928299–9

1 3 5 7 9 10 8 6 4 2

Preface

These notes are published in the hope that they will explain and justify some of the editorial decisions I have had to make. In addition I think it desirable to draw attention to the fact that, however much progress has been made by modern scholars towards reliable editions of Greek authors, there is still much to engage the interest of the thoughtful reader. We are not as near to enjoying definitive editions as is sometimes supposed.

The range of topics discussed is wide. Some details may seem at first sight to be of little account; in particular my concern with such matters as the precise definition of the nuances conveyed by particles and the distinction between stressed and unstressed personal pronouns may be thought to verge on the obsessive. But I make no apology for stating the conviction that they must be taken seriously if we are to achieve really accurate translation and understanding of the text. In the pages that follow some parts of the plays are more densely annotated than others. This fact reflects not only the uneven quality of the transmitted text but the varying success, as any editor is bound to see it, of previous efforts to resolve doubts and difficulties. There are quite long stretches of text where either there appear to be no puzzles or the difficulties are such that I have nothing useful to add. Although Aristophanes certainly presents fewer problems than Sophocles, the greater quantity of extant text still provides plenty of material for debate. Many decisions remain subjective insofar as they depend on a consideration of conflicting pieces of evidence, none of which appears decisive.

I take the opportunity to record here my thanks to two publisher's readers for some helpful suggestions, and to Dr Leofranc Holford-Strevens (H.-S.), whose help has been most valuable. I am also extremely grateful to Dr Christos Simelidis and Dr Kathleen McLaughlin for their assistance in the final stages of production.

Contents

Abbreviations	viii
Introduction	1
Acharnians	15
Knights	39
Clouds	62
Wasps	81
Peace	99
Birds	115
Lysistrata	131
Thesmophoriazusae	149
Frogs	163
Ecclesiazusae	185
Plutus	198
Addenda	213
Index	215

Abbreviations

Complete editions referred to by name of editor:

F. H. M. Blaydes (Halle, 1880–93).
V. Coulon (Paris, 1923–30).
F. W. Hall and W. M. Geldart, rev. edn. (Oxford, 1906–7).
J. Henderson (Loeb Classical Library, Cambridge, Mass., and London, 1998–2002).
J. van Leeuwen (Leiden, 1893–1906).
B. B. Rogers (London, 1902–16).
A. H. Sommerstein (Warminster, 1980–2002).

Other works and editions of single plays referred to by name of author or in abbreviated form:

C. Austin and S. D. Olson, *Thesmophoriazusae* (Oxford, 2004).
F. H. M. Blaydes, *Adversaria critica in Aristophanem* (Halle, 1899).
—— *Spicilegium Aristophaneum* (Halle, 1902).
J. Chadwick, *Lexicographica Graeca* (Oxford, 1996).
H. W. Chandler, *A Practical Guide to Greek Accentuation*, 2nd edn. (Oxford, 1881).
S. Colvin, *Dialect in Aristophanes* (Oxford, 1999).
Cooper–Krüger = Guy L. Cooper III after K. W. Krüger, *Attic Greek Prose Syntax*, 2 vols. (Ann Arbor, 1998).
V. Coulon, *Essai sur la méthode de la critique conjecturale appliquée au texte d'Aristophane* (Paris, 1931).
Denniston, *GP* = J. D. Denniston, *The Greek Particles*, 2nd edn. (Oxford, 1954).
DGE = *Diccionario griego-español* (Madrid, 1980–).
E. Dickey, *Greek Forms of Address from Herodotus to Lucian* (Oxford, 1996).
P. P. Dobree, *Adversaria*, 5 vols. (i–ii London, 1883, iii–v Berlin, 1884).
K. J. Dover, *Clouds* (Oxford, 1968).
—— *Frogs* (Oxford, 1993).
N. V. Dunbar, *Birds* (Oxford, 1995).
Fraenkel, *BzA* = Eduard Fraenkel, *Beobachtungen zu Aristophanes* (Rome, 1962).

J. Henderson, *Lysistrata* (Oxford, 1987).
H. van Herwerden, *Exercitationes criticae in poeticis et prosaicis quibusdam Atticorum monumentis* (The Hague, 1862).
—— *Analecta critica ad Thucydidem Lysiam Sophoclem Aristophanem et comicorum graecorum fragmenta* (Utrecht, 1868).
—— *Studia Thucydidea* (Utrecht, 1869).
—— *Vindiciae Aristophaneae* (Leiden, 1906).
O. Hoffmann, rev. A. Debrunner, *Geschichte der griechischen Sprache*, 2 vols. (Berlin, 1953).
J. Jackson, *MS* = *Marginalia scaenica* (Oxford, 1955).
W. J. W. Koster, *Autour d'un manuscrit d'Aristophane écrit par Démétrius Triclinius* (Groningen and Jakarta, 1957).
P. Kretschmer and E. Locker, *Rückläufiges Wörterbuch der griechischen Sprache*, 2nd edn. (Göttingen, 1963).
K–B = R. Kühner, rev. F. Blass, *Ausführliche Grammatik der griechischen Sprache: Elementar- und Formenlehre* (Hannover, 1890–2).
K–G = R. Kühner and B. Gerth, *Ausführliche Grammatik der griechischen Sprache: Satzlehre* (Hannover and Leipzig, 1898–1904).
Lexbyzgr = E. Trapp (ed.), *Lexikon zur byzantinischen Gräzität* (Vienna, 1994–).
LGPN = P. M. Fraser and E. Matthews (eds.), *A Lexicon of Greek Personal Names* (Oxford, 1987–).
LIMC = *Lexicon iconographicum mythologiae classicae* (Zurich and Munich, 1981–99).
D. M. MacDowell, *Wasps* (Oxford, 1971).
G. Mastromarco, *Aristofane, Commedie* (Turin, 1983–).
S. D. Olson, *Acharnians* (Oxford, 2003).
—— *Peace* (Oxford, 1998).
L. P. E. Parker, *The Songs of Aristophanes* (Oxford, 1997).
M. Platnauer, *Peace* (Oxford, 1964).
P. Probert, *A New Short Guide to the Accentuation of Ancient Greek* (London, 2003).
W. Rennie, *Acharnians* (London, 1909).
H. Richards, *Aristophanes and Others* (London, 1909).
E. Schwyzer, *Griechische Grammatik* (Munich, 1939–71).
Sommerstein 2001 = addenda on pp. 219–321 of his edition of *Wealth*
W. J. M. Starkie, *Acharnians* (London, 1909).
—— *Wasps* (London, 1897).
J. Taillardat, *Les Images d'Aristophane* (Paris, 1962, rev. 1965).
P. Thiercy, *Aristophane: théâtre complet* (Paris, 1997).
L. Threatte, *The Grammar of Attic Inscriptions* (Berlin, 1980–96).

R. G. Ussher, *Ecclesiazusae* (Oxford, 1973).
J. W. White, *The Verse of Greek Comedy* (London, 1912).
Wilamowitz, *GV* = U. von Wilamowitz-Moellendorff, *Griechische Verskunst* (Berlin, 1921).
A. Willems, *Aristophane: traduction avec notes et commentaires critiques* (Paris and Brussels, 1919).
A. Willi, *The Languages of Aristophanes* (Oxford, 2003).

Introduction

Though there are many studies of the textual transmission of Greek authors, Aristophanes must be said to have received less attention than he deserves. There is no overall survey of the manuscript tradition along the lines of those dedicated to the three tragedians by Alexander Turyn, and despite the advances in our knowledge made in recent decades, more work is needed before a full account can be attempted. However, much important information is supplied by recent editions of several plays which give fairly detailed reports about the papyri and medieval manuscripts available for the play in question; a gap that remains to be filled is the evaluation of some of the more recent manuscripts of the *Plutus*. In addition there is a good and accessible recent survey of the history of Aristophanic textual scholarship in Nan Dunbar's edition of the *Birds*.[1] The purpose of the account that follows here is to offer a sketch from the vantage-point of an editor who can claim to be better acquainted than his predecessors with problems of textual transmission, Greek palaeography, and Byzantine studies. The absence of a reference work for Greek texts corresponding to *Texts and Transmission: A Survey of the Latin Classics*, edited by L. D. Reynolds (Oxford, 1983), is to be regretted; my remarks are designed to be similar to an entry in such a volume.

The history of a text begins with the author's autograph or master copy. Such copies do not survive for the text of any ancient author of note. In a few cases inferences can be made about the character of such copies. The incoherent state of certain passages in the text of two comedies, *Clouds* and *Frogs*, forces us to the conclusion that after

---

[1] (Oxford, 1995), 31–51.

the first performance the author decided to modify the text, perhaps with a view to a second performance, which is attested for the *Frogs* by the remark of the Peripatetic scholar Dicaearchus quoted at the end of one of the Arguments. Alternatively, the author may have wished to allow a revised version to circulate through the book trade, which developed gradually in the second half of the fifth century and may have been quite vigorous by the time of the poet's death.

Though I have used the term 'book trade', it should probably be assumed that initially access to the master copy was obtained only by direct contact with the author or his family. There is no sign at this date of authors offering their works to booksellers, who would also have fulfilled the role of publishers. When Aristophanes died it would appear that the text of at least the two plays just mentioned had not been fully revised. He is not the only author to have left some of his work unfinished. When investigating the text of Aelian's *Varia Historia* I came to a similar conclusion.[2] The same explanation will account for some other alleged instances of second or revised editions.[3]

It has been claimed that there is other evidence of disorder in the texts that Aristophanes kept as master copies. The suggestion has been made that in the *Wasps* two sections of text, 290–316 and 266–89, need to change places; also—and less plausibly—1265–91 and 1450–73; similarly that in the *Lysistrata* 1273–94 and 1295–1321 should be read in reverse order. The errors allegedly occurred because the passages in question were written out on separate sheets for the benefit of the actors, and these sheets were subsequently put together in the wrong order. In other words either the faulty order was transferred into a copy made on a papyrus roll, perhaps by or for the author, or the author was content to have a bundle of sheets rather than a roll as his master copy, and the sheets were not numbered. The latter hypothesis seems very implausible, but the former cannot be entirely ruled out.[4] In recent commentaries on the plays

---

[2] See my Loeb edition (Cambridge, Mass., and London, 1997), 18.

[3] For discussion of Isocrates and some other 4th-c. authors who appear to have revised their texts see P. M. Pinto, *Per la storia del testo di Isocrate: la testimonianza d'autore* (Bari, 2003), 153–60.

[4] A recent discussion can be found in the latest version of C. F. Russo's monograph *Aristophanes: An Author for the Stage* (London, 1994), 243–5, 263. These cases were raised in S. Srebrny, *Eos*, 50 (1959–60), 43–5; 51 (1961), 39–43.

the problem is usually discussed not so much in terms of the history of ancient books as the coherence of the context. It is difficult to come to a definite conclusion and the editor should probably err on the safe side by accepting the transmitted text. Yet it is interesting to note that one modern commentator of generally conservative tendency admitted that the first transposition proposed in the *Wasps* is quite possibly right.[5] An uncertain light is thrown on the question by the recent publication of a papyrus (P.Oxy. 4546, i BC/i AD) containing Euripides, *Alcestis* 344–82, but with omissions: the scribe wrote only the lines spoken by Admetus. Was this an actor's copy?

There is not much that can usefully be said about the circulation of texts of the plays between the early fourth century BC and the end of antiquity. But one unexpected testimony to knowledge of our author is provided by an inscription from Rhodes. On the base of a cylindrical column are inscribed ll. 454–8 of the *Frogs*, with the author's name given above. The inscription would appear to be from a dedication by one or more members of a guild of initiates. Their text avoids two errors that occur in most of the medieval witnesses, one a minor detail involving a connecting particle, the other a substitution of ἱλαρόν for ἱερόν, a mistake induced by recollection of a well-known phrase in a Christian hymn.[6] But epigraphic evidence for literary texts is extremely rare.[7]

The papyri have not brought a generous harvest of fragments from plays that failed to survive until the middle ages, and their contribution to the extant plays is also relatively modest.[8] In this latter respect they are on a par with the Sophoclean papyri. They reveal few serious textual divergences, with the possible exception of P. Colon. 14 of *Lysistrata* dating from the fourth century AD, which in ll. 182–99 has a lacuna and some lines in the wrong order. This fact has been taken to suggest that a second authorial version of the scene existed or that

---

[5] D. M. MacDowell in his edition (Oxford, 1971), 169.

[6] See G. Pugliese Carratelli, *Dioniso*, 8 (1940), 119–23, with plate.

[7] Some examples are given in L. D. Reynolds and N. G. Wilson, *Scribes and Scholars*, 3rd edn. (Oxford, 1991), 199–202, 287.

[8] See C. F. L. Austin, *Comicorum graecorum fragmenta in papyris reperta* (Berlin and New York, 1973), 7–32; Th. Gelzer in *RE* Supp.-Band xii (Stuttgart, 1971), cols. 1552–4; P. Mertens in M. Serena Funghi (ed.), Ὁδοὶ διζήσιος: *Le vie della ricerca* (Florence, 1996), 335–43; *The Oxyrhynchus Papyri LXVI* (London, 1999), nos. 4508–21.

an actor or producer wished to abbreviate the scene. But the arguments against these possibilities are strong.[9] We are probably safe in assuming that the text of the comedies was stable and that Alexandrian editors played their part by making their library's exemplar available for transcription, as is supposed to have been the case with Homer. The number of published papyri continues to increase. It is noticeable that many are from late antiquity. This may reflect the influence of the Atticist movement with its interest in many aspects of Athenian life in the fifth and fourth centuries BC, for which Aristophanes was an excellent source. It is possible that as a result Aristophanes began to occupy a larger place in the school curriculum, so as to rival Menander. Some of the quotations which constitute a part of the secondary tradition are a result of the Atticist movement. Educators of late antiquity, unlike many of their modern counterparts, did not expound their principles, and so we have to guess as best we can to what extent and when the syllabus of the schools was modified.

Although statistics derived mainly from papyrological evidence can never be entirely satisfactory, because of the unpredictability of future publications and because almost all the evidence comes from Egypt, where the reading habits of the public were not necessarily identical in all respects with those typical of other regions, it is still worth quoting figures from a recent survey. Among the extant books written in the period from the fourth to the seventh century there are 36 containing Aristophanes and 34 of Menander. For the sixth and seventh centuries the figures are respectively three and four, probably too low to be reliable, and one of the four in any case results from a significant redating. But the general picture is clear.[10]

Aristophanes' place in the curriculum was apparently not affected during the so-called Dark Age. Menander, though a few of his plays seem to have been still available in Byzantium at the end of the sixth century and perhaps figured in the curriculum, can no longer be traced at the end of the eighth century when the first signs of a cultural revival began to appear. The most notable product of that

---

[9] See J. Henderson in his edition (Oxford, 1987), 91–2.
[10] E. Crisci, *Segno e testo*, 1 (2003), 90–3, 113 n. 107, 115 n. 113. The relative popularity of the two poets as attested by the papyri has also been studied by A. Blanchard, *Ktema*, 22 (1997), 213–25.

revival, the patriarch Photius (*c*.810–93), displays in his correspondence a knowledge of *Plutus* and *Frogs*, and he would not have made the allusions if he had not hoped that his addressees would follow them. From that time onwards it is clear that educated Byzantines had read some Aristophanes at school. Since the Byzantines had no theatre their reading of ancient drama can only have given them a limited appreciation of the texts, and quite possibly these were regarded as little more than a quarry for telling examples of rhetorical devices or vocabulary suitable for use in their own archaizing literary compositions. Notwithstanding this unpromising cultural background there are a number of medieval copies of the plays. About thirty-five are datable before *c*.1400. If one adds those transcribed between that date and *c*.1600 the total rises to about 170. Of these the vast majority contain at most three plays, *Clouds*, *Frogs*, and *Plutus*, often referred to as the triad, and some have only one or two, reflecting the reduction of the curriculum.[11]

Very few classical authors are transmitted in more than a handful of manuscripts that date from the middle Byzantine period, which began with the revival just mentioned and continued until the capture and destruction of the capital by the Crusaders in 1204. Aristophanes is no exception to this rule. The witnesses that belong to this period can be counted on the fingers of one hand. Pride of place goes to MS Ravenna, Biblioteca Classense 429 (R), from the second half of the tenth century, which alone (apart from a Renaissance apograph now in Munich) contains all eleven plays. Though it is rather carelessly written, many of its errors are trivial and it often preserves the true reading or something close to it, so that the quality of its text overall entitles it to be considered the best manuscript. It was first used systematically by Invernizi at the end of the eighteenth century.[12] Consultation of the facsimile[13] has enabled me to correct

---

[11] They were listed by J. W. White, *Classical Philology*, 1 (1906), 1–20, 255–78; his sigla are generally accepted. Six others that remained unknown to him are listed by K. J. Dover in his edition of the *Clouds*, p. c n. 2. See also Th. Gelzer (n. 8), cols. 1560–63 and C. N. Eberline, *Studies in the Manuscript Tradition of the Ranae of Aristophanes* (Meisenheim am Glan, 1980).

[12] His edition appeared at Leipzig between 1794 and 1834.

[13] Edited by J. van Leeuwen (Leiden, 1904).

reports of its readings in a few passages. For practical purposes the *Suda* lexicon, compiled at much the same time as the Ravenna manuscript was written, is to be regarded as its incomplete twin. The extremely numerous quotations from the plays and accompanying scholia exhibit an almost identical text.

Not much later is a tiny fragment of the *Birds*, a single leaf surviving in Florence (MS Laurentianus 60. 9). But the only other substantial witness from this period, i.e. one that contains more than the three plays normally read in the schools, is in Venice: MS Marcianus gr. 474 (V) contains seven plays and on palaeographical grounds is to be dated to the second half of the eleventh century rather than to the twelfth.[14] Though I am inclined on balance to rate V as slightly inferior to R overall, it should be recognized that its merits are considerable, and for instance in many passages of the *Wasps* it alone offers the correct readings.

A witness of uncertain date which probably belongs to the twelfth century is now in Madrid, Biblioteca Nacional de España MS 4683 (formerly N 53) (Md1). It contains the triad and *Knights* 1–306, but parts of it, including the fragment of the *Knights*, are leaves restored by its fifteenth-century owner Constantine Lascaris and another unknown hand; the original scribe is responsible for *Plutus* 1–528, *Clouds*, and *Frogs* 1–959. A later date was proposed by W. J. W. Koster on the ground that certain of its readings look like emendations of a kind to be expected from scholars of the Palaeologan period (1261–1453).[15] He was followed by Sir Kenneth Dover in his edition of the *Clouds*. The key point is that at l. 728 Md1 is one of several witnesses that make the metrically necessary change of ἐξευρετέος for ἐξευρητέος, and all the others are of the later date.[16] Could the reading be attributed to a fortunate slip or to superior metrical knowledge displayed by a twelfth-century scholar such as John Tzetzes or his brother Isaac? Although these men did not greatly distinguish themselves as metricians, one or other of these

---

[14] This was the view expressed by T. W. Allen in his preface to the facsimile (London, 1902) and confirmed in my discussion in *La Paléographie grecque et byzantine* (Paris, 1977), 237.
[15] *Mnemosyne*⁴, 9 (1956), 225–31.
[16] See his edition, pp. ciii, cxx.

two explanations may have to be accepted in the light of the palaeographical evidence.[17]

Another important manuscript is in Milan, Biblioteca Ambrosiana MS C 222 inf. (K). It is now in very poor condition, so that collation from microfilm is barely possible. An up-to-date description has been published by C. M. Mazzucchi, who concludes that it is to be dated between 1180 and 1186.[18] His palaeographical analysis, supported by close study of some informative marginalia, results in a substantially earlier dating than was accepted in the past; in my opinion it is correct and this manuscript therefore becomes one of the very few that predate the disaster of 1204. Some of its readings in *Plutus* were reported by Holzinger in his commentary; I examined it *in situ* in October 2003 in order to be able to give a fuller report of its variants in that play, but even so I do not feel absolutely confident that I have extracted every detail that might be useful. For its readings in the other plays of the triad I have accepted the reports in Dover's editions.

As is well known, the return of the Byzantine government to its former capital in 1261 was followed by a notable artistic and cultural revival, especially in the years *c.*1280–*c.*1350. One of the early signs of this is the corpus of classical poetry collected in what is now the Florentine MS Laurentianus 32. 16, produced under the auspices of the monk Maximus Planudes *c.*1280. Manuscripts of classical authors written between that date and *c.*1350 survive in relatively large numbers—no doubt this is due in part to the shorter time that they have been exposed to the hazards of war and natural disaster— and the activities of several scholars can be traced in varying degrees of detail. For Aristophanes the main figures are Thomas Magister and Demetrius Triclinius.

Thomas's contribution is very difficult to assess, as no autograph copy has yet been identified. He may have confined himself to the triad. For the *Plutus* there is no modern study of the transmission which might throw light on his contribution. In his edition of *Frogs*

---

[17] In his edition of *Frogs* (p. 79) Dover contented himself with the remark that the dating is controversial and referred to earlier discussion. The later date has also been proposed by D. Holwerda, *Scholia vetera in Nubes* (Groningen, 1977), pp. vii f., xxxi f., but his attempt to find analogous scripts in MSS of *c.*1320–45 did not convince me.

[18] *Aevum*, 77 (2003), 263–75, with two plates; 78 (2004), 411–40.

8 Introduction

Dover refers to Thomas Magister as the author of some scholia identified as his by Triclinius.[19] But Thomas is not described as having prepared a recension of the text. In Eberline's monograph on the MSS of the play a number of Thoman manuscripts are identified (they are Cr O3 P25 V2 and Ln3 L2 Vv18).[20] It is noted that there are 'gaps and inconsistencies' in this group and Eberline remains uncertain whether Thomas edited the text.[21] If he did, 'it is certain that many of the readings cited above for Th(omas) are not his own conjectures'. This conclusion explains why Dover did not attempt to cite Thoman readings in this play. In his edition of *Clouds* he uses the siglum *f* to refer to one or more Thoman MSS and mentions some good readings that first occur in them, while admitting that the class is difficult to define.[22] They are found at 87 $\pi i\theta\omega\mu\alpha\iota$ in Vv2, 654 ἔτ' in Ct1 P25 V2 Vv2(pc) and 1046 δειλόν in Ct1 O3 P20 P25 V2. Thomas is also cited at 647, 711–15, 733, 811 and 886. Whether we accept any of these readings or not, are we entitled to speak of a Thoman recension? Though he wrote a fresh version of the short life of the poet and hypotheses to the triad plays, it does not follow that he did more. Given the uncertainties about Thomas' work I have found it difficult to be consistent in reporting. In some places, where I know of only one MS carrying an allegedly Thoman reading I record the fact in the form e.g. Vv2 (Thomas Magister); where the attestation is apparently wider, the sigla of the MSS are omitted.[23]

Triclinius is more easily dealt with. His definitive recension of eight plays is represented by Oxford, Bodleian Library, Holkham gr. 88 (L) (almost complete, lacking only the end of *Peace*), its damaged twin, MS Vaticanus gr. 1294 (the three plays of the normal school curriculum of that date, followed by *Knights* 1–270) and MS

---

[19] Edition, p. 81.   [20] Eberline (n. 11), 78.
[21] Ibid. 86.   [22] Edition, pp. cxvii–cxix.
[23] In his essay 'Explorations in the History of the Text of Aristophanes' in vol. ii of his collected papers, *The Greeks and their Legacy* (Oxford, 1988), 223–65 Dover does not deal with Thomas. The Cremona MS has been studied by D. Harlfinger and M. Chantry in their contributions to the proceedings of the 1998 Cremona congress on Greek palaeography, *I manoscritti greci tra riflessione e dibattito*, ed. G. Prato (Florence, 2000), 665–7, 766–8. It turns out to be earlier than previously supposed (a watermark hints at a date as early as c.1320–5); but there is no evidence that it is an autograph, and other Thoman MSS may conceivably be equally early. The forthcoming dissertation on Thomas by Dr Niels Gaul will help to place him clearly in context.

Vaticanus gr. 2181.[24] His earlier edition, of the triad only, is in Paris, Bibliothèque nationale de France, MS suppl. grec 463; the text, which is not in his hand, is said to be Thoman in character. Triclinius attributes some of the scholia to Thomas, which is another matter.[25] Triclinius' understanding of some basic principles of metre enabled him to make a more significant contribution to the textual criticism of the plays than any other scholar in the Middle Ages or Renaissance. We do not know how many copies he was able to use as the basis for his text, but from his work on *Birds* we can make some inferences. At l. 809 it would seem that he depended on a manuscript like Laurentianus 31. 15 (*Γ*), which omits the word χρή, because he there remedied the lacuna of one syllable in a totally inappropriate way, which he would have avoided had he been able to use any better source. It also appears that towards the end of the play he was using a witness akin to MS Vaticanus Urbinas gr. 141 (U) because he shares readings with it at ll. 1437, 1514, 1666 and 1712. At ll. 1543, 1548, 1566, 1575, 1624, 1670, 1693, and 1736 he has a reading shared with both U and *Γ*, and at 1579 his correction presumably derives from a faulty reading found in those two codices.

Approximately contemporary with Triclinius are a small number of other manuscripts that contain at least one play from outside the triad and are of some importance to editors. They are Θ (Laurentianus, Conventi Soppressi 140, triad and *Knights*), U (Urbinas gr. 141, triad and *Birds*), M (Ambrosianus L 39 sup., triad and *Knights*), E (Modena, Estensis 127 = α. U. 5. 10, triad, *Knights*, *Birds*, and *Acharnians*), *Γ* (Laurentianus 31. 15 + Leiden, Vossianus gr. F 52, *Knights*, *Birds*, *Acharnians*, *Ecclesiazusae*, *Lysistrata*, and *Peace*), and A (Paris, grec 2712, triad, *Knights*, *Birds*, *Acharnians*, and *Ecclesiazusae* 1–444). The sum total of what these manuscripts contribute to the text is modest; to put it another way, if they had not come down to us the task of the editor would not have been significantly more difficult. Other manuscripts of this date or a little later

---

[24] M. Sicherl, *Griechische Erstausgaben des Aldus Manutius* (Paderborn, 1997), 125 n. 63, argues that this MS is a copy of the Holkham MS. For the latter see my paper in *CQ*^{2} 12 (1962), 32–47.

[25] A detailed study of this MS is provided by Koster, *Autour d'un manuscrit*; his assertions about the extent of Triclinius' part in the production of the MS cannot be accepted in full.

occasionally need to be cited, usually for no more than an isolated reading; an exception is MS Perugia, Biblioteca Augusta, H 56, a fifteenth-century copy of the *Ecclesiazusae*; there are also manuscripts of modest value containing scholia only (Bodleian Library, Barocci 38, *Lysistrata* and Naples, Biblioteca Nazionale II. D. 49, a copy of Γ which supplies some lacunae in that manuscript).[26] Triclinius does not appear to have had any worthy successor among later Byzantine teachers, and in general it is not common to find much of value in manuscripts copied after c.1350. But it is worth saying that there is some hope of further research enabling us to give a fuller picture of the handling of the text in the Palaeologan period, which might overturn this negative judgement. Progress will depend on detailed study of all the surviving fourteenth-century manuscripts, so as to obtain an assessment of their variant readings. Extra precision may be achieved in two ways: many of these manuscripts are written on Western paper, in which the watermarks often permit a fairly accurate dating, and it may also be possible to identify the hands of some of the scribes.

The next important phase in the transmission of texts begins early in the fifteenth century, when refugees from the declining empire brought their books and their notions of education with them to Italy. Though some parts of the text are far from easy for students, the plays were recommended by at least one of the most eminent humanists of the day. Aldus Manutius' preface to the editio princeps of 1498 reports that Theodore Gaza (1400–c.1476), when asked his advice about the best authors to read, replied 'Just Aristophanes, because he is very acute, fluent, learned and pure Attic.' But at this stage in the history of Greek scholarship no more than a tiny handful

---

[26] I mention in passing a recent article by A. Bravo García in J. A. López Férez (ed.), *La comedia griega y su influencia en la literatura española* (Madrid, 1998), 369–86, which deals with MSS of Aristophanes in the libraries of Madrid. It does not appear to have findings of note for the textual critic, but refers to the work of I. Pérez Martín, *El patriarca Gregorio de Chipre (ca.1240–1290) y la transmisión de los textos clásicos en Bizancio* (Madrid, 1996), 99–113; she discusses excerpts in Escorial MS X. I. 13 (355) which amount to some 17% of *Plutus*, 13% of *Clouds*, 10% of *Frogs*, and 9% of *Knights*. These turn out not to offer anything of importance, in striking contrast to similar excerpts from Sophocles in the same MS. A leaf from A (Paris, grec 2712) which was extant in the 18th c. and then disappeared has now been recovered by Chr. Förstel and M. Rashed, *Museum Helveticum*, 60 (2003), 146–51.

of readers or copyists, whether refugees or their Italian pupils, were expert enough in the niceties of the classical language to be able to make a contribution to the criticism of what was by now a rather corrupt text. It is not wholly surprising that Aristophanes tends not to be mentioned in educational treatises by humanists, who give few specific recommendations about Greek authors to be read.[27] Manuel Chrysoloras might have been expected to introduce Aristophanes to his Florentine audience in the years 1397–1400. The youthful Guarino while studying with him and his nephew in Constantinople had acquired a copy of some comedies (MS Vaticanus Palatinus gr. 116) and equipped it with Latin glosses. But there seems to be no proof that the master on arrival in Italy included this standard text in the range of authors to be studied.[28]

Early traces of an interest in the *Plutus* can be found. It served as part of the inspiration for a work entitled *Fabula Penia* by Rinuccio di Castiglione, composed in Crete in 1415–16. Acceptance of the comedies as essential reading came slowly. In Vittorino da Feltre's celebrated school at Mantua, which flourished in the second quarter of the century, it is reported that the master omitted or toned down passages that seemed to him obscene or otherwise objectionable.[29] In the meantime an attempt had been made, perhaps c.1439, to translate *Plutus* into Latin: Leonardo Bruni, perhaps following up an initial effort by Giovanni Tortelli, produced a version of ll. 1–239. It is worth noting that here again a reference to sexual practices in ll. 153 ff. is suppressed. A later version of the play has been credited to the Paduan scholar Pietro da Montagnana (d. 1478); it is in MS Marcianus lat. XIV. 10 (4659), fos. 41–65ᵛ. Elsewhere one can see the study of the plays being undertaken at a far from exalted level, which I suspect may have been typical, in a MS now in Vienna (phil. gr. 204). This is a copy of *Plutus* and *Clouds* commissioned from a Greek scribe in 1458 by Alexander of Otranto, later a professor of theology

---

[27] See e.g. the useful collection edited by C. W. Kallendorf, *Humanist Educational Treatises* (Cambridge, Mass., 2002).

[28] This is the negative inference I draw from the fact that there is no other mention of our author in the up-to-date surveys provided by R. Maisano and A. Rollo (eds.), *Manuele Crisolora e il ritorno del greco in Occidente* (Naples, 2002); see p. 136.

[29] Platina as cited by E. Garin, *Il pensiero pedagogico dell'Umanesimo* (Florence, 1958), 680.

and vicar-general of the Dominicans in his province. Having obtained his copy Alexander entered in the margins a Latin version and notes on *Plutus* and ll. 1–205 of *Clouds*. But it is clear that though he may have consulted other copies while making his version he did not have the ambition to undertake scholarly work on the text and there is only one passage where he shows awareness of a textual variant. His Latin is literal and not at all elegant, but no doubt he was less concerned with elegance than with the practical requirements of the schoolroom.[30] The use of *Plutus* as a university text is attested by some short extracts in MS Laurentianus 66. 31,[31] the contents of which seem to represent the programme of instruction given by Andronicus Callistus during an academic year at Florence.

There are three exceptions to this general picture of gloom. One is Marcus Musurus, who produced the *editio princeps* for Aldus Manutius. It will be seen from my apparatus criticus that he tidied up details, not, however, achieving nearly as much as he did later in his career when editing some other authors.[32] His edition included nine plays; *Lysistrata* and *Thesmophoriazusae* had to wait until 1515, when they were issued in Florence by the Juntine Press. The second bright light is found in MS Paris, grec 2715 (B), traditionally regarded as mysterious since it contains a number of good readings of unexplained origin. The situation can now be clarified. Not long ago, when examining some photostat prints taken from it I realized that, despite the misleading effect created by a substantial enlargement, the hand must be that of the prolific copyist Andronicus Callistus, and this identification was confirmed by the new standard reference book on Greek scribes.[33] It was already known that this scribe was capable of making useful suggestions for the improvement of texts, and it is therefore no surprise that he should have been able to do the same for Aristophanes.[34] Nor is it necessary to toy any longer with

---

[30] See M. L. Chirico, *Aristofane in Terra d'Otranto* (Naples, 1991), esp. p. 36.

[31] Information kindly provided by Professor G. N. Knauer.

[32] For an account of his career see N. G. Wilson, *From Byzantium to Italy* (London, 1992), 148–55. The materials used by him for the edition have been identified by Sicherl (n. 24), 114–54 with pl. iv.

[33] E. Gamillscheg and D. Harlfinger, *Repertorium der griechischen Kopisten 800–1600*, ii (Vienna, 1989), 34.

[34] On the quality of some of his other proposals see my remarks, op. cit. (n. 32), 117, 182 n. 13.

the hypothesis that B represents, albeit very imperfectly, the result of work undertaken by Triclinius after his completion of the recension that we see in L.

The third figure of some note in this period is an Istrian humanist called Andreas Divus. He was born in Capodistria but it is not clear whether he was Italian or Slovenian and his vernacular name has never been discovered. His Latin version of the comedies was issued in Venice in 1538 and reprinted in Basle in 1542; from time to time it is clear that he has successfully emended the Greek. The version was perhaps made from Zanetti's 1538 text, if the reading at *Lysistrata* 600 is any guide; there Divus has *opportunum est,* corresponding to Zanetti's proposal. But as the translation appeared in the same year as the edition, one may prefer to suppose that there was collaboration.[35]

Other early printed editions of the Greek text issued during the sixteenth century exhibit occasional improvements. It should be noted that few contain all eleven plays; the majority offer only one, doubtless chosen as a set text for school or university use. One such edition, which contains the triad only, is a bibliographical rarity, details of which deserve to be clarified; see my note on *Plutus* 216. It is also interesting to note that the edition of the *Plutus* by the French scholar Girardus, issued in Paris in 1549, arranges the material in an intelligent way: a short passage of the Greek text, anything from four to twenty-two lines, is followed first by a Latin version in ordinary type, then by notes, where the Latin is in italics and a smaller type face. It may be that this arrangement was a didactic innovation.

The progress of textual scholarship since the Renaissance is adequately known in its general outlines. Interesting additions to our knowledge are made from time to time when the work of previously obscure or anonymous scholars comes to light. A case in point is the discovery that Biset, Daubuz, and an anonymous French scholar made useful suggestions which anticipate proposals by Bentley and others.[36] One result of my experience in editing Sophocles was the

---

[35] The interest of Divus' version was noted by Colin Austin, *Dodone*, 16 (1987), 69.

[36] For a convenient conspectus see Austin and Olson's edition of *Thesmophoriazusae* (Oxford, 2004), pp. xcix–civ. Korais's notes in the plays have been published from MSS in the library at Chios by N. Kalospyros in the *Praktika* of the FIEC Congress held at Kavalla in 1999 (Athens, 2001), i. 444–67.

conviction that there is potential for further discoveries if only it were possible to compile a repertory of conjectures. Many of those published in the nineteenth century appeared in pamphlets that are exceedingly difficult to consult, and it can even happen that contributions to well-known periodicals are lost sight of.

Acharnians

Hypothesis I At l. 19 Olson declines to accept Elmsley's conjecture and suggests that the author was confusedly thinking of ll. 676–718. Perhaps so; but in that passage the emphasis is more on the speakers in the courts of law than the jurors. If the reference to the latter is to be retained one might emend to something like ὡc πρὸc δικαcτάc, 'as if speaking to a jury'.

Text 5 This line is more difficult than it appears at first sight because of three interconnected questions: (i) is it an indirect question? (ii) what is the function of γε? (iii) how should one punctuate? Denniston, *GP* 149, cited this line and 60 as examples of γε postponed. At p. 125 he took the subordinate clause to be relative rather than interrogative; so he would not have favoured taking this line as an indirect question introduced by ὅc, for which parallels could be offered from 118 and *Knights* 468, cf. van Daele in the Budé edition and A. López Eire in J. A. López Férez (ed.), *La comedia griega y su influencia en la literatura española* (Madrid, 1998), 139. Whether postponed or not, why is this particle used here? *GP* 123 tells us that relatives are usually emphasized by δή, and the only superficially analogous passage cited there is Dem. 54. 33; in that passage γε emphasizes the first element in a correlative proposition. I think, despite Denniston's doubts, that we should see this as an example of γε in an indirect question of the type seen also at *Wasps* 310–11.

Blaydes considered either punctuating after ἐγὼδ' or reading ἐφ' ᾧ 'γώ because he felt the particle was inappropriate. Most translations are like that of Sommerstein, who renders 'I know—something I rejoiced in my heart to see'. Similarly Thiercy.

11 O. Taplin, *Comic Angels* (Oxford, 1993), 65 n. 25, considers reading ὅδ' instead of ὁ δ', with heavier punctuation at the end of l. 9. The pronoun would be justified as implying a gesture at a member of the audience, e.g. the *archon basileus*. Olson does not mention this proposal, nor does Sommerstein (2001: 226). It is exposed to the objection that ἀνεῖπον is normally used in reference to public pronouncements by a herald.

13 Thiercy 991 prefers to translate ἐπὶ Μόσχῳ as 'sur un veau' and refers to the discussion by M. Landfester, *Rh. Mus.*² 113 (1970), 93–4, which is mentioned with approval by Mastromarco in his edition (p. 73). This was also the view of W. G. Clark, *Journal of Philology*, 8 (1879), 181: 'Dexitheus dressed as a rustic came upon the stage mounted on a young bull or heifer'. Landfester translates 'er sang ein boiotisches Lied auf ein bzw. das Kalb', with approximate parallels in *Knights* 1318 and Dem. 18. 287. A song about a calf is a possible concept here, but I am far from convinced. It is not simply that the preposition in the expression παιωνίζειν ἐπί seems to signify 'in response to, in reaction to', which is not exactly what we have in the present passage. There is another objection. In arguing against the generally received notion that Moschus is a proper name he notes that the scholiast here may just be inventing, which indeed is a frequent fault of scholiasts, but when he says that the description of Moschus as a native of Acragas inspires no confidence he goes too far. If the scholiast were inventing this detail he would not choose Acragas but some town in Boeotia. It ought in any case to be recorded that Moschus is a name attested in Athens and elsewhere in the fifth century BC (see *LGPN* ii).

24–5 The irregular syntax is usually explained as being due to the colloquialism of a very angry speaker. Olson obelizes in 25, but Colin Austin, *QUCC*² 72 (2002), 73 defends the use of ἐλθόντες with a dative of hostile sense. His analogies are from Homer and the Apocalypse, and I would myself prefer something from a genre closer to Old Comedy.

Since εἶτα δ' after a participle is so rare in Aristophanes—*Knights* 377 is the only case cited—I think it best that the participle of l. 24 should be replaced by one of the verbs suggested by Haupt and others; R. J. T. Wagner, *Rh. Mus.*² 60 (1903), 448–9, proposed εὕδουσιν, citing *Lys.* 15 for the antithesis of sleeping and keeping an appointment, and D. S. Robertson, in unpublished lecture notes kindly lent to me by Mr D. Mervyn Jones, similarly suggested ῥέγκουϲιν. This, in conjunction with H.-S.'s transfer of the participle from 24 to 25, gives a good solution.

36 For πρίων as a nickname see Hesychius s.v. Λάμιοϲ = fr. com. adesp. 382. F. Lotz, *De locis quibusdam Acharnensium, Aristophanis fabulae, disputatio* (Programm, Fulda 1866) proposed to read Πρίων as a proper name.

46 ff. Amphitheus has often been taken to be a fictional name; so *LGPN* ii s.v., while Thiercy 992 criticizes as bizarre an identification with Hermogenes, son of Callias. But the name is found on *IG* ii². 2343 and one ought to consider seriously whether the figure on the stage is the man named on the inscription. Sterling Dow drew attention to it in *AJA* 73 (1969), 234–5; see further Th. Gelzer, in *RE* Supp.-Band xii (Stuttgart, 1971), col. 1398 and for a helpful diagram and photograph of the stone H. Lind, *MH* 42 (1985), 249–61. It has the names Philonides, Simon and Amphitheus in a list of sixteen members of a thiasos of Herakles under a priest who is a citizen of Kydathenaion (Simon is the priest). Given that Aristophanes belonged to the same deme, that a Philonides is known to have produced some of his plays and that the name Simon occurs in *Knights* 242, it seems perverse to deny that these men may be friends of the poet and that for some reason which we cannot now guess one of them is portrayed on the stage.

A fourth rare name on the stone is Antitheus. He seems likely to be the man named in *Thesm.* 898 as the father of Kritylla; she is also named in *Lys.* 323, but *LGPN* ii gives no other examples and regards her as fictional—again wrongly, I suspect, as the name, though rare, is found in volumes i and iiiA and could equally well have been known in Athens.

52 A. M. Bowie, *LCM* 7 (1982), 113, may be right to suggest that Elmsley with his emendation ποιῆϲαι 'is rather too keen to standardise the use of active or middle for certain verbs'. Elmsley in his note on 58 said 'Activam igitur formam retinuerim in hoc versu, reposuerim in v. 52, 131' but did not print these suggestions in his text. How do we know that Amphitheus is not one of the parties making the proposed treaty? Does he not think of himself as one of the beneficiaries or at least create that impression? Some editors have thought otherwise: Rennie on 52 says 'Amphitheus is merely the go-between'; Starkie on 52 notes that H. Weber retains the middle 'since Amphitheus was to make peace as the representative of Athens, cp. 268'; but there ἐμαυτῷ seems to alter the situation. I follow Elmsley, but with some hesitation.

53 Do we need the vocative particle? Dickey 199–206 leaves me uncertain. She does say (p. 201), that ὦ is found in 80% of examples in Aristophanes. The question then is whether the exceptions can be taken as instances of Wackernagel's notion, *Vorlesungen über Syntax* (Basel, 1926–8), i. 311–12, that omission indicates disrespect, or are to be explained in some other way. See below on *Wasps* 908.

55 Blaydes thought the sentence incomplete, expecting a participle in the accusative such as ἑλκόμενον. Olson cites Menander, *Perinthia* 6, for the use of περιορᾶν absolute as here. Probably the parallel is valid, but since at least a century separates the two texts and usage could have changed in that time, one cannot be quite sure.

78 Blaydes thought of τοὺς πλεῖστα καὶ φαγεῖν δυναμένους καὶ πιεῖν but he printed Morel's solution, which is very similar. The MSS offer καταφαγεῖν and the scholiast comments on κατα-, which, however, may only mean that the text was already corrupt in his day. Rennie's κἀμπιεῖν would restore the balance of the two compounds and the scholiast's credit. But van Leeuwen pointed out that καταφαγεῖν with its overtones of greed is not the word which the ambassador should use, unless by a slip of the tongue he reveals his true feelings. Since it can also be argued that κατα- was a mistake induced by the last word in the following line, I have adopted Morel's proposal. But one cannot rule out the possibility that καταφαγεῖν was written, in order to be picked up by καταπύγονας in 79.

95–6 Sommerstein follows van Leeuwen in reading τί πρὸς θεῶν for πρὸς τῶν θεῶν, so that two clearer questions result. For most editors 95 must be a question, but to say 'Are you looking like a battleship?' which is the only accurate translation, has little point. An alternative is to read with Page, *Wiener Studien*, 69 (1956), 117–19, βλέπων. The vocative with a participle has an analogy, not cited by Page, in

Anacreon 15 ὦ παῖ παρθένιον βλέπων. See also the examples collected by Wankel on Dem. 18. 17 (p. 420). This is a simple remedy and to be preferred.

97 Though που 'I suppose' can be defended as sarcastic, Robertson's γοῦν is attractive.

100 The Greeks were not notable for interest and competence in foreign languages. Though it is possible that someone in the poet's circle knew Persian or Median, the chances are that this line was not intended to do more than convey an impression of the language. The latest contribution to the debate is by A. Willi, *Mnemosyne*[4], 57 (2004), 657–81.

101 Though the form of the aorist transmitted by the MSS is not securely attested epigraphically until rather later, I am prepared to believe that we have here the first instance of the form that eventually became standard.

104 χρυcό is not in doubt, but R perhaps lapsed into Attic here with χρυcον (unaccented). However, I have not recorded this in the apparatus criticus because the reading is far from certain; the nu is misshapen, and as it is not obvious that the parchment is creased, I am at a loss to interpret the scribe's intention.

108 The corruption into the deictic form ὁδί is at first sight puzzling; in the period before Triclinius scribes will not have given thought to the prosody of ἀχάναc, which if erroneously scanned as an anapaest could have induced a well-meaning emendation. Perhaps a scribe's eye strayed a few lines down the page and saw the deictic forms at the end of 111 and 115. But see below on *Wasps* 877 for a similar corruption; there is another at *Knights* 1270.

112 My apparatus does not record the quotation in Clemens Alexandrinus, *Paedagogus* 2. 108. 5, because it has a corrupt text. cαρδιανικόν was restored there by W. Teuffel; the MS (P = Paris. gr. 451) is reported to have cαρδηνιακόν. Hesychius is very similar, with cαρδανιακόν in the MS, not emended by Latte.

127 The parallel passage in Eupolis 286 does not provide an easy solution. Kassel and Austin are inclined to favour Starkie's adoption of the reading in the *Suda* ι 717 and Olson follows suit. But the position of the particle γε is not ideal; Denniston, *GP* 120, quoted the line with οὐδέποτέ γ' ἴϲχει θύρα, which he did not discuss, and Sommerstein adopts this solution. With the omission of the article we get 'A door never prevents . . .', which seems possible.

136 Elmsley's proposal presupposes a confusion between ἔμειναν/ ἔμεινα ἄν and ἄν ἦμεν. A decision depends on whether one thinks that the singular, used regularly in what follows, should be restored here.

143 Repetition of ἦν is hardly objectionable, but if one wanted to make a small adjustment, γ' for τ' (coincidentally found in HVp2) and ὤν for ἦν would make sense.

146 Olson does not record that A and Γ have the partitive genitive ἀλλᾶντος, which can at least be translated.

165 Dover on *Frogs* 1175 reports that ancient grammarians distinguished between two senses of μοχθηρός with different accentuation. He favours proparoxytone there and at Plato, *Phaedr.* 268 E, with the implication of 'rough, jocular compassion'. But the grammarians were not unanimous: Herodian i. 197, as found in Eustathius 341. 14, took the view that in both meanings the word was oxytone. Olson takes the word as purely abusive and prints as oxytone, which is the accentuation found only in the late MSS. I have preferred the alternative view. Schwyzer i. 380 appears to accept variation of accent according to meaning; see also Sandbach on Menander, *Heros* 6.

176 Though I have accepted one of the simple ways of restoring the metre, I find van Herwerden's suggestion extremely attractive because it coheres so well with the following line. Olson thinks that the loss of the second γε is due to someone objecting to repetition; careless omission is just as likely.

178 Where there is change of speaker I have chosen if possible not to elide; the result is a split anapaest. Cf. *Clouds* 214, 1192, *Wasps* 155, *Frogs* 1220. But at *Wasps* 793 and *Peace* 41 elision is obligatory, and one has to ask how the actors coped.

Acharnians 21

193 Van Leeuwen made the intelligent observation that one would expect here a noun indicating attempts by the Spartans to detach the cities of the Athenian empire from their allegiance to Athens. But the transmitted text has to be translated 'wearing down', i.e. gradual destruction of the allies, as Olson correctly states. ἀποτροπή, whether in active or passive sense, might be worth considering.

194 I do not see any way to determine whether ϲοι or ϲπονδαί is the intrusive word in R's version of the line.

197 Olson takes the infinitive ἐπιτηρεῖν as a kind of epexegetic, quoting K–G ii. 5–6. He dismisses Reiske's transposition, but it is clever and could easily be right. It is rather odd to have an infinitive dependent on a verb like ὄζουϲ᾿. τοῦ μὴ might have been expected, making the line stand in apposition to the preceding nouns. But perhaps Reiske made the mistake of trying to improve a classical text.

ϲιτί᾿ ἡμερῶν τριῶν is best taken as a quotation from the order issued to the hoplites at the time of mobilization. It was so understood by W. G. Clark, *Journal of Philology*, 9 (1880), 5; he is followed by Sommerstein and Olson.

201–3 I feel that Elmsley's transposition makes for a better exchange. ἐγὼ δὲ in 201 in the transmitted order of the lines seems too emphatic; δέ . . . γε is just as good after 200 as after 202. Henderson and Sommerstein (2001: 227) have also adopted this view.

221 The subjunctive ἐγχάνῃ is to be retained if one accepts as adequate parallels Thuc. 4. 85. 2 μηδεὶϲ μεμφθῇ and Theognis 101 μηδείϲ . . . πείϲηι. Many editors have accepted Brunck's slight adjustment to give the optative, but Cooper–Krüger i. 677 (§54. 2. 2C) seem to me to have assembled enough material to justify retaining the subjunctive.

234 The proparoxytone accentuation Βαλλήναδε appears to be confirmed by Ioannes Alexandrinus 34. 4 as quoted by Chandler, *GA* 240 (§§846–7). The reading of the MS (Hauniensis 1965) is Παλίναδε, which W. Dindorf in his edition (Leipzig, 1825) p. xv interprets as Παλλήναδε. In my edition of the scholia on this play I inadvertently followed the practice of editors who had preferred the paroxytone accentuation, which appears to be contrary to the evidence of the MSS of *Acharnians* (I have examined once again REΓL).

264 V. Schmidt, *Sprachliche Untersuchungen zu Herondas* (Berlin, 1968), 68, argued that the form Φάλης, paroxytone, should be read here, citing H. Herter, *De dis Atticis Priapi similibus* (Bonn, 1926), 44. Herter drew attention to Hesychius' entry Φάλης and the title of Aristophanes' play Τριφάλης.

292 Denniston, *GP* 126–30, shows that γε may occur in exclamatory questions. So the reading of L (οὐκ ἴςτε γ') is possible. But γε was Triclinius' universal nostrum, and one must at least consider alternatives. Kock's ἠκούςατ' is presumably based on the assumption that R's οὐκ ἴςατ' is the result of the scribe's mental dictation of two syllables in the wrong order; this hypothesis is ingenious and does not deserve to be criticized as palaeographically difficult; it is not only letter forms that provoke scribal error, but scribal thought processes. Nor, *pace* Olson, do I find the repetition of ἀκούω inappropriate in the highly charged plea of the hero to be given a hearing. Yet P.Oxy. 4510 has ΙϹΤΕ[, which may imply support for Triclinius, or for W. G. Clark's οὐκ ἰϲτέ; (*Journal of Philology*, 9 (1880), 12) or for Handley's ἴϲτε. τἄλλ'. Certainty is unattainable. If R preserves a vestige of the truth, the papyrus, which is of the second century AD, shows that corruption had set in early; was it a case of trivialization? (For a number of syllabic transpositions in Greek texts see Housman's *Classical Papers* (Cambridge, 1972), i. 222, for Latin texts his edition of Manilius, vol. i, pp. lvii f. H.-S.)

307 Elmsley's minor change makes the chorus say 'Given that you have made a treaty with the Spartans, how can you now have anything respectable to say?' The emphasis is on the temporal sequence, and I do not find Olson's objection convincing.

325 Gonis in his notes to P.Oxy. 4510 sees elision of δήξομ' here, but he overlooks the parallel case of *Frogs* 509 περιόψομἀπελθόντ', where crasis is found. I do not believe that the mark of elision which he claims to see in the papyrus has any claim to be taken as authoritative.

347 A. L. Boegehold, *When a Gesture Was Expected* (Princeton, 1999), 76–7, accepts the transmitted text, translating 'So you were all getting ready to shake your shouts at me'. He admits that there is something obscure here, but understands the line as referring to the idea of shaking one's cloak as a gesture of anger, which he has discussed in the preceding pages. Though his interest in gestures is welcome, in this line the difficulty of maintaining his interpretation seems to me to be too great.

Despite Sommerstein's approval (2001: 227) I find it hard to accept W. Lapini's ἀνακείcειν (Dindorf) βοήν (R^pc), proposed at *SIFC* 92 (1999), 3–11. To my way of thinking this is not a very successful example of παρὰ προcδοκίαν. The oddest fact about the transmitted text is that it has βοῆc in the genitive, and I continue to think that Dobree was right to take that as the starting-point for emendation. If one insists on an accusative, the verb ἀναcτήcειν should be considered, even if it leads to a split anapaest.

348 The debate about the correct form of the word meaning 'from Mount Parnes' seemed to have been settled by Dover, *Maia*, 15 (1963), 14–15. But it has been reopened by *IG* i³. 1057 bis. This is tentatively dated 480–460 and reads

[Δ]ιὸc Παρ-
[νηccίo

The editor also cites *SEG* 33. 244c, a vase inscription from Parnes [Διὸc Πα]ρνεcίο ονε. No date is given for this. Pausanias' form (1. 32. 2) Παρνήθιοc Ζεύc is therefore not the only acceptable spelling.

351 Editors do not cite parallels for the compound ἐντιλάω. The alternative ἐπιτιλάω, attested in all three of the *Suda* quotations, is possible, because the preposition seems equally suitable.

376 R. Kassel, *Rh. Mus.*² 137 (1994), 35, thinks that Sommerstein is probably right to revert to ψήφῳ δακεῖν. I incline to the view that Brunck was right to prefer a present to the aorist (Olson did not notice this anticipation of his own decision).

392 The proverbial expression is quoted in slightly differing versions; see fr. 349. The question is whether the verb was simple or compound; it is simple in the earliest version cited with this verb, as opposed to (ἀνα)μένειν, in Plat. *Crat.* 421 D and *Legg.* 751 D. That gives some support to Cobet's reading. Olson's ἐνδέξεται is also worth considering, but probably not everyone will agree with his view that Cobet's proposal is a more violent emendation.

412 Richards 5 pointed out that logically the rags used in Euripidean tragedy ought to be the consequence of the poet's wearing rags, just as the lameness of his heroes results from his composing with his feet up and not using his legs. Perhaps here one is again guilty of improving a classical text; but on this occasion I have been unable to resist the temptation.

415 C. Reisig, *Coniectaneorum in Aristophanem libri duo* (Leipzig, 1816), 175, took the use of the definite article here to be analogous to *Wasps* 1511 ὃc τὴν τραγῳδίαν ποιεῖ, 'id est, malus ille tragicus'. I am not aware that he proposed to take τοῦ as enclitic; Blaydes attributes that idea to Bergk, but W. G. Clark, *Journal of Philology*, 9 (1880), 167, named Reisig. One might ask whether we have here an example of the article used 'almost like a possessive pronoun', to quote Cooper–Krüger i. 371 (§50. 2. 3).

430 Blaydes, doubtless bothered by the lack of a definite article with ἄνδρα, proposed to punctuate after οἶδ'. But that leaves the accusatives without justification. The line is paratragic, similar to Eur. *Cycl.* 104.

434 C. Beer, *Ueber die Zahl der Schauspieler bei Aristophanes* (Leipzig, 1844), 147, argues as follows: if the slave speaks the second half of the line, he would not say ἰδοὺ ταυτὶ λαβέ. That is only appropriate if he were pointing to one of several sets of garments he had with him. Instead he would need to say ἰδοὺ λαβέ, like Xanthias at *Frogs* 483, or at a pinch ἰδού, ταυτί. λαβέ, which seems less suitable. Olson's report is misleading. Beer preferred to give ἰδού, ταυτὶ to Dicaeopolis.

436 Editors are right when they say that 435 can stand on its own as an exclamation. But are they right in claiming that 436 has no place here? Dicaeopolis has finally got the set of ragged clothes he wanted, and as he inspects them with delight he can be imagined as uttering the wish that they will make him look utterly down-at-heel. Brunck (at l. 411 in his numeration) admitted that if either 384 or 436 is to be deleted, then 436 is the line to sacrifice; but he went on to say 'sed utroque in loco sedem suam bene tuetur'. I think he may have been right.

461 οὔπω may be right, even though the temporal nuance is not obviously essential, but Thiersch's proposal οὗτοι is idiomatic; see the parallels in Denniston, *GP* 543–4. I see no need to follow Thiersch's other suggestion, to give the line to Euripides, since then αὐτός would lack point.

D. Kovacs, *Museum criticum*, 29 (1994), 171–2, objects to the transmitted text that the line does not constitute a reply to Euripides' command. He notes that Thiersch's proposal οὗτοι does not remove the difficulty. His remedy is to read οὔπω μὰ Δί'. οἷς᾽ οἷ᾽ αὐτὸς ἐργάζει κακά. He notes also an unexplained variant οἶδ᾽ in the Aldine. I remain unconvinced. (i) It may be part of the deliberate humour of the scene that Dicaeopolis does not respond properly to Euripides; this is not tragic stichomythia, where the sequence of thought has to be taken seriously. (ii) I take the sense of οὔπω in the transmitted text to be '[despite my repeated requests] you still do not realize what danger I face if you do not help'. (iii) The variant in the Aldine is only part of a paraphrase in the scholia. (iv) 'Suffer the trouble you yourself create' is obscure, even if οἶςε can be used in this sense; there is no proper connection between the postponement of Dicaeopolis' departure and the implied threat or wish. I find the effect too staccato.

463 Olson argues that in this scene Dicaeopolis does not ask for objects that are already visible. Rather than punctuate after μόνον and assume ellipse of a verb of begging he marks a comma after μοι. The deictic pronoun needs explanation; I think it could be treated as an extended example of the usage whereby a word just spoken, rather than a visible object, is referred to (e.g. 558, 593); for the deictic applied to a word or words about to be spoken see *Knights* 49.

As to the orthography of cφογγίῳ, Threatte i. 469 cites the Attic spelling cφόνδυλοc from fourth-century inscriptions and cφόγγοc from *IG* ii². 1283. 18 of 263/2 BC. Aspiration at the earlier date is possible. It may even be that the Athenians were inconsistent. Elmsley's note here refers to Pierson on Moeris 360 s.v. cχινδαλμόc, which includes the remark 'cφόγγοc pro cπόγγοc apud Etymologum'; if that is meant to refer to the *Etymologicum Magnum*, it should be noted that Gaisford's edition at 739. 29 suggests the opposite. This kind of detail is very hard to settle; see Dover on *Clouds* 130.

472 κοιράνουϲ has been replaced here by τυράννουϲ in R. The same substitution occurred at Aesch. *Ag.* 549 in MS F, and was put right by Triclinius.

487 'what you yourself believe' looks like a clause in which ϲοὶ should not be printed as an enclitic. But R, Γ and E give the enclitic form. K–G i. 558 say first that in the combination αὐτῷ/αὐτῇ ϲοι it is enclitic, and then go on to allow for the possibility of non-enclitic forms if extra emphasis is intended, citing Stallbaum on Plat. *Euthyd.* 273 B.

508 is a serious difficulty. ἄχυρα appears to be ambiguous; the meanings commonly given are chaff or bran, the edible outer husk of barley; cf. the entry in *DGE*, which adds 'dross' resulting from refining gold. If the first meaning is accepted, the text implies that metics were not present, which is most unlikely; if the second, the metics are compared to an inferior product of grain. That seems a gratuitous aspersion. There is some discussion of the passage in D. Whitehead, *The Ideology of the Athenian Metic* (Cambridge, 1977), 39–40, but it did not enable me to come to a decision.

The matter is complicated by the fact that the late L. A. Moritz, to whom I once wrote asking for advice about the passage, told me that the term 'seems to have meant pretty well all or any of that part of the plant which could not be eaten' (letter of 20 April 1966). 'Any solution suggesting that ἄχυρα is something that remains with the grain when it is περιεπτιϲμένον simply won't do. Nor do I see how we can get out of accepting that Ar. is simply saying that the metics are the "inedible" part which is removed by "peeling"'. Chadwick 56–9 argues for 'straw' as the normal meaning of the word, and in connection with our passage concludes 'This is simply the worthless part of anything'.

For this reason I have taken the bold decision of following Dobree and deleting the line. The proposal was originally made by Valckenaer, who did not state his reasons, and so Dobree tried to reconstruct them. I quote the last of them: 'non tanti erant μέτοικοι, ut coram illis male audire puderet populum Atheniensem'. Of course the presence of the line in our texts has to be explained. It must originally have been a marginal addition by a learned reader who wished to illustrate a rare metaphor by a reasonably close parallel. The marginal note was later incorporated by mistake into the text. More than one example of this type of corruption can be cited. At Aesch. *Pers.* 253 the Medicean MS has in the margin Soph. *Ant.* 277, and this line figures in the text of copies dependent on M. Eur. *Hipp.* 80 appears as *Bacch.* 316. Aesch. *ScT* 601 was deleted by Musgrave for this reason. Theocritus 8. 77 is a wrong insertion from 9. 7, doubtless via the margin.

510 Sommerstein and Olson follow van Herwerden in reading καὐτοῖϲιν αὖθιϲ. Olson says that θεόϲ at the end of the line is 'exceedingly awkward'. That I simply do not believe; there is merely a slight redundancy.

527 The dual form πόρνα is probably right, but it is well to remember that from the second century AD onwards scribes and readers were taught that the dual was a feature of classical Attic which they should use in their own compositions, and they may sometimes have yielded to the temptation of restoring it in a classical text in a passage where it might be expected

553 J. S. Morrison's conjecture ap. Morrison and Williams, *Greek Oared Ships* (Cambridge, 1968), 320 n. 2, is at first sight attractive. τρυπωμένων 'being bored' indicates a noisy procedure like others in the context, and this consideration has convinced Sommerstein, Mastromarco, and Thiercy. Olson disagrees, arguing that not all the activities described need to be noisy, because Aristophanic lists can be incongruous mixtures (which is incidentally why Blaydes was not necessarily right to suggest that l. 549 should contain three accusatives). A further point has been overlooked in the discussion so far: the fleet was already in a state of near-readiness, and I find it hard to imagine that oar-ports needed to be bored then; that is a stage in the construction and initial fitting of ships.

571 Olson rightly notes that τιϲ here is somewhat awkward after its occurrence in 569, but that Elmsley's τι ἀνύϲαϲ produces unusual word-order (cf. e.g. *Knights* 119, *Clouds* 506). Another remedy has been suggested: Blaydes's τάχ' deserved a mention.

575 Olson does not record in his apparatus that R has the error φίλων, which was presumably what spurred Thiersch to propose τῶν πτίλων καὶ τῶν λόφων, which is recorded by Olson. It seems to me that neither this nor Hamaker's deletion of the line is plausible enough to be taken seriously; as Olson rightly says, the remark is intensely sarcastic and the phrasing has a parallel at 1074.

582 The dative of the person affected, though not well attested, is idiomatic.

583–5 In each line νυν occupies the position of an enclitic, but the temporal sense would not be out of place. In 583 I am puzzled by the presence of the emphatic form ἐμοί, which does not seem to be called for. That is doubtless why Meineke replaced it with ἰδού, spoken by Lamachus. One might account for the corruption by noting the presence of μοι in 582(?) and 584. Could cύ μοι be the answer?

591 οὐ γὰρ κατ' ἰcχύν ἐcτιν is said to mean 'it is not a matter to be decided by force'. There is some kind of ellipse; perhaps one should understand ὁ ἀγών. Olson cites Chadwick's discussion of ἰcχυρόc, which seems to me not relevant in this context. What one would like to see is a close parallel. Meineke perhaps had a point when he suggested coύcτιν.

641–2 At the end of 641 one has the impression that the sentence is complete; 642 does not follow on very neatly and Olson notes 'the abruptness of the observation perhaps reflects the loss of a line from the text'. On balance I prefer Richards's solution, which he does not mention.

673 A. C. Cassio, *RFIC* 99 (1971), 55 n. 3, argues in favour of A's reading ἔντονον. He emphasizes the recurrence of the word at 666 and the scholiast's note. Though I think he may well be right, and Olson, apparently independently, takes the same view, I do not see the point of adducing the scholium here (πρόθυμοι γὰρ οἱ ἄγροικοι εἰc πᾶcαν πρᾶξιν καὶ εὔτονοι). Cassio understands the word as related to ἐντείναcθαι in *Clouds* 968.

685 Many modern editors accept Kock's ἐπ' αὐτῷ for ἑαυτῷ and translate 'against him'. I have serious doubts about this. Although it becomes clear in the antepirrhema that one notorious trial is of great concern to the chorus, in the present passage there has not yet been a noun in the singular to which Kock's pronoun can refer, and despite the assertions of the commentators I do not feel easy with this example of oscillation between plural and singular, especially as the immediately preceding reference to the intended victim was in the first person (προcέcταμεν) rather than the third; ἐφ' ἡμῖν is metrically equivalent and would have conveyed the meaning clearly if Kock's solution were right. I take the MSS reading to mean that the young man ensured for himself the role of state prosecutor.

Elmsley detached ὁ δὲ from νεανίαc and made an alternative proposal νεανίαν. But then the prosecutor remains the subject of the main verb παίει whereas the decisive intervention came from the junior.

709 The puzzle of this line remains unsolved. There was a cult of Demeter Achaia at Athens, as attested by Herodotus 5. 61, but he says it was one of a number restricted to the Gephyraioi, in which the rest of the Athenians had no involvement. The priestesses of Demeter Achaia and Demeter Kourotrophos are known from undated inscriptions in the theatre of Dionysus (*IG* ii². 5117, 5153). R. C. T. Parker, *Athenian Religion: A History* (Oxford, 1996), 289 n. 12, thinks the apparent reference in this line is probably corrupt and is attracted by Borthwick's conjecture (see below) Certainly if the text is corrupt the mistake could have been caused by a learned scribe who knew that there was a cult of Demeter Achaia and absent-mindedly introduced it in place of the genuine reading. It is very hard to see what the point could be of referring to a cult apparently of concern to no more than a minority of Athenians. Even if one were to take seriously the information provided by the scholia and Orion about a noisy procession, to say 'he would not even have tolerated Demeter Achaia herself easily' is pretty odd.

Sommerstein comments favourably on but does not adopt E. K. Borthwick's conjecture (*BICS* 17 (1970), 107–10) αὐτὸν Ἀρταχαίην, which introduces a reference to a Persian of gigantic stature and stentorian voice known from Hdt. 7. 117. But it was not so much a stentorian voice as clever rhetoric that defeated Thucydides in the court. A further difficulty which seems not to have been considered sufficiently in recent discussion is the meaning of ἠνέcχετο. As

Hamaker emphasized (*Mnemosyne*, 2 (1853), 163–5), 'tolerate, put up with' is the expected sense. Even supposing that a reference to skill in wrestling is required, as might be inferred from what follows, how can a verb with this meaning be right here? Hamaker proposed to read ᾧ for ὅϲ in the preceding line and then Αὐτοκλῆϲ παλαίων, translating 'Autocles niet ligt in het worstelen zou hebben uitgehouden', but that seems, if I understand it rightly, not to give the exact meaning for the verb which he had earlier stipulated.

If the original text named a formidable opponent, the expected meaning is 'he would not easily have tolerated the threat from X'. A threatening, bullying, or otherwise hostile presence is the concept needed to explain the verb. Now it has to be said that heroes were sometimes thought of as menacing, and as Artachaies had a cult at Acanthus, that is a point in favour of Borthwick's hypothesis. But would one not expect reference to a local Athenian cult? It is hardly credible that Artachaies was a kind of bogeyman figure to the Athenian public.

Hence my tentative approach, recorded by Olson. The antepirrhema begins with talk of Scythia. Note that Artachaies was not a Scythian. But who was the most famous Scythian? Someone who according to Hdt. 4. 77 had been critical of Greeks other than Spartans. There is no other sign that he had made a name for himself as the barbarian critic of Greeks in general, but it may be worth considering αὐτὸν τὸν Ἀνάχαρϲιν. This is a very long shot, even as a diagnostic conjecture.

Colin Austin (*QUCC*[2] 72 (2002), 73–4) reports a suggestion made by Sir Denys Page in 1960. The transmitted text can be taken as an oath by Demeter in which the normal particle μά is omitted. This ellipse is usually confined to Doric; the only Attic example is Soph. *Ant.* 758. If that passage is deemed to be acceptable as a parallel, one still has to account for the unusual choice of oath.

712 With some hesitation I adopt Blaydes's adjustments of this line. The verb in περι- does not seem to be quite in place; a better climax to the three consecutive assertions is provided not only by the use of ὑπερ- but also by the emphatic αὐτούϲ rather than the unstressed αὐτοῦ.

717 I do not share the confidence of recent editors that the transmitted text is sound; as Olson says, the interwoven word-order is difficult. R. S. Conway, *CR* 14 (1900), 359, took the meaning to be τὸ λοιπόν, ἂν φύγῃ τις, χρὴ καὶ ἐξελαύνειν καὶ ζημιοῦν, etc. But I do not feel comfortable with the transposition; καί is adjacent to the wrong word. Paley and Richards contemplated κἂν/ἂν φυγῇ τις ζημιοῖ 'if one is to punish with exile'. This is perhaps acceptable if ἂν or ἢν is read; καί is otiose. If one takes the transmitted text to mean 'and if someone escapes (that punishment, i.e. exile), fine him', that is awkward because in a judicial context one expects φεύγειν to have its technical meaning.

It may be worth making another proposal: κἂν τύχητε 'if you hit on this solution', the usage given by LSJ s.v. τυγχάνω A. 4, cf. Cooper–Krüger i. 862 (§56. 16. 0). A suggestive but not entirely exact analogy is to be found at Thuc. 3. 43. 5.

733 The uncertainty about the verb forms should be considered in the light of *Plutus* 73–6, where dual and plural are seemingly employed indifferently. There Blaydes compared *Peace* 414, *Birds* 641, Soph. *OC* 1435 f., while Holzinger added *Birds* 44 and *Plutus* 446–9.

Deletion of ἐμὶν seems implausible; a dialect form was relatively unlikely to be interpolated. Is the initial dual intrusive? Conceivably, as the Byzantines were encouraged to use dual forms wherever possible in their own compositions and might have introduced them, whether consciously or not, into the texts they copied.

740 Hamaker, *Mnemosyne* 2 (1853), 167, observed that the definite article with χοιρίον has no point. His proposal τὼc is more economical than Blaydes' ᾅ.

755 I do not see why Olson claims that the plural ταῦτ' as an internal accusative is more idiomatic than R's τοῦτ'. In general I do not share his view that R is inferior to the other branch of the tradition, although one has to concede that it has many careless slips.

775 εἴμεναι seems not to be attested. Colvin 213 cites Ruijgh's suggestion that it is an attempt to represent linguistic convergence of εἶμεν and εἶναι, and at p. 223 suggests himself that it 'sounded vaguely archaic and literary, and therefore suitable for a speaker of Doric'. Perhaps; but I am not sure that an ordinary Megarian would be expected to speak in that style, and so have some doubts about the alleged suitability in the present instance. Olson's combination of two previous proposals εἶμεν ἐκ is very attractive. If one retains the transmitted text, perhaps it is best to assume an error on the poet's part.

777 If one wished to preserve χοιρίδιον, it could be done by reading φώνει δὴ τύ, χοιρίδιον, ταχύ.

788 I am prepared to accept the dubious form τράφεν as a slight error of dialect on the poet's part, like ἦμεν at 771.

790 One can hardly decide whether R's τωὐτῶ is to be rejected in favour of the strictly correct τωὐτοῦ. There is no guarantee that Aristophanes was entirely consistent in his use of dialect forms.

791 αἴ κα is attractive, as proposed by Blaydes and Meineke, but one would expect a connecting particle. That can be obtained by Blaydes's further suggestion καί κα. Ahrens' ἀλλ' αἴ is at least close to the reading of the papyrus and R, but perhaps we do better to assume that the poet did not use the correct forms.

The second verb is problematic. Olson does well to note that the uncompounded form elsewhere is χνοάω/χνοάζω, and so Bothe's – χνοιανθῇ is open to objection, unless one wishes to suppose that in dialect the form in -οια was characteristic of the noun.

803 It is usually assumed that each 'piglet' is addressed in turn, which makes αὐτός hard to account for. Olson adopts a suggestion by Douglass Parker and Dover: it is not the second piglet but the Megarian who is addressed, and he writes τρώγοις καὐτὸς ἄν;, to which the Megarian responds with a porcine squeak. That is funny to us, but it makes the Megarian enter into the humour of the scene in a way which seems to me not consistent with his other utterances. So with much hesitation I follow Brunck and Elmsley.

809 Should οὐχὶ be rendered as οὐκὶ in Doric? Colvin does not deal with this. W. Pökel, *Neue Jahrbücher für Philologie und Paedagogik*, 137 (1888), 246–7, says that οὐκὶ is not confined to Ionic, citing Theocritus 25. 81, 178 and Moschus 4. 90. If his inference from R's reading at 809 is correct, he would make the corresponding adjustment in 785 and *Lys.* 1171. His view was adopted by Coulon. But it is based on a false assumption: the passages he cited from the pastoral poets are from compositions in epic style and dialect and naturally they use Ionic forms. R's οὔτι is probably a slip; we do not expect to find it except in expressions such as οὔτι χαίρων κτλ.

826 The suggestion of παθών in the Amsterdam edition of 1670 is assigned to 'quidam' and is not therefore Scaliger's.

830 Olson accepts Handley's ἀπεδίδου, an imperfect being superior to an aorist. H.-S. queries the use of the present stem of this verb in preference to πωλεῖν. On consulting Greek grammars, e.g. Weir Smyth (p. 154), I find it stated that in -μι verbs the second person singular middle retains the -co termination in the imperfect. That being so, I prefer Page's ἀπεδίδουc (*Wiener Studien*, 69 (1956), 122–3); *pace* Olson, Page shows that the active in the sense 'sell' is far from inexplicable.

833 is difficult. The abstract noun must refer to some intrusion or uncalled-for activity. Not all translations get that right, doubtless because it is not immediately obvious how such an interpretation can be put on the dialogue. What is Dicaeopolis apologizing for? Perhaps Willems was right: 'Am I intruding into your troubles?' But if that is a legitimate rendering of the noun, van Herwerden's πολυπραγμοcύνη νῦν εἰc κεφαλὴν τράποι' ἐμοί also seems attractive by reason of its pseudo-tragic implication. Page proposed πολυχαρμοcύνη, which is clever and cannot be excluded.

843 Prepis is sometimes said to be totally unknown; see e.g. Mastromarco 177 n. 2 and Thiercy 1018. But he is presumably the person already listed in Kirchner's *Prosopographia Attica* as no. 12184, and *LGPN* ii cites the inscriptions which mention him, *IG* i^3. 79. 1, 3; 391. 7. The first shows him acting as grammateus in 422/1, a decree about building a bridge near Eleusis, and the second is from the same year, dealing with the 'traditiones primitiarum' at Eleusis. As the name is well attested I have removed from the apparatus mention of the faulty variant Premis found in the *Suda*.

879 Since πικτίc is apparently not attested elsewhere, Rennie wondered if πηκτίδαc 'bird-cages' or 'nets' is worth considering. He cited Oppian, *Ixeutica* 3. 7. This work is now better known as Dionysius, *Ixeuticon*, edited by A. Garzya (Leipzig, 1963), where the word occurs at 3. 1 and 3. 7. Garzya takes it as meaning 'cavea' or 'rete'. i.e. πηκτή, comparing the scholion on *Birds* 528, which defines πηκταί as nets; he cites also Arist. *Hist. An.* 614ᵃ12.

Recent discussions of the word are worth mention. C. Morenilla-Talens, *Glotta*, 64 (1986), 216–21, would accept πυκτίc in the sense 'Schreibtäfelchen'. The result is an incongruity in the list, which of course is not excluded in this author. What would the point be here? If we suppose that the Athenians thought all Boeotians illiterate, could it have seemed funny that a Boeotian offered writing-tablets for sale? I am not at all sure that this would be effective here, but one should not rule out the notion. O. Hansen, *Philologus*, 134 (1990), 158–9, is aware of the form πυκτίc found in B and the Aldine but accepts the form with iota in the first syllable. He suggests that this is a foreign word referring to timber imported from the Caucasus and cites words from Armenian and Georgian which he believes may be cognate. I find this rather far-fetched, and note that the two languages do not belong to the same family.

893 Borthwick, *Mnemosyne*⁴, 20 (1967), 411–12, has been followed by Mastromarco, Thiercy, and Olson in his preference for ἔκφερ', the point being that this is appropriate in a context where the *Alcestis* is being parodied. If this is right, action would be needed on stage to make the point clear, especially as the parody proper is in the following line and a half. I wonder if it is not better to have the object removed, i.e. taken into the house.

894 Olson reports the defence by Taillardat of the transmitted ἐντετευτλανωμένηc by analogy with words for culinary wrapping such as cτεγανόω, but the verb would have to be ἐντευτλ(ι)ονόω or -λ(ι)όω. It is far more likely that Blaydes was right to restore a regular form. The mistake could have been prompted by -αν- in θανών just above.

900 Elmsley restored a dialect form of Ἀθήνηcι with elision. Olson claims that elision is impossible. If the locative is really a dative, then his claim would not be valid in all dialects. Colvin 185 accepts Ἀθάναιc as dative plural and notes that it could be written with -αιc or -ηc. I do not see the need for Olson's intervention; Ἀθάναιc could be a dative of possession, which is what he posits for Βοιωτοῖcιν.

916–17 Though some editors print the plural θρυαλλίδαc in 916, the

Acharnians 35

singular is by no means unacceptable; in fact it might be regarded as a nice point that the informer has only detected one offending object but makes the most of the fact. Olson suggests that there is some doubt about the reading of the papyrus.

927 Rennie's ἐνδήϲω καλῶϲ, following a basic idea propounded by Elmsley and others, is worth considering. He notes that καλῶϲ occurs in the scholion on 928. That of course may result from its occurrence in the text in 930; but he was right to note that φερόμενοϲ in 928 may have induced a scribe to write φέρω.

938, 949 I follow Parker, *Songs*, 143, in believing that the overall metrical shape of this passage favours deletion in 949. In 938 τά presumably implies 'our affairs' or 'the affairs of the city'.

951 If πρὸϲ πάντα 'for all purposes' is found difficult O. Schroeder's suggestion, *Hermes*, 68 (1933), 467, τὸν πάντα may be considered. This type of expression is exemplified by LSJ s.v. πᾶϲ D. II. 4. πρὸϲ could have displaced the article, being repeated from πρόϲβαλλ' above. Olson cites Xen. *Mem*. 4. 6. 9 ὃ οἶϲθα πρὸϲ πάντα καλὸν ὄν, which is not quite precise as a parallel.

959 If Dicaeopolis says τίϲ ἐϲτι he is to be imagined as not having looked up to identify the new intruder. This is intelligible; Elmsley's τί ἐϲτι as in *Knights* 150 is of course an easy change.

993 The accentuation of ἠ is open to doubt; but ἦ, though rare in Aristophanes, is found several times in its affirmative sense, as listed by Denniston, *GP* 584, in his Addenda and Corrigenda to p. 280. See further the note on 1111–12 below.

994 Modern editors have not asked what the particle γ' is doing in this line. It is not part of the combination ἀλλά . . . γε. I have little doubt that Blaydes saw the truth and that the line is if anything improved if both pronouns are repeated from 993.

997 L's ὄρχον is by our standards a most inelegant repetition after 995, and of the various conjectures ὤϲχον is the best. It could well be right, but I note that in the imitation of this passage by Aelian, *Letter* 4, there is no phrase corresponding to this line. That could mean that Aelian had a text with repetition of ὄρχον and chose to eliminate it. Of course it is also possible that the text of Aelian is faulty.

1037 Olson defends the transmitted text by taking ταῖc cπονδαῖcιν as instrumental; on balance I prefer the slight emendation by Dobree.

1055 The accentuation of χιλίων is a puzzle. It looks to me as if the MSS here and at *Knights* 660, as well as at Dem. 22. 21, 28, have paroxytone accents. At *Peace* 1237 R and V have perispomenon and the scholia are silent, while the scholia on the other two Aristophanes passages and the *Suda* entry χιλιῶν recommend perispomenon, as does Herodian i. 426. 11–12 = Iohannes Alexandrinus according to Lentz; this is not the medical writer who composed commentaries on Hippocrates and Galen some time between 550 and 650 AD, but the author of an epitome, ed. W. Dindorf (Leipzig, 1825), who is identified (wrongly?) with the well-known grammarian and philosophical commentator John Philoponus; see *RE* ix/2, s.v. Ioannes no. 21, cols. 1781–2. J. Vendryes, *Traité d'accentuation grecque* (Paris, 1945), 210, accepts Herodian's doctrine as valid 'sans doute à cause de l'emploi fréquent de l'adjectif à côté du substantif δραχμῶν'. One does not see why mere proximity should have had any effect, if the noun itself is included in the statement rather than being understood. So I remain sceptical about the validity of Herodian's rule.

1080 The symmetry of the dialogue in the following scene makes it virtually certain that a line is missing here. Cf. on 1142 below.

1093 can be accepted as it stands if we assume that it is a squib directed either at the—perhaps not very frequent—heterosexual adventures of the famous Harmodius, or at the proclivities of one of his descendants, of whom we know nothing else. Of the many conjectures made by scholars uneasy about taking this view none is convincing; it is all very well to introduce a quotation from the famous skolion, but what then follows at the end of the line?

1111–12 Chadwick 129 discusses the affirmative use of ἠ (no accent printed). *Birds* 162 and 1397 show it used in initial position of its clause. He links it with ἀλλ' ἠ in the sense 'to be sure', citing *Lys.* 928 and *Knights* 953. But the first of these passages is printed as a question by recent editors and the latter passage would be a puzzle if printed as an affirmative; when one has said 'the seal looks different', to continue 'to be sure, I can't see' leaves something to be desired.

Chadwick also says that 1111–12 are 'sometimes regarded as

Acharnians

interrogative'. He does not bother to say that Denniston, *GP* 28, rejected the view of K–G ii. 145 that ἀλλ' ἤ corresponds to the Latin *at profecto*, which was based only on Eur. *Alc.* 816. This is a difficult question; Denniston does also refer to Neil on *Knights* 953; cf. *Thesm.* 97, *Knights* 1162, *Lys.* 928.

1142 Given that almost every remark of Lamachus in this scene is capped by Dicaeopolis with a response of equal length, it seems extremely unlikely that the pattern was abandoned for the final exchange between them. A. Müller's 1863 edition entertains the idea of supplementing *exempli gratia* καὶ βάδιζ' ὦ παῖ λαβών | ἰοῦ παπαιάξ. This is a variation on an earlier proposal. Blaydes cites R. Klotz, *Jahns Jahrbücher für Philologie und Pädagogik*, 73 (1856), 550–1 with κνῖcα in place of ἰοῦ. Van Herwerden (1862, p. vii) had the same idea, offering cίζει instead of ἰοῦ.

1150 The form ξυγγραφῆ is very dubious. Threatte ii. 234 says that the many hundreds of examples of ἱερέα, demotics in -(consonant)έα, φλυέα, and especially the very frequent γραμματέα never show any variation from the normal -έα termination; the contraction is quite foreign to Attic. Although Parker, *Songs*, 151, notes that the responsion of choriamb and iambic metron is possible, and Sommerstein cites as parallels Eur. *Alc.* 25, *El.* 439, I doubt if they are acceptable; in the former passage Diggle's text now has ἱερέα and in the latter we have the proper name Achilles in elevated lyric.

1168 Rennie's neat and simple conjecture should not go unmentioned. I suspect the same easy transposition of consonants should be made at *Birds* 56.

1182 Olson seems unwilling to contemplate the possibility that πεcὸν is corrupt and I find it hard to understand what view he takes of the sentence. Despite Cooper–Krüger i. 841 (§56. 9. 6C), who think that we have here a comic extension of a known construction, I do not believe that an accusative absolute is admissible and think it far easier to assume that the last word of 1080 has caused a corruption here. Bergk tried λιπών and Weber, *Aristophanische Studien* (Leipzig, 1908), 114–16, κλάcαc, which Sommerstein, *CQ*[2] 28 (1978), 392, objected to as a word not found in our author or in tragedy. Weber's proposal leads me to suggest either θλάcαc, another verb known from epic but apparently not from tragedy, or φλάcαc, which has the advantage that Aristophanes uses it elsewhere, and though it is absent from tragedy it appears at Pind. *Nem.* 10. 68.

1185 If γε is right, it is to be explained as an instance of reinforcement of apposition, as in Denniston, *GP* 138–9 (noted by Sommerstein in *CQ*² 28 (1978), 393). R omits the particle; if this were a partial preservation of the truth rather than a minor slip, one would be tempted to have recourse to A. Palmer's τοὐράνιον (*The Quarterly Review*, 158 (1884), 365); though he does not say so, the assumption lying behind his proposal is that the adjective derived from the *nomen sacrum* οὐρανός was corrupted. This ingenious notion is more plausible than recent editors have been willing to allow.

If γε is wrong one needs to explain its presence in MSS which derive from a hyparchetype that is presumably earlier than Triclinius. Whereas his use of the particle as a supplement was based on a respectable level of metrical knowledge, other Byzantines might conceivably have employed it as a means of creating a twelfth syllable in the line in accordance with contemporary practice (though strictly speaking, if they wished to follow the rules fully, they should also have found a way of making the penultimate syllable accented).

1222 Olson notes that if the name Pittalos is to be given in the genitive, the formula with εἰc and the definite article is unusual, and he hesitates to accept *Eccl.* 420 as a satisfactory parallel. But the usage can perhaps be justified by Plat. *Rep.* 328 B εἰc τοῦ Πολεμάρχου. Blaydes's ὡc τοὺc has the minor advantage of making the utterances of the two characters match more closely.

Knights

Dramatis personae Whether the two slaves should be named Nicias and Demosthenes has been discussed frequently. I have nothing to add other than to record my feeling that Sommerstein's commonsense approach (p. 9 of his edition) is right. In CQ^2 30 (1980), 46–7 he concluded that a definite answer to the puzzle cannot be given, but made the important observations that (i) in 87–8 and 97 the second slave is portrayed as abstemious, which is highly unusual and may be intended to reflect Nicias' ascetic and unsociable character, (ii) if portrait masks were used, the issue would be settled. A slight doubt arises from 358. Although, as Sommerstein says, the slaves are not named in the text, Nicias is mentioned as the Sausage-Seller's target in 358. If 'Nicias' was on the stage at that point, the phrasing of the line would be open to objection; but Sommerstein rightly suggests that his last utterance at 234 was made from inside the building.

4 εἰςήρρηςεν is the reading of the MSS and is found elsewhere in Aristophanes. But the scholiast records a variant εἰςέφρηςεν from the much rarer verb εἰςφρέω, and the future of that verb is attested at *Wasps* 892, where it is transitive. LSJ say that it can also be intransitive and quote Polybius 21. 27. 7 and Alciphron 3. 17 (3. 53). In those passages the text appears to be sound and the meaning is to 'slip in'. Was this usage confined to Hellenistic and later authors? Perhaps not, since Alciphron pillaged Attic comedy for material and vocabulary.

If the MSS are correct, the variant has to be explained as a gloss, which is unlikely in view of its rarity, or as a suggestion for improvement made by a learned reader. If the variant is right, the MSS reading is a gloss.

8–12 Sommerstein (2001: 239) reports W. Kraus's observation that the usual order of the speakers should be reversed so as to avoid a prima facie inconsistency between 8b–9 and 11–12. If the conventional arrangement is retained, Demosthenes has a change of mind.

8 Though Denniston, *GP* 216–17, accepted δή without discussion, R is not here supported by the *Suda* as it usually is, and its reading may be an aberration. The papyrus sides with the rest of the tradition.

32 Was Blaydes right to punctuate after ἐτεόν? Postponement of γάρ is possible, so his choice is not obligatory.

49 Deictic iota is used for citations, not just to point at something; *Wasps* 55 is another good example. LSJ fails to make this clear. At 492 below the deictic pronoun refers to what has just been said; cf. 721 and 820. At *Birds* 1599 it introduces a specification of the terms to be agreed between Zeus and the birds.

56 It is hard to choose between the variants here. The prepositions περί and παρά are so easily and so frequently confused in medieval MSS, because they were abbreviated in almost identical fashion. Either compound would make sense here. Sommerstein cited *Wasps* 837 in favour of παρα-, while περι- gets support from 65.

61 Most MSS have εἶθ' ὁ, but the temporal sense seems less satisfactory. How is the error to be explained? Perhaps κᾆτα in 64 influenced the scribe. Bergk suspected that εἶτ' should be restored in 62 for ὁ δ', and I incline to this view. The second δέ in 61 then falls into the category exemplified by Denniston, *GP* 169–70, equivalent here to γάρ in a parenthesis.

66 Blaydes here proposed cείει for αἰτεῖ because it is used with ταράττω at 840 below and perhaps αἰτεῖ seemed to him a trifle colourless by comparison with the other expressions in this sentence. He also cited fr. 228 ἔcειον, ᾔτουν χρήματ', ἠπείλουν, ἐcυκοφάντουν, which may be a hint that he would have preferred a construction of αἰτεῖν with an explicit object. Cf. also *Peace* 619 with Olson's note. The corruption is not easy to explain unless one assumes that αἰτεῖ is a gloss on a rare word. A conceivable alternative might be ᾄττει 'he dashes about', for which there are parallels in ps.-Dem. 25. 52, Plat.

Theaet. 144 A, 190 A (cf. also Isaeus 4. 10, Plat. *Alc. 1* 118 B, *Legg.* 709 A).

At the end of the line editors may have been right to restore the deictic form.

89 D. D. Heath, *Journal of Philology*, 5 (1874), 183–4, explained the adjective in the light of his experience while waiting for a steamer at Reggio Calabria. He was near a fountain where a man 'made it his business to amuse the ladies, young and old, by jokes and grotesque tricks, as by lifting up a water-pot full of water, and in a manner simulating drunkenness pouring the water down his throat from a distance of a foot or so above his head'. He thought a similar buffoon might have existed in Greece.

Blaydes put forward the view that the element -ληραῖοc appears more likely to derive from a feminine noun than a masculine one and so he preferred to adopt a suggestion made by Bentley, to emend to -λημαῖοc, which he printed in his text. It seems that this linguistic argument is not cogent; -αῖοc can be used to form the adjective of masculine nouns, e.g. κηπαῖοc from κῆποc. But does the proposal deserve approval on grounds of sense? And did the poet write an adjective or a neuter noun here? Some support for the change may come from *Plutus* 581, where Κρονικαὶ λῆμαι seems to indicate old-fashioned prejudice, and from the fact that at least in later antiquity there was a proverbial expression λημᾶν χύτραιc ἢ κολοκύνταιc (Diogenian 3. 10 in Leutsch–Schneidewin vol. ii (5. 63 in vol. i).

Van Herwerden (1869), 163, repeated in *Mnemosyne²*, 30 (1902), 40, tried κρουνοχυτο-, rendering 'e fonte manans'.

As far as the accent is concerned, the MSS have proparoxytone, which Neil retains. This appears to be correct, cf. Chandler, *GA* 109 (§355) for the rare exceptions and p. 153 (§536); but simple adjectives in -αῖοc with more than two syllables are properispomenon with very few exceptions; cf. ibid. 116–17 (§§378–80). That is presumably why Dobree altered the accent here.

173 Though R's present imperative could be right here, the aorists in 169 and 170 tip the balance in favour of the majority reading.

174 The reference to Carthage can stand; see Neil's note. A Byzantine scribe might have absent-mindedly introduced the name of

Chalcedon because of the Church Council held there in 451 (this mistake is attested in a Byzantine author: Theophanes, *Chronographia*, 301. 12 and 15, where the correct reading is Carthage and has been restored from the Latin version of Anastasius Bibliothecarius). The same variant occurs below at 1303. However, in Photius, *Bibliotheca* 38^{b}20 ('codex' 72, Ctesias) the correct reading Χαλκηδονίων is found in MS A, whereas M has Καρχηδονίων, and it is not obvious that the context induced the error. Other passages where the names are variants or require emendation are Herodotus 4. 144. 2, Arrian, *Anabasis* 3. 24. 5, Diogenes Laertius 2. 106, and Athenaeus 7. 320 A.

175 For γ' see Fraenkel, *BzA* 47–8. The sarcasm gives a better effect than δ', when the sentence becomes a question.

184 The notion of good or bad conscience is not often expressed in classical Greek; is this the first occurrence? With this line one may compare *Wasps* 999. See the article 'Gewissen' by H. Chadwick in *Reallexikon für Antike und Christentum*, x (1978); at col. 1035 he quotes these passages and *Thesm.* 471–7, referring also to Eur. *Hipp.* 271–317, 1290–2, *Bacch.* 1259–62, *Andr.* 805–10, *Or.* 396. To have a bad conscience seems to be the meaning of the verb at Lysias 7. 36 and Isocrates, *Demonicus* 16. Later examples I have noted are found at Pausanias 7. 10. 10 and Porphyry, *Vita Pythagorae* 40. cυνεπίcταμαι with the same meaning occurs at Gorgias, *Palamedes* 36.

190 See Fraenkel, *BzA* 45–7, for the word-order. He is followed by Sommerstein in recognizing here a case of Wackernagel's law about the tendency of enclitics, particles, and unstressed pronouns to take second position in a clause. Henderson differs.

193 Neil here observed: 'It is hardly credible that the text is right, but I know of no good correction.' Both Meineke and van Herwerden (1862: p. vii) tried to put the syntax right by inserting ἧκεν and ἥκει respectively after βδελυρόν. More recent scholars seem strangely unworried. The meaning ought to be 'affairs have now come into the hands of an ignorant and repulsive man' or perhaps 'everyone now turns to an ignorant and repulsive man'. The damage to the text is probably more serious than hitherto supposed, and I wonder if the equivalent of one line has fallen out after βδελυρόν.

218 The accentuation of ἀγόραιος is problematic. B. I. Wheeler, *Der griechische Nominalaccent* (Strassburg, 1885), 118, differs from Chandler and cites evidence from three sources, Ammonius, Philoponus, and Zonaras, purporting to show that the accent varied according to the meaning. Though all three sources make a distinction, they do not agree about what it was. One is tempted to ask whether the distinction is just a figment of grammarians' imagination. On Ammonius 11 Nickau in his Teubner edition of 1966 notes that different doctrine is to be found in *Etymologicum Gudianum* 16. 6d. According to this the properispomenon is used of Hermes Agoraios, proparoxytone when the word refers to a day. Provisionally I follow R, without much confidence, but in the hope that it here has a remnant of the truth.

220 Van Herwerden, *Mnemosyne*², 30 (1902), 41–2, felt that hendiadys was not an acceptable explanation of the line. τὸ Πυθικόν can hardly refer to anything but an oracle from Delphi, and there has been no reference to one. Hence van Leeuwen's κατά for καί does not really remove the difficulty. Van Herwerden argued that the line interrupts the flow of Demosthenes' thought, but he did not suggest a reason for the interpolation. Sommerstein wondered if the line could be a quotation from tragedy because of the lack of a definite article with χρηϲμοί. My suspicion is that it was a marginal addition, a parallel that occurred to a learned reader, that entered the text.

247 In the scene beginning with the chorus' entry at 247 there are various difficult, perhaps insoluble, puzzles about the attribution of lines. One way of looking at the question is to consider whether Demosthenes has any part to play. It was his summons in 242–6 which brought the chorus into the action. Editors tend to give him little or no part in the action for a while after this; nearly all bring him back at 282–3. But as he has shown some initiative, is it likely that he then recedes into the background during a lively conversation lasting from 255 until 281? Coulon gave him 274 and Gomme 258–60, noting that this makes the plural ξυνεπίκειϲθ' of 266 more pointed.

255 Threatte ii. 117 confirms that φράτηρ is the only form attested in Athens.

260 A. W. Gomme, *CR*² 8 (1958), 1–2, argued against taking μὴ πέπων as 'ripening', no parallel having been offered. So either ὠμός or μὴ πέπων must go. 'Large and juicy' is the meaning he would have expected. Instead of ὠμὸς ὠχρός 'pale with anxiety' is a possibility, with χλωρός a less plausible alternative.

μὴ πέπων is taken as 'not quite ripe' by Blaydes and Rogers, 'not yet ripe' by Sommerstein. Though this is perhaps better than trying to extract the sense 'ripening', which was favoured by Neil, I am not sure that in Greek it was possible to omit the adverbial modifier; hence Kock's μηδέπω.

266–8 Here Paphlagon reacts with annoyance as he realizes that it is not just the other slaves but the chorus who are against him. His first two words are usually now printed as a question, following the suggestion of Casaubon (Mastromarco's edition is an exception). Editors then treat the following sentence as a statement: 'I am being beaten up on your account, gentlemen, because I was on the point of proposing that it is right and proper to set up on the Acropolis a monument to your bravery.' This statement makes no sense. No one reacting with injured innocence to what he claims is an undeserved attack would say that the attack has occurred because he was trying to help the aggressor; it is not a causal connection between these two elements of the context, the aggression and the help, that would be alleged. The complaint only becomes plausible if the speaker says 'I am being beaten up at a time when I was on the point of doing you a good turn' The causal element is latent, not explicit. Read ὅτε, not ὅτι. And probably the whole sentence is a question, which conveys better the feeling of surprise or outrage. This use of ὅτε with latent causal sense is not rare in the plays and several instances occur as part of a question (*Clouds* 717, *Wasps* 1134, *Thesm.* 707, *Frogs* 22).

266 For R's omission of the vocative particle see above on *Acharnians* 53.

268 Elmsley's restoration of a transitive verb seems an improvement; it suits a speaker who is trying to claim credit for his own initiative.

269 εἶδες in the singular is presumably addressed to a fellow member of the chorus or Demosthenes. Blaydes (1902: 129) wondered if the plural might be more appropriate. E. W. Whittle, *CR*² 22 (1972), 362, in his review of M. Kaimio, *The Chorus of Greek Drama within the Light of the Person and Number Used* (Helsinki, 1970), summed up by saying: 'In Aristophanes the collective aspect of the chorus is, by contrast, more predominant; the plural is slightly more frequent in all contexts except choral lyrics, and even there the proportion of singular passages is much smaller than in tragedy.'

271 Sommerstein (2001: 239) suggests γ' ἐνιῇ for γε νικᾷ, adapting P. T. Eden's proposal ἐνῆται. This technical term of cavalry warfare is used in the active in the two Xenophon passages he cites, *Cyr.* 7. 1. 29 and *Hell.* 2. 4. 32. Palaeographically γ' ἐνιῇ is most attractive if we may imagine a mistake arising from a minuscule archetype: eta and kappa were easily confused, and one letter was added to create a form of a well-known word. But the assumption is far from secure; and if an uncial archetype is assumed, the corruption is not much more difficult.

276 Denniston, *GP* 404, is prepared to accept the paradosis here, assuming that ἀλλά ... μέντοι introduces the main clause while γε goes with ἐάν. But I do not feel happy at this interweaving of two particle formulae. Porson's slight change seems on balance better. It creates a good antithesis between the two accusative pronouns. R. E. Harder, *Hermes*, 124 (1996), 35–6, noted the absence of a pronoun in 276 as transmitted by the MSS and used this as an argument to support the attribution of 274 to the Sausage-Seller. But she was unaware of Porson's proposal.

295 As λαλεῖν tends to mean 'chatter' I prefer to see in the text a more vigorous term that can be traded as an insult.

301–2 See Parker, *Songs*, 37, for the metrical effect intended here. The scansion of ἱεράς is a problem; cf. *Birds* 373, 1113, *Eccl.* 1156. Hermann, *Elementa doctrinae metricae*, 2. vi. 3, proposed ἱράς but later offered ἔχοντά c' ἱεράς.

310–11 Whereas in 310 the genitive of the personal pronoun is obviously natural and correct, in the following line a dative of the person concerned seems more idiomatic.

327 *LGPN* ii does not list Hippodamos, and there is no suitable

bearer of the name Hippodamas. Hermann and Kock proposed to read Hippodamnos, but this too fails to receive support from *LGPN*. The identification with the famous town–planner is controversial; see Gomme, CR^2 8 (1958), 2–4, Sommerstein, CQ^2 30 (1980), 47–8, P. Benvenuti Falciai, *Ippodamo di Mileto architetto e filosofo* (Florence, 1982), 119–21.
But the metrical problem here is serious. We have a choriamb instead of the expected trochaic metron. Olson on *Peace* 1154 cites as parallels Aesch. *ScT* 488 and 547, which are generally accepted as examples of anaclasis (cf. Maas, *Greek Metre*, §107, West, *Greek Metre*, 82). Iambo–choriambic equivalence is one thing, but is it what we have here?

339 αὐτὸ is difficult. Sommerstein does not translate it, whereas Ribbeck offered 'grade'. The nearest parallel I can find is *Lysistrata* 286.

347 ξένου μετοίκου is accepted by D. Whitehead, *The Ideology of the Athenian Metic* (Cambridge, 1977), 21 n. 34, 139 n. 61. If it is right, this is a technical term which sounds rather formal. Perhaps something colloquial is more appropriate; rather than von Velsen's ἀξένου one might try Εὐξένου, which is well attested in *LGPN* ii. Müller-Strübing's ἀπρόξενου is ingenious enough to be worth a mention in the apparatus.

353 Thiercy 1039 reads δ' ἄρ' and translates 'À ce que je vois, tu n'as trouvé qu'un simple homme à m'opposer?' I confess to not understanding what is wrong with γὰρ in a question of this kind. It would fit into the category V (6) (ii) in Denniston, *GP* 77–8.

357 ἐκπιὼν may be right here, even if R and the *Suda* have ἐπιπιὼν as in 354. The speaker caps his rival's remark with a more emphatic expression.

358 'I shall ruffle Nicias' boasts the Sausage-Seller. As Nicias was notoriously diffident, this is no achievement to boast of in competition with the Paphlagonian, and I cannot believe that the text is right. Bentley made a different objection, that Nicias is on stage in the person of one of the slaves, and wondered if cφηκιὰν ταράξω should be written. A slip on the part of the dramatist? No, because we may assume that Nicias disappeared into the stage building at 154 and speaks from within at 234.

But it is essential to find a word that matches κατακλβάcω for vigour and vulgarity. Although ἀράξω is palaeographically close and is vigorous, it is hardly vulgar (the uncompounded verb is plausibly restored at *Clouds* 1373 and *Lys.* 459; cf. also *Eccl.* 977). My preferred solution is λαπάξω, 'I'll evacuate his bowels for him'. Sommerstein (2001: 239) seems to be on the right track when he tentatively suggests translating 'make Nicias shit himself', since ταράττω occasionally refer to gastric disturbance, as at *Clouds* 386 and in the Corpus Hippocraticum. It is not, however, a sufficiently vulgar expression to be right here.

359–60 The punctuation is not quite certain. τὸν ζωμὸν τῶν πραγμάτων seems more attractive as a locution than ἐν τῶν πραγμάτων and with some hesitation I prefer it, despite the objection that ὁτιὴ cannot occupy its normal position of first in its clause. Blaydes even wondered if τῶν ῥημάτων should be written.

370–4 are difficult. Ideally the threats of both speakers should reach a climax. Various transpositions have been suggested, the latest being that of Henderson, who favours 373, 370, 372, 371. I am not entirely convinced by this, since it is not clear to me that the leather-worker would end his task by pegging the hide on the ground. Perhaps Sommerstein (2001: 239) is right to suspect the loss of a line after 369 and 370.

The accusation of theft in 370 at first sight looks as if it should be directed at Paphlagon; but note that he too uses it later at 828.

394 It is difficult to be sure of the exact form of the verb to be adopted here. Some light is thrown on the problem by the presentation of the evidence in the new edition of the comic fragments. In Ar. fr. 308 (Pollux 10. 187) from the second *Peace* the reading ἀνεῖτ' was proposed by Kaibel; the MSS oscillate between ἀν- and αἰν-. Pherecrates fr. 197 (cited from Pausanias the grammarian in Eustathius 801. 57) has ἀνεῖν. But Hesychius α 4819 has ἀνεῖν and Herodian, *Π. μον. λεξ.* ii. 930. 28 L αἴνειν, while Aelius Dionysius ap. Photius α 603 gives the contracted form αἰνεῖν with smooth breathing.

Here ἀφανεῖ as in R could be right. The grammarians did not agree about the form of the word or its meaning, since some thought it was a process for steeping barley in water, others equated it with πτίccειν. Schwyzer i 694 and *DGE* accept this reading; the latter cites Hesychius α 8647–8 ἄφηνα: ἔκοψα and ἀφῆναι: τὸ τὰc ἐπτιcμένας κριθὰς ταῖc χερcὶ τρῖψαι. But cutting and winnowing are not the best notions to import into this context.

E. K. Borthwick, CQ^2 19 (1969), 243–4, was willing to accept either Ribbeck's conjecture or R's reading, continuing the metaphor of 392–3. The central point in his note is that the scholia appear to refer to the process of winnowing, since they speak of the threshing-floor. The rare word could therefore be a synonym for πτίccω, meaning to separate the wheat from the chaff; Cleon is alleged to have selected the best of the Spartan prisoners from Pylos to be exploited financially. I have wondered exactly how this was to be arranged with prisoners from a society which did not have its own currency; it is not hard to imagine that the Spartans already operated in the way suggested by Plato for his Utopia (*Legg.* 742 AB), with the government holding foreign currency or bullion for military and diplomatic purposes; presumably this derived from booty or other ill-gotten gains. The present passage is not discussed by S. Hodkinson, *Property and Wealth in Classical Sparta* (London, 2000), 167–70, but he does helpfully refer to Androtion, *FGrH* 324 F 44, which records the ransom of prisoners for one mina each in 408/7. Whether this was private or state money is not clear.

397–8 μεθίcτηcι is transitive and would require us to take the following genitive as partitive. Hirschig's μεθέcτηκε avoids that difficulty, but I feel it is easier to follow van Herwerden and restore the rarer verb μεθίηcι so as to create more normal syntax.

454 ἀνδρικώτατα καὶ creates a metrical oddity for which there is only the dubious parallel of *Acharnians* 849. Dindorf's ἀνδρειότατα is commended by Bentley's emendation at *Peace* 498.

474 ταῦτ' here is not very forceful, and indeed Sommerstein (2001: 240) recommends translating 'this' with emphasis. So Blaydes may have been right to suggest πάντ'. These words are often confused. At Isocr. *Areop.* 20 πάντα was proposed by Korais for ταῦτα of the MSS and Richards 226 later made the same suggestion; he claimed to

Knights 49

know of other examples of this confusion but did not list them. In Dem. 8. 13 Tournier plausibly tried πάντα for ταῦτα, and the MSS are divided between these two words at 18. 69, 125. In comedy the question recurs repeatedly; see the proposals at *Clouds* 588 (Bentley), 631 (Blaydes), 697 (Wilson), *Wasps* 798 (Reiske), *Frogs* 703 (van Herwerden), *Plutus* 471 (Blaydes). Note also that at *Wasps* 346 R has πάντων for τούτων, while at Aesch.(?) *PV* 505 ταῦτα is found in some MSS for πάντα. Further examples are cited by J. Diggle, *Euripidea* (Oxford, 1994), 494. Similarly αὐτά and πάντα may have been confused; see *Frogs* 1466 and *Eccl.* 807. For τἄλλα at *Wasps* 939 Blaydes tried πάντα; cf. *Lys.* 1273.

526–7 are problematic. The occurrence of ῥεύcαc and ἔρρει so close together is far from elegant by modern standards, and I am not sure if it is protected by the examples cited in the Addenda A of Jackson, *MS* 220–2. But that is not all. ῥεύcαc is not well attested in Attic at this date and might easily be a gloss which has taken the place of a still more vigorous expression; many suggestions have been made. Threatte ii. 515–16 has no example of ῥευ- because the aorist is evidently not found in inscriptions; but Schwyzer i. 685–6 suggests the passive ἐρρύην as the normal Attic form. Van Herwerden, *Mnemosyne*², 30 (1902), 43, objected to the aorist and reckoned that our text probably results from a desperate attempt to fill a lacuna. He saw some merit in van Leeuwen's πλήθων, cf. Iliad 5. 87, 11. 492, where it is used of a river flowing over or into a plain.

ἀφελῶν is translated 'the broad plains of artlessness' by Sommerstein, 'les plaines uniformes' by Thiercy, 'les plaines unies' by van Daele. 'Through the level (open) plains' says Blaydes. Such renderings do not inspire complete confidence, nor do emendations convince immediately. Van Herwerden, who had tried ὁμαλῶν (loc. cit.) later suggested ἀφνεῶν (1906: 21), which is not ridiculous; Thuc. 1. 13. 5 uses it of a χωρίον. The *Supplement* to LSJ has a useful suggestion: 'in apparent allusion to Cratinus' style', which if correct can be used to support the view that the poet was creating the vocabulary later used in formal literary criticism. O. Imperio, *Parabasi di Aristofane: Acarnesi Cavalieri Vespe Uccelli* (Bari, 2004), 195–6, cites Hesychius α 8593 πεδία ἀφελῆ· τὰ cύνδενδρα and renders 'pianure boscose, piene di alberi'. I suppose that flat country, thickly wooded, can be so described; but what is the relevance of this concept to Cratinus or Attica?

536 The transmitted text means that there was a statue of Dionysus in the front row. C. F. Russo, *Aristophanes an Author for the Stage*, rev. and expanded edn. (London, 1994), 48–9, says that a statue in this position is attested for the theatre at Priene. But the helpfully illustrated guide to the site given by E. Akurgal, *Ancient Civilisations and Ruins of Turkey*, rev. edn. (London, 2002), 196–201, states that the centre of the front row was occupied by an altar rather than a statue. If there is no evidence for a statue we need to give consideration to Elmsley's simple conjecture, which introduces a reference to the priest of Dionysus and his well-known seat.

539 κραμβοτάτου in the superlative is not attested otherwise except in Hesychius, who took the word to refer to laughter. -οτάτου might well be an error of assimilation to the following word cτόματοc, and I strongly suspect that E. J. Kiehl, *Mnemosyne*, 1 (1852), 49, was right to propose κραμβοφάγου. Van Herwerden, *Mnemosyne*^{2}, 30 (1902), 43, defended the paradosis by reference to Hesychius' entries κραμβόν and κραμβότατον. The form of the adjective as transmitted is perhaps supported by the existence of κραμβαλέοc 'dry': M. G. Bonanno, *Studi su Cratete comico* (Padua, 1972), 36–8. It is amusing to note Korais' defence of the paradosis: 'simili ὑποκοριcμῷ scorta Parisiis amasios appellant *mon choux*': see N. Kalospyros in *Praktika* of the 1999 FIEC Congress (Athens, 2001), i. 444–67.

540 μόνοc is not easy; 'il a été le seul à tenir bon' says Thiercy, i.e. the only person to survive the whims of the Athenian public. But as Sommerstein points out, this makes the catalogue of the poet's predecessors end on the wrong note; the fate of Crates has to be represented as a strong deterrent. His proposal μόνον 'only just' seems to me not fully satisfactory; I would translate 'he merely survived' and wonder if it is sufficiently forceful. Better is van Leeuwen's μόλιc.

545 cωφρονικῶc is not a common word; this may be its first occurrence and one must ask why cώφρων ἦν was not the poet's choice of wording, as Halbertsma suggested. Perhaps the novelty of the word used added a humorous touch. The suffix -ικοc was popular at the time, cf. 1378 ff. and *Clouds* 483, 728, 1172–3. Its use in Aristophanes was the subject of an article by C. W. Peppler, *AJP* 31 (1910), 428–44, but he did not dwell on this passage.

There is another difficulty here. I think F. Ademollo, *Atene e Roma*, 39 (1994), 177–80, is right to insist that in order to achieve the required translation of the transmitted text a verb has to be supplied after the first adverb, and no suitable matching verb can be extracted from the context. If that is so, an emendation has to be sought. Sommerstein (2001: 240) agrees with Ademollo.

546 The figure eleven has not been explained. Is there any chance that this numeral had a special significance? J. MacQueen, *Numerology: Theory and Outline History of a Literary Mode* (Edinburgh, 1985), gives no hint that could justify such a hypothesis.

580 I follow van Leeuwen and Sommerstein in accepting 'tiara' as the meaning of cτλεγγίc with the consequent minor emendation of ἀπ- to ἀν- (the latter compound is not recorded in *DGE*). Henderson translates 'our use of luxurious bathing utensils', but the adjective is hardly to be extracted from the Greek. Van Leeuwen adduced as verbs of parallel formation ἀναδῆcαι and ἀναcτεφανῶcαι.

589 Here Sommerstein translates 'Victory the companion of our choral songs, who strives with us against our foes'. Apart from the fact that χορικὰ is more naturally taken as an adjective than a noun, it may be asked whether 'our' can legitimately be extracted by anticipation from ἡμῶν. Wilamowitz, *Hermes*, 14 (1879), 186 = *Kleine Schriften*, iv. 22, clearly thought not, and he was followed by Kock (in his third edition of 1882); the essential point is that 'non omnium ... sodalis Victoria est sed alterius partis' (he might have said 'of only one among several competitors'). A word is needed which indicates the divinity's good will towards the poet and the chorus.

Sommerstein (2001: 244) cites Zimmermann's remark that mention of Athena bringing Nike would remind Athenians of the cult-image of Athena Parthenos, who held Nike in her hand. One might add that they should also have been reminded of the temple of Athena Nike, on which work had begun again in 427.

628 Thiercy 1040 proposes ἐρέccων for ἐρείδων, comparing *Clouds* 1367 and Soph. *Ajax* 252. The former passage includes the word κρημνοποιόν, and I cannot see how that supports his proposal; but the latter describes how the Atreidae make repeated threats, ἐρέccουcιν ἀπειλάc. Aesch. ScT 854–6 could also be quoted for ἐρέccω, the object there being a πιτυλὸν γόον; also Soph. Ant. 158 ἐρέccων μῆτιν. The objects in these three examples are less physical than κρημνούc.

The argument from *difficilior lectio* may still be thought to favour Brunck's notion; after ἤρειδε a rare verb was more likely to be corrupted and κρημνοὺc ἐρέccων seems unduly bold an expression even for Aristophanes.

637 Neil noted that three MSS give the form γλῶccαν, which is more in accordance with the paratragic style. According to Blaydes that reading is to be found in 'BCpr. X[=Laur. 31. 13]Ald.' Its presence in B might be thought a lucky accident, but it does seem preferable.

648 Is the point of ταχύ 'I at once advised them, in secrecy, in order to . . .' or 'I advised them, in secrecy, immediately, in order to . . .'? In the latter case the separation of the adverb from the verb it modifies is not easy, and the awkwardness could be avoided by placing 650 before 649, as suggested, but without a statement of the pros and cons, by Wilamowitz, *Hermes*, 14 (1879), 185 = *Kleine Schriften*, iv. 22.

651 The emphatic form of the pronoun ἔμ' is a trifle surprising; the important fact was that the audience gaped, not that they looked at him rather than Paphlagon (contrast 663). Conceivably one might read πρὸc ἐπεκεχήνεcαν 'and what's more they gaped in my direction'; the compound verb is rare but attested in Lucian, who read his classical authors with care.

666 An amusing example of the desire to add obscenity to Aristophanes' text is Scaliger's proposal (see p. 920 of the 1670 Amsterdam edition) to read ἐcτυκότεc. This was noted by Daubuz in his copy of the Gelenius edition (British Library 1348 i. 1) and Casaubon had had the same idea, marking above the line in his copy of the same edition (British Library C77 g. 12) 'f. *v*.', i.e. ' *fortasse* ἐcτυκότεc'.

694 Here again one has to ask whether the emphatic pronoun ἐμοὶ can be justified. Sommerstein's translation is 'if any of my old mendacities is left in me', and Thiercy appears to take the same view. Should one italicize 'my'? Or might it be possible to give a closer rendering as follows: 'assuming any of the same mendacities is within *my* powers'? Paphlagon would then be saying 'if I can lie as well as you did just now before the Council'.

711 What is the best way for the Sausage-Seller to cap his opponent's threat 'I'll bring you before the Demos . . .'? 'And I'll bring *you*, and slander you to greater effect' would seem appropriate. I think emphasis should fall on the pronoun. That could be achieved by writing κἀγὼ δέ ϲ', but the elision of the pronoun might be thought to weaken the effect slightly. There is also the consideration that the γε transmitted in most MSS after διαβαλῶ has not generally been accepted by modern editors, and one may conjecture that a muddle caused this particle to be misplaced.

722 Is Paphlagon momentarily pretending to be polite? Editors take ὠγάθ' to be ironical; yet van Herwerden was not stupid to wonder if ὥϲπερ should be read. In the second half of the line he shared van Leeuwen's doubts and the emendation he suggested is not drastic. Olson on *Ach.* 296 cites Dickey 119, 139, for the view that ὠγαθέ has neither friendly nor unfriendly connotations. The present passage makes me wonder if the generalization is correct.

724 Sommerstein prints the normal reading but translates 'here I go' as if he accepted βαδίζω from B[ac] and Blaydes.

742–3 are extremely difficult. (1) Suppose we retain ἐκ Πύλου. The phrase could refer to the preceding or following words: (*a*) if the former, the syntax will need adjustment, since I cannot believe that ὑποδραμών took a genitive; it would be easy to read ἀποδραμόντων, 'the generals ran away from Pylos', which is a gross exaggeration of their cautious conduct; (*b*) if the latter, 'I sailed there and brought back the Laconians from Pylos', ἀποδραμόντων is again an easy change. (2) Suppose we retain ὑποδραμών. The adjacent genitives cannot stand but a construction with the accusative is possible: 'to get in ahead of' is the sense at Eur. *IA* 631. The singular τὸν ϲτρατηγὸν as given by one of the correcting hands in Γ is palaeographically easy to justify; but as there were two generals serving at Pylos Brunck's τοὺϲ ϲτρατηγοὺϲ would be needed (cf.

355), and it is hard to avoid Brunck's and Weise's further change to ἐν Πύλῳ.

If there is something wrong with the rare word ὑποδραμών it would be better to substitute for it not a commoner word like ἀποδραμόντων but another rare one; Kock's ὑποτρεμόντων is worth considering.

774 The punctuation raises a question about the correct form of the pronoun. The emphatic cοί seems too strong, as the quantity of money in the treasury is apparently the notion to be stressed. If an enclitic is preferred, the punctuation after cοι as given by Blaydes and Neil yields the sense 'when I was serving in your interest on the Council'. Though it removes the expected diaeresis at this point in the line, it should not be ruled out; see White, *Verse*, 126–8.

Punctuation before cοι, as in Sommerstein, leaves an enclitic following punctuation when the preceding words are more substantial than a mere vocative. Though this seems questionable there are a few examples which are extremely difficult to emend away; see Olson on *Peace* 20–3. The most striking example is Eur. *Cycl.* 676. The combination of that line and 774 may be thought to justify a still more awkward case at 851 below.

786 For the form ἔκγονος see Barrett on Eur. *Hipp.* 447–50.

803 Blaydes was exercised by the position of cου, not liking to understand the phrasing as equivalent to τὰ πανουργήματά cου, which is what Neil recommended, citing as parallel Plat. *Gorg.* 517c ἀγνοοῦντες ἀλλήλων ὅ τι λέγομεν, 'misunderstanding each others' statements'. That may explain the genitive; other parallels, not all equally persuasive, are assembled by Cooper–Krüger i. 205 (§47. 10. 8A). I continue to have doubts, even if none of Blaydes's suggestions carries conviction. One might wonder if πως 'somehow' was appropriate to the context. Was cου mistakenly introduced partly as a result of cε in the next line?

805 εἰ with the subjunctive was noted by K–G ii. 474 Anmerkung 1, as occurring in Homer, the poets and Herodotus, but rare and doubtful in prose. Thuc. 6. 21 and Plat. *Legg.* 761c were cited, and both these examples have survived in some modern editions. At 698 and 700 above R has εἰ and I have accepted this. A fuller treatment in

Cooper–Krüger i. 741 (§54. 12. 3) reveals the complexity of the situation; their examples from Thucydides have not survived in Alberti's authoritative text (Rome, 1972–2000).

808 τὴν ψῆφον seems regularly to be translated 'a voting pebble', but the definite article needs to be accounted for; could one say 'his voting pebble', i.e. his usual weapon? A. Palmer, *Quarterly Review*, 158 (1884), 365, believed that it should be replaced by τε and cited *Birds* 255 as a sentence of very similar structure, where τε links the third item in a sequence of the kind 'A, B, and C'. Blaydes tried ψῆφόν τιν' ἰχνεύων and ψῆφον κατιχνεύων. Is it by synecdoche the institution of the jury vote (H.-S.)?

814 The latest attempt to deal with the crux here is that of Thiercy 1051–2, who substitutes πύργων for εὐρών. He sees a contrast between Themistocles' elaborate fortification of Athens and the internal divisions caused by Cleon's policies mentioned in 817–18. This is ingenious, and he has a point when he notes that Themistocles' main achievement was not the improvement of the water supply, to which Sommerstein sees an allusion. Neil noted from Pollux 5. 133 that ἐπιχειλής means 'nearly full'. That seems to offer insufficient contrast to μεστήν. One would prefer a word meaning 'half full'. Could Blaydes' ὑποχειλής (*lexicis addendum*) mean 'not full to the lip'?

835 As the sum of money named is surprisingly small, Zacher wondered if the difficulty could be remedied by reading μυριάδας. Neil in his apparatus criticus suggests how the corruption might have arisen. μύριοι could have been abbreviated by the letter mu, and the noun derived from the same root would only need to be made explicit by adding the termination in question. But the regular use of such abbreviations is much commoner in MSS of technical content than literary texts. Despite that his idea has a certain attraction.

851 See on 774.

858 Since πονηρέ here means 'villain' I print it oxytone. If it meant 'poor wretch' proparoxytone might be considered. See above on *Acharnians* 165–6. I find it odd that here the tradition appears to favour the proparoxytone; I have checked RVMΓΘL.

877 Dover, *CR*² 22 (1972), 24, made the case for reading Γρῦπον 'Hooknose' by analogy with Simos, properispomenon, derived from the adjective, which is oxytone. The corruption of pi to double tau could easily have occurred in a capital letter script. But as the name is not attested in *LGPN* ii one might wonder whether an alternative such as Gryllus may be worth considering. Yet another suggestion by Blaydes is Grin(n)os, found in Hdt. 4. 150; this too fails to receive support in *LGPN* ii, which has Γρύπων from the fourth century BC and Γρῖποc from the second–third century AD.

891 πόνηρ' with proparoxytone accent is possible here, though hardly obligatory; cf. above on 858. (Neil was wrong to say that R does not have the proparoxytone.)

892 Lenting's minor change is very easy; but I cannot entirely dismiss the feeling that it is overlogical to claim that Paphlagon himself cannot be the addressee because Demos would by now be accustomed to his odour. That is not a consideration which will necessarily occur to members of the audience. On that subject it is worth drawing attention to D. Bain, *Greece and Rome*, 26 (1979), 132–45, a valuable paper on the apparent inconsistencies in Sophocles' *Oedipus Rex*, which will probably have gone unnoticed in the theatre.

921 Bentley proposed two remedies for the metrical fault, δᾳδίων and δαλίων. Neil rejected the latter on the ground that it is a ritual word for the brand dipped in the holy water. But its use may not necessarily be so restricted, and at *Peace* 959 it is probably to be accepted. Olson there refers to Headlam on Herondas 1. 38, who suggested that the Greeks used a brand of wood, kept alive under ash on the hearth, instead of matches, and their word for this was δαλόc.

δᾳδίον ought to mean a lighted torch. One usually thinks of them being brandished, which would make ὑφελκτέον inappropriate. δαλίον is more likely to have given rise to the variant ξύλον, which appears to be a gloss.

937 I am not at all sure that ἀνήρ without the definite article is idiomatic; Lenting added it so as to refer to the official in question. He was followed by some editors. Otherwise one would expect τιc to be used, and cέ τιc would have been satisfactory.

Knights 57

940 Neil was disinclined to emend, reckoning that the lengthening of omicron before mute and liquid, being possible in tragedy, might add a note of burlesque to the curse. True, but I do not see any signs of elevated style in the context, and so have opted for Elmsley's conjecture 'may you choke on it'. He compared ἐπιδιαρραγῶ in 701.

953 Chadwick 129 takes this passage and *Lys.* 928 as examples of ἀλλ' ἦ in affirmative sense, 'to be sure'. But I feel bound to dissent; here the translation can be 'But am I failing to see clearly?'

974–5 Editors seem to agree that the contrast is between residents and visitors. But is οἱ παρόντες Greek for 'residents'? 'Audience' is how one would naturally take it. In the context it would not be amiss if the Greek meant 'for the present generation and for those to come', which is in fact how one of the scholiasts wished to interpret the lines. Bentley proposed the future tense τοῖς ἀφιξομένοισι. Parker, *Songs*, 174–7, obelizes. Neil supports Cobet's εἰςαφικνουμένοις in the sense of 'visitors' and seems to assume without discussion that παροῦσι means 'residents'.

1018 λάσκων, though suitable enough, duplicates the sense of κεκραγώς. δάκνων, found in v and Φ, is less likely to be a gloss than a mistake arising from assimilation of ideas.

1023 Blaydes asked why the form ἀπύω, not otherwise found in Attic except in tragedy, is used here instead of ἠπύω. There does not seem to be any parody in what Paphlagon says here. So perhaps the best answer is that supplied by W. Schulze, *Kleine Schriften* (Göttingen, 1934), 707 n. 2, reviewing P. Kretschmer, *Die griechischen Vaseninschriften ihrer Sprache nach untersucht* (Gütersloh, 1894) in *GGA* 1896, 228–56. He wrote: 'Die Sklavensprache charakterisiert Aristophanes in den Rittern mit Absicht durch ἀπύω 1023 (meine Quaest. ep. 332 [actually 338], ταγέ 159, sowie durch das nichtattische πέρναται 176.' However, one has to ask whether the three words listed are all signs of the same kind of language, and whether they are sufficient to characterize the speaker as a vulgarian. This puzzling question is not addressed by Willi. I note in passing that περνάντα occurs at Eur. *Cycl.* 271, which is not a guarantee that the word was a part of ordinary Attic colloquial vocabulary.

1024 Can Coulon, Sommerstein, and Henderson be right to print cώζεcθαι 'μ' ὁ Φοῖβος, treating 'μ' as the emphatic form despite elision and prodelision? If the emphatic form is required, perhaps 'μέ without ὁ might be considered. But the sentence already has the emphatic pronoun coί, which appropriately contrasts with ἐγώ in 1023.

1026 Thiercy 1040 proposes τυροῦ for the MSS reading θύρας. He has overlooked that the upsilon is long. Sommerstein (2001: 240) proposes to retain θύρας, noting Nemesianus, *Cynegetica* 168, as evidence that dogs damage doors. Dog-owners confirm this. It might be added that the compound παρεcθίει seems less suitable with ἀθάρης, since a dog was likely to be accused of consuming the whole dish, not just nibbling at it.

1062 Many modern editors reject this line, following the lead of Zacher and Kappeyne van de Koppello; the latter had proposed to mark a lacuna before 1063. Since the line is now extant in two papyri, it would be an example of a very early interpolation. The argument brought against it was that it was originally an explanatory note on 1060 and/or 1061. But if that were so, one would expect the same future tense as in the verse(s) being explained; which is not the case in the extant MSS. Neil says that Zacher deleted the verse and gives no further help. If we adopt Bothe's restoration of the future, the line need no longer be condemned as 'weak, repetitious and anticlimactic' (Sommerstein). I find it acceptable as a response to Demos.

1131 χοὔτω is the majority reading, but the construction of the whole period is odd, and the proposal to read καί for the transmitted εἰ in the next line restores good sense by means of the easy supposition that the word was mistakenly transposed.

1158 Porson's εἴcομ' ἦν φράcῃc is tempting, but Blaydes, followed by Neil and Henderson, rejected it. The best parallels are Plat. *Gorg.* 470 D and Xen. *Oec.* 3. 12, whereas *Peace* 262 is a difficult line and the conversational context not quite the same.

1162–3 J. C. B. Lowe, *Glotta*, 51 (1973), 46 n. 17, approves of Neil's division of the lines into two sentences but insists that the second must be an assertion, 'By Jove, I shall play the coquette', as in *Birds* 1397, where the text does not admit of any doubt. Sommerstein takes both sentences as assertions with 'either ... or'. Chadwick 129 appears to have overlooked this passage, which he might have used to support his view that the affirmative use of the particle, though rare in prose, can be seen occasionally in Aristophanes (he referred also to *Birds* 13 and 162). See on *Acharnians* 1111–12 above.

1177 Dindorf as cited in Bekker's 1829 edition extracted Φοβεcτράτη from the scholia, and Dübner so printed the lemma, but it is not clear which MS if any actually has this form. Ribbeck's 1867 edition notes Φοβέcτρατοc Ἀθηνᾶ from *Etymologicum Magnum* 797. 54.

1239 ἐναντία in R, the less obvious reading, seems to be protected by the occurrence of the same usage at Plat. *Symp.* 194 B.

1242 If we could accept Neil's view that καί τι καὶ was precious in tone, the use of βινεcκόμην without the augment would enhance the comic blend of vulgar and tragic language; cf. Aesch. fr. 312 κλαίεcκον, perhaps from a messenger's speech, *Pers.* 656, Soph. *Ant.* 950 and fr. 546 (text very uncertain), adespota 268 τίεcκε μύθουc. But Denniston, *GP* 294, doubted Neil's claim, and his doubt is to be taken seriously.

Willi 247 calls the verb 'para-epic' (and translates 'I used to fuck', an imprecision avoided by Sommerstein and Thiercy). According to Schwyzer i. 710–11 verbs of this formation never have an augment (a fact which he does not explain) and are only used in the third person; so in this latter respect the present instance is peculiar. Threatte ii. 453 adds no epigraphic evidence to alter the picture. Willi notes that βινεcκόμην is the only example of an omitted augment in Ar.'s dialogue; he neither explains it nor recommends emendation, although in a footnote he recommends removing the prima facie example at *Ach.* 754. Dover, *The Evolution of Greek Prose Style* (Oxford, 1997), 87 n. 36, says that the humour of the verb 'lies in the Homeric tone given to a very obscene word'. Since he quotes on the same page θύεcκε from an obscene passage in Hipponax I am tempted to speculate that there may be here an allusion to a known vulgar expression from that author.

In the present passage the augmented form is given by M and not by V, as Blaydes stated.

1331 Editors usually accept Porson's τεττιγοφόρας, which is a lemma in Hesychius. The MSS, supported by Procopius Gazaeus, *Epp.* 57 G.–L. (18 H.), offer τεττιγοφόροc, which if right would necessitate another correction, easy enough in itself, e.g. κἀρχαίῳ Bentley or τἀρχαίῳ Brunck). Although cαμφόραc in l. 603, *Clouds* 122, 1298, looks like a borrowing from Doric, the termination -φόραc is attested for Attic by Menander, *Perikeiromene* 294, used of a πτερ- οφόραc χιλίαρχοc. It was probably rare and easily corrupted. Yet in our passage it cannot be regarded as absolutely certain; Hesychius is not quoting explicitly from Aristophanes, and his explanation refers to people (in the plural) who decorate their hair with brooches (quite a number of his lemmata are in oblique cases). Other compounds in -φόραc are listed in Kretschmer–Locker.

1373 ἐν ἀγορᾷ is the reading normally adopted here. The absence of the definite article here is legitimate in view of e.g. 293 and *Ach.* 21. The only snag is that MSS which do not reflect the activity of Demetrius Triclinius, in other words, which represent the paradosis, have the unmetrical ἐν τἀγορᾷ. Perhaps that is only a slip, but one wonders if there could be something wrong here, and Kock's transposition is not really such a violent change as might be thought. He proposed ἐν τἀγορᾷ τ' ἀγένειοc οὐδεὶc ἀγοράcει.

1392 Jackson's ἐλάβετ' αὐτὰc is an attempt to extract the truth from R. He suggests that Demos addresses both Agoracritus and the attendants of the Spondai. Ingenious, but I doubt whether there were any such attendants.

1399 Ribbeck in his edition of 1867, p. 302, noted 'statt πράγμαcιν wird ein Wort mit der Bedeutung von κρέαcιν erwartet. Hunde- und Eselfleisch, was Kleon in seine Würste stopfen soll, zu essen muß nicht unerhört gewesen sein, wie auch aus Erwähnungen bei Aerzten hervorgeht'. Similarly Neil remarked, 'πράγμαcιν is something of a surprise and would be more in place if politics were still to occupy Cleon with the material and audience on a lower scale than before'. I am not at all convinced by Sommerstein's attempt to justify the word: '... *pragmata* (either "things, stuff" or "public affairs") suggests that a demagogue who becomes a sausage-seller, like a sausage-seller who becomes a demagogue (213–16), has only to learn to practise the same techniques on different material, namely "mixing things together and stirring them into a hash" (214)'. More recently (2001: 249) he has suggested that πρᾶγμα is here being used to denote the genitals, referring to Henderson, *The Maculate Muse* (New Haven, 1975), 116, 134. I do not believe the passages cited there are adequate support. Similarly E. Spyropoulos, Ἑλληνικά, 33 (1981), 12, takes the word *sensu obsceno*. No parallels are cited other than a modern Greek expression το πράμα του γαϊδάρου.

My own view is that these attempts to deal with the problem are unsatisfactory interpretative gymnastics which have enjoyed far greater credit than they can possibly deserve. It is better to suppose that the true reading here has been displaced by a common word. τρώγμαςιν, otherwise known only from Philoxenus, *PMG* 836 (e) 12, is satisfyingly ironical.

Students of gastronomy will doubtless be aware that ass-meat figures on the menu in Lombardy and Sardinia. Gibbon, *Decline and Fall*, ch. 41 n. 88, speaking of the besieged Romans in AD 537, says 'They made sausages of mule's flesh: unwholesome, if the animals had died of the plague. Otherwise the famous Bologna sausages are said to be made of ass flesh'.

Clouds

47 Dover remarks that the phrase ἐξ ἄϲτεωϲ functions as an adjective, and demotics can similarly consist of an ἐκ-phrase. Nevertheless I wonder if we might remove the comma which seems to be standard in modern editions, or put it before the phrase instead of after, so that the words are more closely attached to ϲεμνήν and the accompanying adjectives. I find that van Leeuwen preferred this articulation of the sentence.

62 Sommerstein reverts to Reisig's conjecture δὴ 'νταῦθ', although Dover had said 'it is . . . unnecessary to consider the most obvious emendation' and had cited *Lys.* 838 and *Frogs* 652 as containing examples of a split anapaest comparable to the one transmitted here. Dover admits that the position of δή is not quite normal, but that difficulty, if it is one, is not removed by Reisig. The latter's idea has perhaps the merit of explaining the origin of ταῦτ' as the reading of most MSS. Rather unexpectedly Triclinius, as represented by L, has an unmetrical line here; probably an error has crept in, because even if L was copied directly from his autograph, which is not certain, a few errors were unavoidable.

ἐντεῦθεν and ἐνταῦθα are so similar in meaning that either could easily be substituted for the other. One wonders if δή might be deleted as an erroneous repetition from the preceding line. It was omitted, doubtless accidentally, by some late MSS of no obvious significance; Dover cites Par19 (Paris, suppl. grec 135) and Blaydes in addition mentions 'S' = Marc.gr. 475, now known as G, 'T' = Marc. gr. 472, now cited as V2, and an Elbingensis; this last has now disappeared according to J.-M. Olivier, *Répertoire des bibliothèques et des catalogues des manuscrits grecs de Marcel Richard*, 3rd edn. (Turnhout, 1995), 277–8.

73 If L accurately reflects Triclinius' considered views, it may be worth noting that he does not adopt the variant ἐπίθετο, attested in allegedly Thoman MSS, which he might be expected to follow, as above at 62. But here again one cannot exclude the possibility that error has crept into L; this would be a very minor aberration.

74 The dative μοι offered by E^pcKNΘ^ac is less obvious than μου and I doubt whether scribes would wilfully have introduced it; the principle of *utrum in alterum* seems to apply.

75 Richards proposed to read ὁδόν with punctuation after ηὗρον. This is ingenious, but unnecessary if one accepts as valid Blaydes's parallel of *Frogs* 117, which Dover does not bother to cite.

88 With some hesitation I follow Sommerstein in accepting ἔκςτρεψον. The metaphor from turning one's clothes inside out is very forceful, but I feel that Dover goes too far in claiming that it will not do. ἔκτρεψον as read by EU could be right; it might equally well result from the loss of a single letter.

95 Lenting's suspicion that the scholium θᾶκος δὲ καλεῖται ἀττικῶς ὁ τόπος ἔνθα πολλοὶ ςυνέρχονται ςκεψόμενοι implies the reading θακοῦς᾿ is very implausible. θᾶκος is cited as an Attic word for a place of assembly, and readers of late antiquity or later periods usually welcomed any information that would increase their knowledge of Athenian language and customs; so that is probably why the scholiast mentioned the word, not because he saw it in front of him in his own copy. Holwerda in his edition (Groningen, 1977) deleted the sentence, I think rightly, as an interpolation.

99 Since ἀργύρια in the plural means 'silver coins', e.g. at *Birds* 600 (Dunbar's note there lists other examples), I have wondered whether the singular could have retained its original sense in some expressions that were part of colloquial usage. If that were the case it could have an effect on the interpretation of this line, which is normally taken as proof that Socrates is being accused of charging fees. The clause ἀργύριον ἤν τις διδῶ occurs again at *Thesm.* 937, where the context is of bribing an official. Is it possible that 'If you give him a coin' meant something like our 'If you give him a tip'? This is a passage where a gesture might have been a useful adjunct to the spoken word.

130 Here I follow Dover's lead in accepting the spelling cκινδα-λάμουc; at *Frogs* 819 he adopted the alternative cχι-, without comment.

146 The scholiast in RV alleges that Chaerephon had massive eyebrows and Socrates a bald head. Dover cites Tzetzes' remark that reference to portrait masks is irrelevant, as Chaerephon is not a character in the play. But Sommerstein brings him on at 1497, as does Thiercy, and even if this view is rejected there is a question whether he appeared in the first version of the play.

A scholium in VM Vat. Barb. gr. 126 and Md1 on 146 begins ἰcτέον ὅτι αὐτοπροcώπωc εἰcῆγον τοὺc κωμῳδουμένουc, which does suggest portrait masks. These words from the old scholia were cited by Tzetzes, who queries the interpretation put on them by his predecessors (p. 419, ll. 16–25 ed. Holwerda). He takes αὐτοπροcώπωc to mean 'in person' rather than 'with portrait masks' and contrasts public vilification of convicted malefactors by the heralds with τὸ κατά τινων ἀπόντων λέγειν κωμῴδημα. Though this contributes nothing to the understanding of the play, it gives an interesting insight into how one Byzantine scholar read ancient drama.

155 Since φρόντιcμα is not listed in the index of Diels–Kranz, *Fragmente der Vorsokratiker*, commentators might have been expected to suggest that it is another comic coinage like φροντιcτήριον in 94, with a nuance that should ideally be reflected in translation.

161 Dover correctly says that the absence of an accent on διά in R is not important, since the scribe of this MS often failed to write an accent on prepositions. One may add that the same is true of many other Byzantine scribes. διαλέπτου is perhaps the result of readers' unease at the word-order, and the sentence would run much more easily if it began δι' αὐτοῦ. But Blaydes usefully cited Thuc. 7. 84 ἐν κοίλῳ ὄντι τῷ ποταμῷ . . . ταραccομένουc as a parallel for the participial expression.

διάλεπτοc seems to be first used by Eustathius 1157. 18, in a different context, and van der Valk ad loc. wondered if he invented it; he might well have assumed that the form found in the majority of MSS here was correct. (*DGE* cites also Tzetzes, p. 423.17).

169 Further to Dover's note about πρῴην with an iota, preserved in

Clouds

R and stated by Herodian to be correct, it should be made clear that already in antiquity many scribes were careless about this type of iota, and in medieval MSS it is only erratically preserved. Threatte offers no further information.

182 Sommerstein attributes the correct form of the accusative Cωκράτη to the Aldine edition, Dover to an unspecified partially Triclinian MS (it is not found in L), and Blaydes to 'Bodl. 8', which is Bodleian Library, Rawlinson MS G. 89. This last statement is correct; the MS is very recent, probably of the early sixteenth century and therefore likely to be more recent than the Aldine edition, which appeared in 1498.

248–9 Without much confidence I follow Blaydes and Sommerstein in accepting ἦ with a circumflex (wrongly accented in most MSS) at the end of the line and introducing a fresh question. Dover says that this reading is given by Vv4^ac X 'followed by Triclinius'. But these two MSS are dated respectively 1362 and to the late fourteenth century; so in all probability they do no more than reflect a Triclinian solution.

292 Dover did not venture to print his own excellent adjustment of Wilamowitz's θεόсεπτα. The internal accusative seems to me right; and I confess to not understanding what he means by saying that the emendation 'cannot be supported by adequate stylistic evidence'. Corruption by assimilation would be easy (it is probably the commonest of all forms of error in MSS), and the internal accusative of an adjective in the neuter is surely a well-attested syntactical feature. Is it his objection that this particular adjective is not found in this usage elsewhere? That would be a consideration, but hardly decisive.

294 τετραμαίνω is attributed by Dover to an unspecified partially Triclinian MS. Blaydes's usually extensive reports do not help here. It is not the reading of L nor Rawlinson G. 89, which had a correct form at 182 above. Dover overlooked Coulon's correct statement that the *Suda* has the true form of the verb.

324 Dover notes that Triclinius' remedy ἥсυχα ταύταс is not Attic. But is it in fact Triclinius' remedy? It is not the reading of L (nor for that matter of Vv5; see S. Benardete, *HSCP* 66 (1962), 242). The Triclinian scholia make no reference to the matter; the MSS which have the reading in question are apparently Vc1, Par8, and Ct2, and W. J. W. Koster, *Scholia recentiora in Nubes* (Groningen, 1974), p. cxxvi, classifies the first two of these as 'mixti et contaminati', the third as exhibiting the second edition by Triclinius. I think the attribution is unlikely to be correct.

335 The case and therefore the accentuation of στρεπταίγλαν have been discussed. Blaydes stated that both possibilities could be found in the MSS and are attested in the scholia. The modern edition of the latter by D. Holwerda (Groningen, 1977) indicates that the old scholia give the paroxytone form without discussion, while the Thomano-Triclinian commentary considers the alternative as well. Triclinius noted the paroxytone form as occurring 'in the older copies' ἐν τοῖc παλαιοτέροιc τῶν ἀντιγράφων, which is consistent with the evidence of the old scholia and perhaps indicates that Thomas was responsible for raising the question. Sommerstein prints the genitive plural form. But I slightly prefer the word-order with the other reading.

337 Coulon, *REG* 66 (1953), 44, accepts Reisig's διερᾶc, taking ἀερίαc to be a noun, on the pattern of *Wasps* 678 πολλὰ μὲν ἐν γῇ, πολλὰ δ' ἐφ' ὑγρᾷ πιτυλεύcαc, which recalls the Homeric usage of ὑγρά. Sommerstein (2001: 255) notes that Thiercy takes the same view, and I have come to think that they are right; each of the citations then consists of a nominal phrase with adjectival description. Then one does not need to resort to the insertion of τ' as found in Par9 (Paris gr. 2822) and also proposed by Bentley.

340 Sommerstein (2001: 255) prefers now to read λέξον νῦν μοι, taking δή to be a gloss on νῦν rather than vice versa. In this he is following a view expressed by Blaydes in his apparatus. It appears to gain further support from Koster, *Autour d'un manuscrit*, 233, which shows that in several late MSS of *Plutus* δή is frequently written above νῦν or νυν. On the other hand Denniston, *GP* 216, says that δή is exceedingly common with imperatives in our author and accepts it here. Did νῦν come in from l. 345 just below?

343 Reisig preferred ἐρίοιc διαπεπταμένοιcιν in the light of the use of this compound of the verb at *Lys.* 732–3 and the rarity of the uncompounded verb.

403 I have not identified the MS(S) which added the necessary nu ephelkustikon.

407 Threatte ii. 503 shows that καίω is a possible form and κατακαίων is here reported by Blaydes as the reading of RVA and some later MSS. I can confirm what he says about R and V.

431 I suppose the deictic form is used here because the speaker makes a gesture or snaps his fingers. The passage is not discussed by A. L. Boegehold, *When a Gesture was Required* (Princeton, 1999).

439 Though the supplements suggested by Reisig and Sommerstein are tempting, I agree with Dover that the resulting asyndeton is awkward and would prefer to suppose that χρήϲθων was added as an explanation of ὅ τι βούλονται.

480 Probert 144 casts doubt on the existence of the combination πρόϲ ϲε where the pronoun is enclitic. But as she admits that πρόϲ με does occur, I find it hard to understand why πρόϲ ϲε should not have been acceptable usage. Both here and in 475 Blaydes printed the pronoun as enclitic. Dover pays no attention to this; Sommerstein accepts the enclitic in 480, and I follow him, feeling that in 475 ἄξιω ϲῇ φρενὶ perhaps entails a degree of emphasis on ϲοῦ at the end of the sentence.

512 Whereas correption can hardly be avoided, the resolution of ὅτι could be remedied by Blaydes's ἐπεί. That would result in an aristophanean which is not a clausula—perhaps unlikely but just conceivable. For that metre see Parker, *Songs*, 82–4.

523 ἀναγεῦϲ' is a hapax legomenon and has caused difficulty. However, the uncompounded γεύω is attested in the active (see *DGE* s.v., and add to their references Eubulus 136, Clement of Alexandria, *Protreptikos* 99 and Iamblichus, *De vita Pythagorae* 5. 21), and the word here could mean 'give a fresh taste of' or 'display for tasting'. I do not entirely agree with Dover's note about the word. His agnostic remark 'if Ar. coined it for this occasion we cannot know (and I do not see how his audience could know) what he intended' seems to me too pessimistic; I do not think such a neologism, if it was one, needed to be obscure in a language which lent itself so easily to the invention of new words, and Dover himself suggests two obvious meanings for it. The two resulting translations differ slightly. The second, 'I have displayed it for tasting again by you first', changes the syntax and would be better with the emendation πρώτοιc ... ὑμῖν. It also runs into the difficulty that this makes the text refer to the second version, whereas the poet's object is to complain of what happened to the first. But in any case if we wish to assume that Aristophanes was precise in his use of words a serious objection has to be dealt with: as Richards observed, 'the idea of a *taste* is quite out of place. A taste of a play would be given by the performance of one scene or the recital of one ῥῆcιc. To exhibit a play entire is not to give a taste of it.' There is a further difficulty in πρώτουc. Why should the poet emphasise that his audience is the first to see the play? Whatever inferences one draws from the South Italian vases showing scenes from or relating to Old Comedy (see especially O. Taplin, *Comic Angels* (Oxford, 1993), 5 and passim), I have yet to be convinced that in the years immediately following 423 it was already established practice for the plays to be performed outside Athens, and—what is more—to be performed so often that an author might seriously consider where to put them on stage first. Both Dover and Sommerstein (1982) take the passage as humorous: the poet pretends to have given the Athenian audience a treat, as if he had had the option of conferring his favours elsewhere. I find that too feeble for a passage that is carefully written and expresses the poet's feelings of wounded pride on a serious issue. Sommerstein (2001: 259) thinks it unlikely that an Athenian at this date would have chosen to have a play performed for the first time outside Athens. I agree.

Is there any other possibility, such as a revival of a play in revised version at, say, the theatre in the Piraeus? Although the evidence about revised versions and performances in theatres other than that of Dionysus is too scanty to provide much help, one might infer from A. W. Pickard-Cambridge, *The Dramatic Festivals of Athens*, 2nd edn. rev. J. P. A. Gould and D. M. Lewis (Oxford, 1968), 47–8, on the strength of *IG* i^3. 970 = ii^2. 3090 that Eleusis was another possible venue. This is accepted by Sommerstein in his edition of *Plutus* (p. 31 n. 126) as evidence of a victory of Aristophanes at Eleusis. The editor of the inscription (fasc. 2, p. 661) notes 'utrum ad Dionysia agrestia

Eleusine celebrata an ad Dionysia in urbe pertineat, diu disputatum est. siquidem recte iudicavit Capps, *Hesperia*, 12 (1943), pp. 5–8, synchoregiam in urbe in usu fuisse solum a. 406/5, illud probabilius videtur.' Not that I think the revised version of this play was destined for Eleusis. Though I find slightly odd the emphasis on the mysteries rather than rites in honour of Athena in the song of the chorus at 299–300, which might at first sight seem significant, the word ἐνθάδ' in 528 puts paid to the notion.

F. G. Welcker, in his translation with notes dedicated to Wilhelm von Humboldt, *Des Aristophanes Wolken* (Giessen and Darmstadt, 1810), thought (p. 146) that the play could not have been intended for any other venue and supposed that the right reading must be πρώτην, implying that the poet had more than one play ready to offer to the public and chose this one. His proposal was accepted in many nineteenth-century editions. A new twist was given to the discussion by O. Kaehler in the critical appendix to the second printing of W. S. Teuffel's edition (Leipzig, 1887), 196–7. He thought the poet should be stating a claim that his play deserved the first prize and proposed ἀναδῆϲ(αι), comparing *Plutus* 589 and 764. Similar thoughts occurred to E. C. Yorke ap. J. G. Griffith, *Festinat senex* (Oxford, 1988), 133–4. Without knowing of Kaehler's emendation he proposed ἀνακηρύττεϲθ(αι), with deletion of ὑμᾶϲ. This is less elegant and is based on some rather elaborate inferences from a scholium on *Plutus* 585, which can be seen from the modern edition to be Thomano-Triclinian and of very doubtful utility in the present context. But the basic idea needs to be taken seriously.

It may be observed that on the usual view of the passage εἶτ' has to be linked to the preceding relative clause. I find this awkward, since the clause is not much more than a parenthesis and ἀλλ' would provide a more natural continuation. However, with the proposed emendation εἶτ' is linked to ἠξίωϲ' which seems to provide a more logical sequence of thought.

I take the opportunity of referring to a minor oddity in the passage. The verb ἀνεχώρουν is in the imperfect. I am puzzled by the use of this tense. M. Sánchez Ruipérez, *Estructura del sistema de aspectos y tiempos del verbo griego antiguo* (Salamanca, 1954), 84 ff. (a French version was issued in 1982) admits that in some passages the logic dictating the choice of tenses remains obscure to us. The aorist that one expects would have been metrically equivalent. Other lines exhibiting an alternation of aorist and imperfect are *Birds* 114–16 and *Thesm.* 794.

528 Dover was right to say that the transmitted text οἷc ἡδὺ καὶ λέγειν cannot be accepted. He and Sommerstein accept Blaydes's οὖc. Though this yields sense I think Blaydes was wide of the mark here. A far better point is made if the poet says that praise came from people who had a tendency to be critical. Hence van Herwerden was right with ψέγειν. This verb has to be restored in place of λέγειν at Soph. *El.* 1423; cf. also *OC* 594, where Lloyd-Jones and I took the same view. For other examples of confusion between these two words see Garvie's note on Aesch. *Cho.* 989, where—and this is very surprising—the reverse corruption has taken place; one does not often find a much rarer word being introduced, since trivialization is one of the commonest faults of scribes.

538 Why did Dobree favour cκυτίον? He says 'legendum puto cκυτίον cum MS. ut forsan scholiastes, et καθημμένον. Idem vitium tollit Valck. not. MSS. e Schol. Ran. 1242'. I have not been able to follow up Valckenaer's point; but the scholium, known to Blaydes from the *copiae Victorianae* (on which see Koster's prolegomena to his *Scholia recentiora in Nubes* (Groningen, 1974), p. cviii), is now edited by Koster (ibid. 310); some late MSS appear to have cκύτιον (also proparoxytone, whereas Sommerstein records the paroxytone as the reading of Laur. 31. 13 and Harley 5725, which he adopts in his text). Is the word to be accepted on such dubious authority? Dover does not even mention it as a variant.

557 Most MSS have the erroneous πεποίηκεν, induced by the wording of 556. V gives the right tense, and no Byzantine scribe can have known enough about eupolidean metre to be able to make the required correction. There is no need for Bergk's conjecture ἐπήδηcεν, which Blaydes liked, while admitting that ἐπί rather than εἰc might have been expected to follow.

619 Sommerstein quotes Threatte i. 500 for the non-aspirated form of ἑορτή that he adopts, but my reading of Threatte ii. 758 is that the traditional form can be justified.

638 The reading of R and some *recentiores*, plus the secondary tradition (scholia on Hephaestion) is ἢ περὶ ἐπῶν ἢ ῥυθμῶν. The rest of the tradition offers a text which can be made acceptable with the benefit of Hermann's ἢ ῥυθμῶν ἢ περὶ ἐπῶν. A. Tessier, *Eikasmos*, 9 (1998), 475–9, supports G. Morelli, *Una testimonianza del Petrarca sul verso saturnio. Con una appendice su Aristoph. Nub. 638 e Plat. Resp. 400B* (Padua, 1996), in preferring R's reading, and the meaning will then be 'metres, the verse of epic, various types of lyric cola'. The analogy with Plat. *Rep.* 399 E–400 C, he argues, justifies this view of the passage; a neutral translation of ἐπῶν as 'verses' is not adequate. The question is whether so much can be extracted from the word ῥυθμοί and whether ἔπη could mean just 'words' in 423. The argument may be too subtle. Sommerstein (1982) translated 'measures, words or rhythms'; his revised view (2001: 255) follows E. Degani, *Giornale filologico ferrarese*, 11 (1988), 55–6 (cf. *Eikasmos*, 1 (1990), 131–2 = *Filologia e storia* (Hildesheim, Zürich, and New York, 2004), 399–400) in accepting Hermann's conjecture, with the meaning 'measure or rhythms or words'. He does not mention Tessier's discussion.

647 Thomas Magister's reading τάχα δ' is rejected by Dover on the ground that it makes Socrates too optimistic. Blaydes had observed that the sarcasm of ταχύ γ' in the *veteres* sits less well with Strepsiades' question in the next line, and so he favoured the Thoman reading. With some hesitation I incline to the view that Blaydes's objection is not decisive; Strepsiades simply fails to understand the sarcasm.

680 Dover obelized and stated that δ' has no place here, which has not convinced Sommerstein or me; he noted proposals by Blaydes involving ἄρα; West, CQ^2 27 (1977), 74, denied that ἄρα was appropriate and proposed δύναμαι for δ' ἦν ἄν. Sommerstein accepts the paradosis and renders 'And what I said would then have been . . .' Might the text be more satisfactory if—again a suggestion by Blaydes—Strepsiades said 'And what I said *ought* to have been . . .'? On that basis ἄρα could be accepted in the sense 'So, I see . . .' ἐκεῖνο χρῆν ἄρα is not, however, attractive palaeographically.

Sommerstein's preference for the dative of Cleonyme is presumably based on 674–5, and I think this simple solution is the best.

696 The reading c' ἐνθάδ' in KNL and the lemma in the scholium of U could be the result of a Byzantine reader's desire to restore at all costs a line of twelve syllables (even if it would not have conformed to all the requirements of a dodecasyllable). Perhaps this possibility tilts the balance in favour of Dobree's deletion of c'.

697 Blaydes' ταὐτὰ ταῦτ' is attractive and Somerstein's rendering 'the same thinking-out' at first sight implies that he accepted it. 'Those very things' is presumably the literal meaning. But I am tempted to conjecture that this is yet another place where ταῦτα and πάντα have been confused.

737 Two words in this line are uncertain. (i) RV have ἐξευρών, other MSS ἐξευρεῖν. The principle of *utrum in alterum* suggests that the proximity of βούλει might have induced a change to the infinitive. (ii) πρῶτος is the reading of almost all witnesses; Tzetzes and the late MS Par14 (Paris, grec 2827) alter to the adverb πρῶτον. Dover argues from Thuc. 6. 88. 8 (I do not follow his reference to the earlier passage in this play at 636 f.) that αὐτὸς πρῶτος is an established expression. If that is so, one may still suggest that the separation of the words here creates a less than perfect example of the idiom. I wonder if πρῶτος ἐξευρών is justified by the existence of the phrase πρῶτος εὑρετής.

876 R and V are alone in adding γε after καίτοι. The resulting text is metrically unusual but not impossible; hence Reisig preferred to shift the particle and read γ' αὐτό, winning the approval of Blaydes and Sommerstein. This is a valid approach on the assumption that RV preserve the truth or something very close to it. The alternative is to assume that the particle intruded from l. 878.

I believe that the interpretation of this line is not quite as certain as is usually supposed. Dover remarks 'Socrates is a clever salesman.' I think the emphasis may be not so much on financial gain for Socrates as on the effort required by the stupid Hyperbolus to acquire skills, comparable to that which will be required by the new and equally stupid pupil. Sommerstein says that this is the only place in comedy where Socrates is accused of being the teacher of a hated politician. From the wording of the line it does not automatically follow that Socrates was the teacher; he could be referring to a notorious fact that Hyperbolus had paid some other sophist, or perhaps more than one, an enormous sum.

894 I am puzzled by the present tense of νικῶ. Sommerstein (2001: 256) now suggests rendering 'I can beat you'. Is the meaning perhaps 'I do beat you' (i.e. in our regular arguments)? Blaydes's conjecture is useful to the extent that it forces us to think about a precise translation. H.-S. points out a later parallel for the sense 'be bound to win' in Gellius' reading νικᾷ for πείςει in Eur. *Hec.* 294 (*NA* 11. 4. 2).

901 R's reading ἀλλ' ... γ' αὔτ' is not certain but receives some support from passages cited by Denniston, *GP* 119.

953–4 Wilamowitz, *GV* 325, declared 'Alles ist in Ordnung bis zu dem dritten Vers, in dem etwas zuviel ist; αὐτοῖν ist ja auch unerträglich.' He did not say why; Dover rejects his view, again without giving reasons. Though the pronoun does not strike me as 'intolerable', it could be an addition; a gloss in the dual is quite conceivable, as the Byzantines were all too alert to this feature of the ancient language and the form had occurred in the text shortly before at 886, which might have been a contributory factor.

Dover's preferred solution is to alter the antistrophe, which looks acceptable in its transmitted form (cf. Parker, *Songs*, 203); he is forced to make a transposition and delete another phrase as a gloss, giving a responsion of – – ⌣ ⌣ to – ⌣ – ⌣ – ⌣ – (see his note on 1029). In his apparatus Dover says that Wilamowitz favoured a solution incorporating Blaydes's emendation λέγειν. The latter was retracted by its author in his *Adversaria* (1899), 20; but in any case Wilamowitz does not say this in the passage cited above, where he concludes 'λέγων ἀμείνων πότεροc heilt sicher, denn direkte Frage ist so gut wie die indirekte'. Parker cites Bergk's solution *exempli gratia* and I find it the most reasonable suggested so far.

954 The variant in Θ^2 γε φανήcεται is quoted by both Dover and Sommerstein, but I decided to omit it from the apparatus. It looks like the result of the following sequence: (i) the scribe of a lost MS wrote γε above φανήcεται because he had become aware of V's reading γενήcεται and was able to indicate the existence of the variant in this economical fashion; (ii) someone transcribing from that copy thought that γε was part of the text, not just a variant.

981 Hall–Geldart took seriously Blaydes's objection to the definite article τῆc and printed καί in front of κεφάλαιον. But 'the radish (on the table)' is to be understood.

985 Though I accept Kedeides as the right form of the name, I do not share Sommerstein's view that it is attested in the *Suda* at κ 1500. His citation of the reading of the single codex V is misleading, since all the other MSS have Κηκιδίου, and in V the variant Κηδίου amounts to nothing more than the careless omission of a syllable by a single scribe. *LGPN* ii lists six known bearers of the name Kedeides, all from the late sixth to the late fourth century BC, whereas there is no name beginning Κηκ-.

995 There are various difficulties here, and I do not feel at all confident of having found the right solution. (i) Henderson prints οὗ for ὅ τι, which looks like an adaptation of one of Blaydes's numerous suggestions; he translates 'or do anything disgraceful that might infect the image of Modesty'. If this is the right approach, might it not be better to write the dative ᾧ? (ii) Dover does not mention the possibility of accepting μέλλει rather than μέλλεις from the scholium in E and *Suda* α 4716. Although the attestation is extremely tenuous, Sommerstein accepts it and the syntax is eased thereby. (iii) Dover and Sommerstein reject the transmitted verb ἀναπλήcειν. Van Leeuwen accepted an ellipse of the expected genitive, citing Thuc. 2. 51. 4, where τῆc νόcου is to be understood with ἕτεροc ἀφ' ἑτέρου θεραπείαc ἀναπιμπλάμενοι. Very hesitantly I follow him. But the verb may well be corrupt; I note its occurrence at 1023, which could possibly account for its intrusion here (suppose a scribe was distracted for a moment and looked at the wrong column of text). (iv) Can the statue of Aidos be understood literally? There was a cult of Aidos on the Acropolis, and an admittedly much later inscription *IG* iii/1. 367 shows that proedria was given in the theatre to a priestess of this divinity. The cult appears to go back to at least the fourth century, if we can rely on ps.-Dem. 25. 35. The article in *LIMC* is helpful.

998 The syntax of καλέcαντα is not discussed by most editors; Blaydes and van Leeuwen were hesitant about the accusative; the latter thought the poet had lapsed into assuming he had said καί cε διδάξω instead of ἐπιcτήcει. Another explanation would be as follows: the nature of the desirable forms of behaviour is such as to suggest that they are recommendations which would normally be dependent on a verb of obligation like χρή.

1006 The colour of the reed is not discussed by Dover, but white has seemed implausible to many scholars. Sommerstein (2001: 256) refers to the useful paper by J. Jouanna, *BCH* 118 (1994), 35–49. Van Leeuwen had cited Ar. fr. 53 in support of λεπτῷ; Jouanna adds Theophr. *HP* 4. 11 and rejects Cantarella's γλαυκῷ (which had been accepted by Sommerstein in 1982) on the ground that its application to the leaves of the olive makes it inappropriate here. It has not been observed hitherto that the two similar words λευκός and λεπτός are both mentioned as variants by the scholium in EM at 1016. The word being explained there is μικρούς (ὤμους) and while 'slender' and 'white' could be understood as possible variants at that point in the text, I think it much more likely that the note has been misplaced, as can easily happen with scholia, and then adjusted. In its original form it related to 1006 and preserved the true reading.

1007f. φυλλοβολούσης was obelized by Dover on the ground that poplars do not cast their leaves in spring. He rejected Meineke's attempt to restore the sense by φυλλοκομούσης because -κομεῖν means 'tend' in classical Greek; but he did not comment on Blaydes's φυλλοφορούσης, which seems more plausible if this approach is to be adopted. Willems's defence of the traditional text (i. 413) is 'Les chatons mâles de cet arbre (et avant les chatons, les écailles qui sont de vraies feuilles) tombent au premier printemps, avant l'apparition de la frondaison, et forment sur le sol une épaisse couverture.' Mastromarco follows him: 'all'inizio della primavera, i pioppi bianchi producono delle infiorescenze che cadono prima della fogliazione, coprendo abbondantemente il terreno sottostante, con un forte odore (ὄζων) di resina'.

But Sommerstein follows the lead of Jouanna, as cited in the preceding note, accepting that the reference is to autumn and taking *smilax* to be green briar, which flowers in October/November. This entails emendation; the reference to spring that follows in the text has to be separated from what has just been said, e.g. by ἦρός θ' ὥρᾳ.

Professor W. G. Arnott has kindly confirmed for me that *smilax aspera*, which has fragrant flowers between August and October, is the plant in question; he draws attention to J. Raven, *Plants and Plant Lore in Ancient Greece* (Oxford, 2000), 68, who states that the common translation 'bryony' is not correct but does not say what is right.

R. Campagner, *Lessico agonistico di Aristofane* (Rome and Pisa, 2001), 331–2, reports with approval Borthwick's φυλλοβολούντων, the reference being to the custom of showering athletic victors with leaves. But in this context there is no mention of any contest; the young man is out jogging with a friend.

1012–18 Why are the parts of the body not given in the same order in each sequence? A little transposition would achieve this effect, and Meineke and others preferred this. But the second sequence as transmitted has one extra item. Should we delete something to restore parity? Dover does so, objecting to the presence of a large κωλῆ, which he thinks cannot mean 'penis', and if it means 'haunch' should be underdeveloped. Sommerstein does not consider this. However, Mastromarco deserves credit for pointing to Colin Austin's approach (CR^2 20 (1970), 20); he suggested that κωλῆν μεγάλην might be an interpolation to achieve more precise correspondence with πόcθην μικράν. The lists are then of equal length and a point is achieved with the final item in the second list.

1028 Though it is not beyond the wit of editors to restore responsion, there are difficulties here: (i) Is Dover's objection to τότ' ἐπὶ τῶν προτέρων valid? In strict logic I suppose it is; but I wonder if we should be so rigorous; the Greek is pleonastic, but is it worse than that? Sommerstein disregards this point. (ii) B. Zimmermann, *Untersuchungen zur Form und dramatischen Technik der Aristophanischen Komödien* (Königstein, 1985), ii. 126–7, proposes εὐδαίμονεc ἄρ' ἦcαν οἱ ζῶντεc ἐπὶ Κρόνου τότε, which scans – – ⏑ ⏑⏑ – ⏑ – – ⏑ ⏑⏑ ⏑ – ⏑ ⏑. Despite Sommerstein's approval (2001: 256) there is a serious drawback to this: it introduces cretics into a song which otherwise has none, and was accordingly not taken into consideration by Parker, *Songs*, 200–3.

1046 δειλότατον is the paradosis. Most modern editors follow Thomas Magister and heal the metre with δειλόν, presupposing an error of assimilation provoked by the superlative at the beginning of the line. This is not difficult. They then accept τὸν ἄνδρα, despite the doubts of Reisig and Blaydes as to the appropriateness of the definite article; the latter suggested τιν' for τόν, accepting Thomas' reading. Perhaps the right way to take the line is indicated by Sommerstein, who translates 'the man who takes them . . .'. Might one also hazard the guess that, since the reply begins with ἐπίςχες, the sentence is interrupted and incomplete?

1066 Threatte i. 463, 505–6 gives the aspirated form εἴληφε.

1073 καχαςμόν was thought by Blaydes to be a gloss on κιχλιςμόν, whereas Dover thought the latter resulted from 'accommodation to 983'. Both words are fairly uncommon; the choice is not easy, as neither looks like a suitable word to serve as a gloss on the other. In a case like this I tend to prefer R's reading on the ground that overall it is the best MS.

1119 I am pretty sure that Sommerstein (2001: 256) has hit the mark with his simple emendation of τάς for τόν. The point, which he does not explain in full, is that once the vines have formed their fruit, extreme weather brings with it the danger that the vintage will fail to live up to its promise. The summer of 2003 in most European countries has shown all too clearly the reality of this risk. The previous remedy for the difficulty in this line was to follow Korais and write τε καὶ τάς for τεκούςας, but it is so much inferior that, however much one admires Korais, it cannot merit inclusion in the apparatus any longer.

1203 νενημένοι is the form preferred by Bentley (and Sommerstein; not accepted or discussed by Dover). Threatte ii. 584–5 deals with perfects in -ςμαι; his evidence tends to support Bentley.

1206 To Dover's examples of the heteroclite vocative H.-S. adds Εὐρίπιδες at Gellius, *NA* 15. 20. 10.

1208 Dover's apparatus is incomplete insofar as it fails to record that Θ has ἐκτρέφεις, as I have verified *in situ*. So also does V.

1254 Elmsley's proposal, not mentioned by Dover but adopted by Sommerstein, is ingenious. *KAITAEY* or *KAITEY* was corrupted into *KAITOYT(O)*. It may be right, but does not seem to me essential. The same may be said for Reisig's καὶ ςοί γ', which is very close to the reading of $E^{ac}\Theta$ καίτοι γ'. That is also the reading of the early printed editions, doubtless because E was one of the MSS used by Musurus for the Aldine.

1262 Sommerstein rightly draws attention to the plural in βούλεcθε and considers that the addressees probably included the audience. I am uneasy about this, since there is no obvious reason to involve them here. Could one think of the chorus instead? Or does the same objection apply? Presumably such thoughts induced Blaydes to propose βούλει μανθάνειν, since it is not classical Greek usage to address a single person in the plural.

1275 Dover does not mention in his apparatus or commentary the emendations proposed for this line. In his note he simply comments on the emphatic personal pronoun αὐτόc 'as distinct from your money'. This train of thought is not suitable in the context, as it would suggest that the creditor, whatever the outcome of his injuries, may recover his money, which is certainly not Strepsiades' intention. Van Leeuwen noted 'αὐτόc codd., cui pronomini nullus hic est locus, cum non habeat cui possit opponi'.

1310 I follow Dover here in thinking that τι κακὸν λαβεῖν is a gloss that has ousted the original text. His suggested emendation strikes me as better than alternatives recently proposed, because ἀποcτραφῆναι and ἄποινα τεῖcαι were less likely to be glossed with the words that have found their way into the text.

1312 Parker, *Songs* 211, notes the use of ἐπαιτεῖν = 'request' at Soph. *OT* 1416; so Bergk's proposal seems acceptable.

1352 The difficulties of this line are well analysed by Dover. But he does not mention van Herwerden's ingenious proposal, which not surprisingly found favour with Blaydes, (1902), 132: ἤδη λέγειν χρή. πρὸς χάριν πάντων δὲ τοῦτο δράcειc. This obviates the awkwardness of πρὸς χορόν without the article and brings in a welcome reference to the audience. The postponement of δέ would seem to be possible (cf. Denniston, *GP* 185–8). The resulting sense seems to me better than the break of dramatic illusion, unique of its kind, which Dover describes.

1360 With the transmitted text Pheidippides complains that he was being forced to sing in order to entertain cicadas, who were thought of as singers. This has been supposed to yield good sense; but (i) singers might be thought of as entertainers rather than the entertained; (ii) cicadas were believed not to eat, so ἑcτιῶντα is not the verb we expect. This may be logic-chopping; but Blaydes noticed that if the complaint is to match Strepsiades' remark in 1358, τέττιγά μ' would be better, and he also pointed out that τέττιγά, without the personal pronoun, is the reading of the *Suda* at α 454. The sense is then 'as if I were a cicada entertaining'.

1371 For a summary of recent debate about the verb in this line Mastromarco's discussion on p. 90 of his edition is helpful. He cites in particular R. Renehan, *Studies in Greek Texts* (Hypomnemata, 43; Göttingen, 1976), 88–92, for the view that λέγειν and ᾄδειν can be used indifferently; cf. esp. Plat. *Tim*. 21 B. V. Tammaro, *Museum criticum*, 15–17 (1980–2), 107–9, drew attention to Ar. fr. 101 and Eupolis 39.

In support of Borthwick's emendation ἦγ' Dover cites Theophr. *Char.* 27. 2. This is not borne out by the Leipzig edition, *Theophrasts Charaktere*, published in 1897 by eight members of the Leipziger Philologische Gesellschaft. In fact the Vatican MS (V = Vat. gr. 110), the most, and almost certainly the only, authoritative witness, reads λέγων, as I have verified myself from a photograph, whereas ἄγων is cited only from the dubious authority of some late MSS; J. Diggle's edition (Cambridge, 2004) has no mention of the variant.

1373 For the readings of the Strasbourg papyrus (inv. 621) I have relied on the report given by Koster and Holwerda in *Mnemosyne*[4], 15 (1962), 267–8.

1427 The deictic form ταυτί is not metrically guaranteed. Olson on *Ach.* 129 refers to Isabel Martín de Lucas, *Emerita*, 64 (1996), 157–71, but I found no explanation of the use of the suffix in this passage. However, at p. 167 n. 31 she reports a suggestion by Dr Julia Mendoza about demonstratives in -ί: 'proponía interpretarlos no como variantes expresivas de las formas base sino como verdaderos actualizadores'. Dover on l. 83 above cites Dem. 23. 211, 212 as examples of a later and less restrictive usage. Probably we should accept the present passage as evidence that it was already current in the 420s.

1444 Most modern editors accept τί δ᾽ ἦν ἔχων from E^pc and N, treating δῆτ᾽ in other good witnesses as an interpolation. Hermann deleted ἔχων and Dover thought that interpolation of this word was unlikely; but as glossators and paraphrasts were active at many periods, one should not rule out the possibility. His objection to the syntax resulting from Hermann's emendation is that the hypothetical τί ... ἄν should not be coordinated with ἦν and an aorist subjunctive. There is force in that, since a curious mixed conditional sentence results.

1456 Since enclitic pronouns have a tendency to cluster with particles as near the beginning of a sentence as possible, the word-order in this line as transmitted seems open to question. One could read τί δῆτά μοι ταῦτ᾽ οὐ τότ᾽ ἠγορεύετε; The negative would then be adjacent to the adverb, a further slight advantage.

1470 There has been discussion of how ἔcτι should be accented. Whereas Chandler 267 (§§938–9) was willing to allow that it may not have been enclitic when signifying existence or possibility, recent opinion has favoured the view that it is always enclitic, as argued by Barrett in the appendix to his edition of Eur. *Hipp.*, p. 426, on the ground that Greek verbs will originally have been treated in the same way as they were in Sanskrit. But Barrett in n. 2 noted that there is slight evidence for a different practice. It could be that a distinction was gradually developed. The latest contribution to the debate is by Probert 144–6, who argues in favour of Hermann's position, i.e. that a distinction can be observed. What has not been noted, so far as I am aware, is the curious fact that there appears to be a partially analogous phenomenon in Serbo-Croat (I persist in using this term despite the linguistic consequences of recent political upheavals). Unfortunately experts in Slavonic philology are not clear about the origin of this feature of Serbo-Croat, which also has complex rules about the position of enclitics near the beginning of the clause, and it is probably too far-fetched to suppose that the similarity of the phenomenon exemplifies survival on the periphery of a linguistic family.

Wasps

3 Elmsley saw that a present tense is needed instead of the highly dubious transmitted form, and it looks as if he was anticipated by Divus, who has *praedebes*. He may have invented this compound; I have not succeeded in tracing it in dictionaries of classical or medieval Latin. (Though a present is natural in translating the Greek idiom, it may be noted that Frischlin's Latin version of 1586 has *debebas*.)

61 The compound ἀνασελγαινόμενος has been doubted by Hermann and others; Blaydes quotes Dindorf as saying 'verbum neque alibi inventum neque aptum huic loco'. Their preference is for the compound beginning ἐνα-, and it perhaps receives some support from the appearance of this form in several passages of Photius' letters and *Amphilochia*: see the index in L. G. Westerink, *Photius: Epistulae et Amphilochia*, vi/2 (Leipzig, 1988), 89. Neither this compound nor the form given by the MSS is found in Photius' lexicon or the *Synagoge*. ἐνα- seems not to occur again until Diod. Sic. 34/5. 2. 12.

68 Van Herwerden, *Mnemosyne*^{2}, 10 (1882), 85–6, asserted without giving examples that μέλας and μέγας are often confused. His argument in favour of the change was that the son as a young man presumably had dark hair in contrast to the elderly father. Perhaps one might add that this makes just as good a point as emphasizing the stature of the man seen on the roof. Examples of the confusion between the two words can be seen at Soph. *OT* 742 μέλας **rp**: μέγας L**pat** (in the OCT the former is preferred) and at Nicander, *Theriaca* 327, where the reading μέλας applied to a snake's venom presented by the MSS MR is clearly preferable to μέγας, found in the other MSS. At Dem. 21. 71 μέλας is the reading of the MSS to describe

Sophilos the pancratiast, whereas the three known sources of indirect tradition give μέγας, which doubtless seemed a more appropriate epithet for a pancratiast.

98 The accepted text is υἱὸν Πυριλάμπους and is translated 'the son of Pyrilampes', despite the absence of the definite article, which might have been expected. Most MSS supply the article τόν in place of υἱόν, which makes the line unmetrical; Bentley proposed τὸν τοῦ, which appealed to Blaydes. It has been objected that one does not find the genitive of the article used with the father's name.

113 Sommerstein (2001: 266) says that the reading of P.Oxy. 4512 (P75)]ήcαντες is more likely to represent the (faulty) reading of RV ἐνδήcαντες. I think he is right. As the scribe of P75 elsewhere employs the iota adscript when appropriate it is less likely that he intended -ήcαντες, and in his period it would have been more normal to write -κλείω if that was the verb he intended.

147 If Philocleon is being told 'Won't you go back down?' the introductory particle ἀτάρ seems out of place. Rather than an adversative we would expect οὔκουν in this kind of question, which amounts to an order. For this reason I suggest that the various compounds of ἔρρω printed by most editors are not the best solution to the problem. ἐς- is the wrong preposition (we expect εἰς- anyway), and Sommerstein does better with his proposal of κατ-. Although the verb is idiomatic in some contexts like the present, it may have been substituted for a much rarer one. The meaning I would expect is 'But after this you will not slip out'; so read οὐκέτ' ἐκφρήcει, future middle. Other forms of the verb occur in this scene; it has survived at 156 and needs to be introduced by emendation at 162. Blaydes had already tried οὐ γὰρ ἐκφρήcω ce, which is a bit further from the MSS reading, whereas Elmsley suggested οὐκέτ' ἐρρήcεις. φρέω is discussed by Barrett on Eur. *Hipp.* 866–7 and Mastronarde on Eur. *Phoen.* 264.

151 If νῦν (RV) is adopted, the scansion of Καπνίου implies paratragedy. Sommerstein accepts this reading; P. Rau, *Paratragodia* (Munich, 1967), 192 did not include this line in his list of passages. MacDowell prefers νυνί.

188–9 E. L. Bowie's conjecture ψωλίῳ appeared in E. M. Craik (ed.),

Wasps 83

Owls to Athens (Oxford, 1990), 33. Though the word would be *lexicis addendum*, at the very least it deserves inclusion in the apparatus.

220 A comic adjective filling the whole line seems appropriate; but R separates the first element ἀρχαῖα. MacDowell is right to conclude that the scholia are not clear enough to support the view that Aristarchus had the same reading as R.

230–4 *LGPN* ii is inclined to treat some of the names in these lines as fictional. I am pretty sure that this is a mistake. Sommerstein correctly pointed to the occurrence of the very rare name Strymodorus in Aegina (Dem. 36. 29), where the poet appears to have had connections, and the almost equally rare Euergides in a casualty-list (*IG* i³. 1190. 30) of *c*.411. Cf. below on 401 and 1201.

Bearing in mind the appearance of Amphitheos in *Acharnians*, who would seem to be a man with a personal link to the poet, one is tempted to ask whether here too Aristophanes is enjoying some kind of private communication with friends and acquaintances. Was there a joke that they appreciated and we cannot? Would the friends have taken such a mention as a compliment? I find this very puzzling.

240 Commentators here seem content with the syntax, but they do not offer good parallels. Florens Christianus thought it necessary to supply a word such as δίκη or τιμωρία. The implausibility of that approach needs no comment. Blaydes as usual made some fairly radical suggestions, but he also noted *Knights* 87, which is some help; however, it is not an exact parallel because of the prepositional phrase found there. One may note also ps.-Dem. 25. 51 οὗτος ... οὐδ' ἂν ἔχοι δεῖξαι πρὸς ὅτῳ τὸν βίον ἐςτὶ τῶν μετρίων ἢ καλῶν, where again the prepositional phrase makes a difference.

As a very long shot, I wonder if the right reading could be ἧπται. This diagnostic conjecture would yield the sense 'Laches has been attacked', with the alternative possible meaning 'A start has been made on Laches'. *Eccl.* 581 is perhaps a parallel for this latter usage.

281 MacDowell notes that the transmitted reading χθεςινὸν appears to have a parallel in an unspecified passage of Aristophanes cited by Phrynichus, *Ecloge* 295R (294 Fischer). Since the apparent occurrence of the word at *Frogs* 987 is unacceptable for metrical reasons, he wonders if the reference is to our passage. That is uncertain, given the large number of lost plays; alternatively one might suggest that Phrynichus had a copy that was already corrupt. In any case the metrical argument in favour of Hermann's χθιζινὸν is strong.

319 Thiercy is the latest editor to be dissatisfied with the paradoxical joke, and for ᾄδειν substitutes ᾄccειν, which he renders ('je ne puis) bondir'. But, as MacDowell points out, if any emendation is to be attempted here, the meaning would be 'come out', a not very fortunate anticipation of the next sentence.

342 Δημολογοκλέων is problematic and many emendations have been proposed. The word is clearly meant to be abusive, but it is spoken by someone who is presumably favourable to Cleon; perhaps that gives an extra twist to the humour, in that the speaker's excitement causes him to say something inconsistent with his usual attitudes.

The formation of the word raises doubts. Is the second element designed to produce a metrical substitute for Δημηγορο-? Perhaps we should accept that; one alternative would be to try to insert the concept of 'deceit'. Hermann's suggestion Δεινολογο- also deserves mention.

399 Most MSS read πρύμναν, and MacDowell's confident assertion that the alpha is proved to be long by the parallel in Soph. *Phil.* 482 is not one that I can subscribe to. For the difficulties of that passage see H. Lloyd-Jones and N. G. Wilson, *Sophoclea* (Oxford, 1990), 189–90. Here one should probably follow C and Elmsley or transpose the noun after the verb (H.-S.); but in the parallels listed by Blaydes the noun precedes the verb.

401 Two of the names in this line invite comment. (i) Teisiades. *LGPN* ii gives him as the first of four bearers of the name and treats him as fictional, quite without justification as far as I can see. Inscriptions apparently confirm the spelling preferred by van Herwerden. (ii) Chremon with eta in the first syllable is not found in any of the volumes of the *LGPN* so far published, but curiously the spelling with an epsilon is known from Lysias 30. 12 and 14 and Xenophon, *Hell.* 2. 3. 2. Do we have here a comic distortion of the name?

446 The paradosis is ὥϲτε μὴ ῥιγῶν γ᾽, with R diverging slightly (ῥιγόντ᾽). Dindorf and others, most recently Sommerstein, delete the particle γ᾽. I have followed them, but with a slight hesitation, because Denniston, *GP* 140, quotes consecutive clauses introduced by ὥϲτε γε, which is close without being exactly parallel. If the deletion is right it may be argued that the particle was erroneously duplicated here, but is in place in the following clause.

447 οὐδ᾽ ἐν κτλ. The meaning appears to be 'not even in their eyes (let alone their behaviour)'. MacDowell preferred to read οὐδέν 'not at all', because the eyes are a normal place to show αἰδώϲ. But whether this usage of οὐδέν is idiomatic in Aristophanes may be doubted. Blaydes went so far as to read τοῖϲιν for οὐδέν.

460 If initial ἆρα here is not interrogative, it would appear to be the first example of the usage otherwise cited a century later from New Comedy (Menander fr. 129, etc.) and characterised by Denniston, *GP* 48 n. 2, as standing 'in a sentence of gnomic or reflective character, marking the realization of a universal truth'. But *Wasps* 460 is not a sentence of that type, and in any case one might observe that the transition from a question asked with a certain degree of confidence to a statement of the expected answer is not a difficult change to imagine, so that it is not clear at what stage the interrogative intonation was felt to have been lost. MacDowell wondered if a better parallel was *Birds* 797, but Dunbar ad loc. takes it as a relatively rare example of ἆρα expecting an affirmative reply, and that is how I would prefer to deal with 460, admittedly with considerable hesitation. Blaydes was willing to contemplate the transposition ἀποϲοβήϲειν ἆρ᾽ ἐμέλλομέν κτλ.. I take the line to be a self-satisfied sneering question, better on the lips of the young master than coming from a slave.

466 See below on *Lys.* 350.

471 The examples of the omission of ἄν in clauses of this type cited by MacDowell are all from tragedy; so perhaps van Herwerden was right to propose ἂν ἐκ for ἄνευ.

522–5 I find it odd that recent editors do not even consider Halbertsma's proposal to transpose 522–3 after 525, which would appear to achieve a better climax. Is it perhaps an objection that then the transition from 521 καὶ μὴν ἐγώ to 524 εἰπέ μοι is a trifle abrupt? With the transmitted order Philocleon's melodramatic threat is ignored; was it delivered as an aside, so that Bdelycleon did not hear it?

534–7 By punctuating at the end of 534 and making a slight adjustment of the conjunction introducing the conditional clause, Sommerstein has enhanced the parallelism in this scene; just as 529–30 interrupted a statement by the chorus, so too 538–9 now do the same.

Emendation is necessary in 536, as Sommerstein (2001: 267) agrees, and the result is that his articulation of the passage gives a mixed conditional sentence, but one of a perfectly acceptable kind. More than one emendation has been tried; I agree with him in preferring Blaydes's cε λέγων κρατήcει to Starkie's c' ἔθ' ἕλοι κρατήcας, even though the latter looks neater palaeographically. However, one may doubt whether ἔτι is in place (Soph. *Ant.* 69–70, cited by Starkie, is a statement designed for a slightly different situation).

554 The transmitted text has a clumsy change of subject from plural to singular, easily removed by Blaydes, who plausibly assumed that μοι was inserted as a gloss. The alternative remedy is to read προcιών τιc in the preceding line, which is possible, but I prefer to retain the sequence of ἕρποντ' and προcιόντι.

555 The formation of the compound οἰκτροχοοῦντες worried Blaydes, since other compound verbs in -χοεῖν have a noun in the first element. He wondered if a compound in οἰκτο- should be substituted. But perhaps the text can stand, as there is an entry in Hesychius ο 282 οἰκτρογοοῦντας, glossed οἰκτιζομένους, ἐλεουμένους. Latte's edition records no attempt to emend this entry. As it is a quotation in the accusative, it cannot be taken as a variant reading for l. 555. But the difference in meaning between -χοεῖν and -γοεῖν, the former being transitive, leaves a nagging doubt.

565 In this very difficult passage MacDowell and Sommerstein accept Paley's emendation. MacDowell does, however, admit that this usage of εἶμι is not paralleled in an uncompounded form without prepositional prefix. The change of subject from plural to singular seems more awkward here than in 568, even though many scholars accept it, as they do at 554 above. I think it likely that ἀνιών, found in V only, is a mistake arising from a kind of dittography. The assumption by Erfurdt and others that κακοῖϲιν was inadvertently omitted after κακά is not extravagant. On balance, in order to provide a readable text, I have preferred the Blaydes–Erfurdt solution. The change in the verb of theta to sigma was an easy corruption.

588 Sommerstein, CQ^2 27 (1977), 267–8, was inclined to accept the transmitted text, though not with much confidence. He noted that 'if we retain ϲεμνόν, then τούτων must have the same reference'. But the change from singular to plural τουτί/τούτων is difficult, a fact which is disguised in his translation. The omission of the personal pronoun, for which he offers a partial parallel in expressions with ἀπολεῖϲ (με), could very easily be remedied by τούτων <ϲ'> ὧν εἴρηκαϲ μακαρίζω, which gives excellent word-order, the unstressed pronoun occupying, as it should, second position in its clause.

Reiske's ϲε μόνον with removal of the punctuation is also attractive, even if it leads to a slightly unexpected construction with a double accusative. Hence Blaydes's proposal for further alteration to τούτου ... μόνου. But at that point one begins to wonder if the changes are becoming too drastic to be plausible.

599 Blaydes deserves credit for noticing (as apparently Meineke also had) that names in -ιοϲ tend to be late, so that one should consider reading Εὐφήμου γ'. LGPN ii confirms his instinct; there is no other example of the transmitted name in the fifth and fourth centuries, whereas Euphemos is well attested. Meineke proposed Εὐφημίδου, which is a trifle easier palaeographically, and two fifth-century bearers of that name are revealed by LGPN ii. It was W. Schulze, *Orthographica et Graeca Latina* (Sussidi Eruditi, 14; Rome, 1958), 95–6, who showed that names in -ιυϲ/-ιοϲ became popular from the third century AD onwards.

601 MacDowell cites *Clouds* 1071–2 as a parallel for the word-order, but I do not find that wholly convincing. The syntax is perhaps to be explained as reflecting the excitement of the speaker; of the various suggestions for making it more regular that of Blaydes is plausible and not drastic.

634 Dawes, *Miscellanea critica* (p. 231 in the Oxford edition of 1781) preferred οὗτος to the 'plane inepta vocula οὕτω', and Blaydes says that it is in fact the reading of B, C, and G (his S). This is not so. The confusion is easy and *pace* Dawes there is little to choose between the readings.

651 Reiske's ἐντετακυῖαν is a very simple adjustment and appears to gain support from Soph. *El.* 1311 μῖσός τε γὰρ παλαιὸν ἐντέτηκέ μοι and Plat. *Menex.* 245 D ὅθεν καθαρὸν τὸ μῖσος ἐντέτηκε τῇ πόλει. The alpha in place of eta is perhaps an objection, as Sommerstein noted; but Blaydes offered as parallel forms ἀραρυῖα λελακυῖα γεγαυῖα τεθαλυῖα μεμαυῖα ἐμπεφυυῖα besides Eupolis 472 πεπαγοίην. While this last example is insecure, as it might be a Doric form, at least some of the others appear to be sound.

680 Denniston, *GP* 120, lists this line as one of the few instances of γε used with a numeral. The particle is transmitted in the principal MSS but not printed by MacDowell or Sommerstein. It is far from clear why in this context the speaker should wish to emphasise the numeral. Does the particle make him seem ridiculous because of pointless emphasis or exaggeration? Self-importance and insistence could create this effect. Blaydes wondered if the particle was misplaced and tentatively suggested γ' αὐτός, throwing the emphasis on the name of the greengrocer or whatever Eucharidas was. I suppose the implication would be that the man was an unsatisfactory supplier with whom people preferred to avoid dealing if possible; in other words, Philocleon was very hard pressed.

The other point to note in this line is καὐτός. 'I too (like others)' can probably stand, but Zacher's κἀχθές should be noted.

704–5 Both the compound verbs in ἐπι- are problematic. Uncompounded σίζω is intransitive, as is presumably ῥύζω. In the present passage we need at least one verb to be transitive, and LSJ appear to treat both as such. For ἐπισίζω they compare Hesychius ε 5129 ἐπιρροιζεῖν, which is glossed ἐπισίζειν, ἐπισεύειν, ἐπεγκελεύειν; here the second explanation is transitive. In the scholia Eratosthenes and Lycophron are cited as treating ἐπισίζω as transitive, which is also the implication of Hesychius ε 5165/6. With the particle γ' as transmitted the translation requires 'he' to be italicized as in

Sommerstein. Though that is possible I feel that the emphasis is unnecessary and the substitution of the pronoun c' as proposed by Meineke gives a better balance to the sentence.

ἐπιρύζω is another rarity; LSJ compare ῥύζω 'growl, snarl', which again is uncommon and presumably intransitive. The scholia, for what it is worth, regard this verb as transitive.

As to the tense of the verb, the MSS divide, with RLVp3 offering the present and VΓ the aorist. In a clause beginning with ὅταν a present has much to commend it and the confusion of xi and zeta was easy.

735 The repetition of παρών needs to be examined. Not that repetition as such is out of the question: Jackson, *MS* 220–2, showed that it is commoner in ancient texts than is consistent with modern taste. The transmitted text is usually defended either by arguing that Philocleon is to play his part in the ensuing action, for which *Birds* 548 is offered as a parallel, or that he is to respond to the god's kindness by not absenting himself. Sommerstein's gloss 'Do not withdraw yourself' is perhaps possible.

πρόφρων, as Dunbar on *Birds* 930 remarks, is used of gods or mortals graciously granting requests (she quotes four parallels from poetry). Though she says that the *Birds* passage is the only place where the word occurs in our author, she has not taken account of the conjecture by Reisig at *Lys.* 316. There is a good chance that Kock was right to introduce it here.

788–9 Commentators assume that a drachma was handed to each pair of jurors, who then had to get change in order to receive their individual fee. This notion is supported by the scholia, where, however, no ancient authority is cited. It may be that this was the regular practice to save the clerk of the court the bother of having to keep a lot of small change. But I wonder if the explanation may be that the mint was unable to maintain an adequate supply of small change.

804 What is the correct spelling of the word for the shrine of Hekate found by the front door of an Athenian house? The MSS offer Ἑκαταῖον (or the proparoxytone variant suggested by the scholia in V and Γ on the authority of Callistratus). Morphologically this is possible, as is shown by the proper name and by Ἡραῖον. But *temenika* are often formed in -εῖον. The Aldine scholion supports this by saying ἔν τισι γὰρ εὕρηται Ἑκαταῖον. But as Koster notes in his edition of the scholia this may simply be an addition by Musurus from the *Suda* entry ε 361 (where Adler prints the word as proparoxytone). That entry, however, relates to *Lys.* 64, as Blaydes saw, but which Sommerstein fails to make clear; from his apparatus it might be inferred that the *Suda* was quoting l. 804. LSJ were inclined to accept either spelling as valid, but the *Supplement* gives -εῖον as the form in l. 804. E. Simon, *Athenische Mitteilungen*, 100 (1985), 271–84, uses the form Hekataion without discussion; she is referring to statues rather than shrines. Threatte does not help us to solve this problem.

834 E. L. Bowie's conjecture φιλοχοιρία allows an attractive interpretation of the rare word χοιροκομεῖον in 844. But I do not see anything in the immediately preceding context to justify it.

877 I accept Elmsley's adjustment because the first vowel in λίαν is long in Aristophanes and these lines are not parody of tragedy, which sometimes has a short vowel (e.g. Aesch.(?) *PV* 1031). It is none the less a trifle odd that the deictic form τουτί was erroneously introduced into the text, unless we may posit an ancient reader with incomplete metrical knowledge influenced by his acquaintance with tragedy. However, for the intrusion of deictic forms see the apparatus at *Ach.* 108 and *Clouds* 847.

878 This line is puzzling. I take the essential fact here to be that honey is the sweetest of all substances, and infer that there is reference to something less sweet. Sommerstein's rendering 'like sweetening boiled wine' therefore seems inappropriate. One way to understand the text would be to suppose that boiled must was commonly used as a comforting sweet drink, but in the present case a still sweeter substance is needed in order to mollify Philocleon. cιραῖoc is mentioned by late medical writers (Dioscorides 5. 6. 4, Aretaeus 5. 1. 17 etc., Galen x. 403K), and a variant of the word is attested in Nicander, *Alex.* 153.

890 Rather hesitantly I accept Meineke's supplement to promote exact responsion. Some scholars think the invocation appropriate in 874 because of the vocative in 869, but reject it here. However, in 885 the antistrophe begins 'we pray', and I think that may justify Meineke's proposal.

897 In *CQ*² 25 (1975), 151 I suggested that there may be an additional joke here if it was the custom for the expelled scapegoat (φαρμακός) to wear such a collar. See L. Deubner, *Attische Feste* (Berlin, 1932), 179. I repeat the observation here, since it appears not to have been noticed and I still think it has a chance of being correct.

908 The prosecuting dog begins to address the jury and one would expect him to use the polite formula in order to cultivate their good will. But the transmitted text seems not to have the vocative particle. Contrast 950, where Bdelycleon begins the speech for the defence. See above on *Ach.* 53.

939 Blaydes's conjecture πάντα for τἄλλα is doubtless based on the plausible assumption that a scribe could have been distracted by the occurrence of ἀλλ' at the beginning of the next line. Thiercy 326, translates 'tous les autres ...' without comment.

942-3 The syntax is open to question here. A construction of the type οὐ παύcει ... ἀλλ' ...; is an invitation to stop performing one activity and begin another. But ὀδὰξ ἔχει refers to a continuation of the activity being complained of. Hence Blaydes proposed ὧν for ἀλλ', and I think he was right.

967 Most editors seem content with the traditional text here, which entails either a proceleusmatic or unusual scansion of the imperative. Neither of these explanations is at all attractive. It is far easier to follow Triclinius in removing the definite article. Though this results in intelligible wording, I have come round to the view that Richards and Starkie were right to suppose that ἐλέει is a gloss which ousted αἰδοῦ.

983 Hirschig's alteration of a single letter is very attractive, since it is supported by the parallel in 882 and the scholiast's ἐπιδακρύcαc. Of course the scholia may be in error: ἀποδακρύειν with γνώμην ἐμήν as its object can be understood, even if a precise parallel is yet to be found.

1024 ἐκτελέcαι is taken as intransitive by MacDowell in the sense 'end up/turn out/become', with a possible parallel in Simonides

86W, cf. LSJ s.v. τελέω I. Sommerstein similarly translates 'he didn't end up getting above himself'. This is not convincing, even if it has the support of van Herwerden, *Vindiciae Aristophaneae*, 50; he thought the usage analogous to Latin *absolvere* with no object stated. Blaydes as usual has various conjectures to record. A. Palmer's οὐχὶ τρυφῆcαι is not easy to explain palaeographically. ἐκγελάcαι seems closer to the paradosis but has less relevance to the context; it could be an allusion to the behaviour of another poet, not recorded elsewhere.

For these reasons I proposed in *CQ*² 50 (2000), 597 ἐκχαλάcαι. This makes the poet say that he did not slack off, i.e. relax in his efforts, because he had got above himself; the idea is expanded in 1029–37. The word is very rare, but is found in the Corpus Hippocraticum, *De septimestri partu* 1, vii. 436. 11 L. = *De octimestri partu* 4. 5. 2 *CMG* I 2,1, p. 90. 6 ed. H. Grensemann (Berlin, 1968) = *De octimenstri partu* 1. 2 in the Budé series, xi. 164. 14 ed. R. Joly, who concludes (p. 161) that the treatise does not need to be dated any later than the end of the fifth century.

1029 Even a critic of generally conservative tendency such as MacDowell is prepared to admit that the text may be corrupt because the active of ἄρχω in the sense required has no parallel, and B's restoration of the metre by the insertion of γ' is suspiciously facile. Hirschig tried ἤρξατο ποιεῖν. I wonder if the verb should be ἐπῆλθε, which could be either impersonal 'it occurred (to him) to produce' or in the sense 'came forward', as in Thucydides and elsewhere; if the latter, perhaps one would need to make the further adjustment διδάcκων or διδάξων rather than accept an infinitive of purpose.

1030 Meineke's change to a finite verb in the imperfect tense is easy; the present infinitive jars in the context.

1040 I am not satisfied with the transmitted text. Why are the villains said to lie on beds? MacDowell seems to take the same view as Sommerstein, who translates 'on the beds of the peaceable folk among you'. This picture of cuckoos in the nest seems inappropriate. Mastromarco and Thiercy have attempted to reflect more precisely on the articulation of the Greek.

Is lying on a bed a sign of luxury, in this case the result of ill-gotten gains? Or is there meant to be a contrast between their recumbent posture and the terrified activity of their victims? But that only becomes apparent two lines later, which is not satisfactory. Hamaker thought that the people in bed were the unfortunate victims of the crimes named in the preceding line. His proposal κατακλινομένουϲ ἐν followed by ἐπὶ τοῖϲί τ' restores the sense needed.

1091 There are two difficulties here. (i) *Pace* MacDowell and Sommerstein, and despite a possible parallel at 460 above, I feel uneasy about seeing inferential ἆρα in initial position. If the sentence is to be taken as a question, the articulation of it needs to be examined. The continuation καὶ κατεϲτρεψάμην may be in order, but the sentence runs more smoothly if one replaces καί with ὅϲ. (ii) The MSS here offer πάντα μὴ δεδοικέναι, accepted by MacDowell without comment; Sommerstein regarded it as a possibility, translating 'I was not afraid of anything'. But the normal way of saying that was surely μηδέν με δεδοικέναι. This is no doubt why Dobree suggested πάντα μ' ἄν, 'so that anyone would have feared me'. But the potential particle introduces the wrong note into what should be the confident boast of a character in Old Comedy. The right sense is obtained with Hirschig's πάνταϲ ἐμέ. But this too has a drawback: the reason for the corruption is not obvious, nor is the emphatic form of the pronoun suitable. A less drastic approach is to see the fault in πάντα; so read ταῦτα, cf. above on *Knights* 474.

1128 Threatte i. 560 says that the change from κν- to γν- begins to appear *c.*400. Does that mean that γν- is impossible in a text written about twenty years before the turn of the century? Or could this be accepted as the first instance in literature of the new pronunciation? Despite these doubts I have followed editors since Dindorf.

1138 The deme Thumaitadai and the phratry Thumaitis are discussed by C. W. Hedrick Jr. in *Hesperia*, 57 (1988), 81–5. I confess to being puzzled as to why the adjective in the text appears to refer to the phratry rather than the deme, which was presumably the source of the cloaks. But perhaps it is wrong to insist on the distinction; R. C. T. Parker, *Athenian Religion: A History* (Oxford, 1996), 105, remarks: 'the phratries to a considerable extent had the character of local associations, most members of a given phratry belonging to the deme in which its altar lay'.

1141 MacDowell accepts τοίνυν because 'it is regularly used when a speaker admits his ignorance of a piece of information just given to him; cf. *Peace* 615, *Birds* 511', and he rejects Wilamowitz's conjecture οὐδὲ νῦν. Blaydes too thought the particle 'ineptum' and proposed οὐκ ἔγωγ' or οὐ δῆτ', οὐχ. It is right to query the text as the passages cited by MacDowell are not identical parallels, and Denniston, *GP* 573, also singled out this passage as curious. He noted two further suggestions: οὗτοι νῦν γ' by Starkie, and οὐ τανῦν γ' by A. Palmer. I have little doubt that Starkie was right.

1150 ἀναμπιϲχόμενοϲ is from a verb not otherwise attested. Presumably the meaning is 're-dressed'. But it is tempting to adopt von Holzinger's ἅμ' ἀμπιϲχόμενοϲ, which is slightly easier than other proposals.

1158 Some editors keep ὑπόδυθι 'get down into' followed by an accusative without preposition. That usage is found in Homer; I am not sure that it is appropriate in the dialogue of Attic comedy. Hirschig preferred to restore a form of ὑποδεῖϲθαι and tried ὑποδοῦ λαβών (om. τάϲ), following Meineke, and van Herwerden preferred ὑποδοῦ δ' ἀνύϲαϲ τι. A simpler remedy is to accept Hirschig's basic idea, with the pronoun ϲύ to supply the short syllable required.

1184 καὶ ταῦτα is puzzling. Commentators assume that Theogenes was a rude man. If λοιδορούμενοϲ is active in sense, the meaning is that he used the expressions given in the text rather than stronger language; presumably he is being laughed at for his failure to find the *mot juste*. If instead the participle is passive, the meaning is that he failed to find the stronger language which, as the victim of abuse, he could justifiably have used. But the passive would be compatible with the view that he was a polite man, who restrained himself under provocation.

1190 Dobree's conjecture seems worth a mention because the imperfect tense is not what we expect (cf. 1383). Denniston, *GP* 444, gives examples of ἀλλ'οὖν (... γε) 'still, at least', but none is from Aristophanes. There is a further reason for doubt: one may reasonably ask whether γ' as transmitted here is in the right position; would one not expect it to follow χρή?

1191 Ascondas is attested as a Theban name (*LGPN* iiiB s.v.) with two other examples. Ephudion (ibid. s.v. Ἐφωτίων) is unique.

1193 Blaydes, MacDowell, and Sommerstein retain χέρας. But Wilamowitz had declared (*Kleine Schriften*, i 327) 'χέρας muß weg'. It is misleading of MacDowell to say that this form can be justified in comedy as an alternative to χεῖρας because it is found at *Lys.* 1317 and *Frogs* 1142. In both passages the tone is different, one being a lyric, the other paratragedy. Blaydes had wondered if something was wrong with χέρας, thinking perhaps an adjective desirable here to match the other adjectives in the clause and suggesting e.g. κρατίστην or κραταιάν. A further step in this direction was taken by Starkie, who proposed χἠρακλείαν with λαγόνα. Both Blaydes and Starkie doubted whether the hands should be mentioned between the ribs and the flank. Richards suggested a transposition καὶ λαγόνα/-νε/-νας χεῖράς τε καί, and it has to be said that a dual or plural might be expected. It is not easy to choose between the various solutions. From a palaeographical point of view Richards's is perhaps the simplest, but it does not meet the objection that an epithet is lacking. Starkie's is not as drastic as might be thought at first sight; once the crasis had been misunderstood, unsuccessful attempts to put the text right could have led to the reading of the MSS.

1201 The commentators assure us that Ergasion is a fictional name. But reference to *LGPN* ii proves them wrong; though the compilers of that volume follow the *communis opinio* with regard to the present passage, they themselves demonstrate that it is ill founded by citing three occurrences of the name from the period in question and four others of later date.

1223 I accept the usual solution of the textual problem here, but feel bound to observe that the explanation of the corruption has one strange feature: it assumes that δεδέξεται was a gloss. A plain future would of course serve as a gloss, but hardly the future perfect. Are we to suppose that a further corruption, dittography of the first syllable, occurred?

1251 Wilamowitz's conjecture Κροῖσος acquires some plausibility from the existence of this name in Athens in the fifth century. But neither of the two men listed in *LGPN* ii was a slave.

1262 Though at first tempted to retain the paradosis in the light of J. C. B. Lowe, *Glotta*, 51 (1973), 34–64, I now incline to the view that in this passage the emphasis given by γ' to μαθητέον seems wrong; the stress should rather be on πολλούc, and τοι can be understood as applying to the whole line.

1286 Eric Handley points out to me that με may have ousted an original τι, which could have been partly responsible for the erroneous κακίcταιc. The repetition of the pronoun is certainly unnecessary.

1310 ἀχυρόc with long second syllable finds support in Ar. fr. 234, Photius α 3470, and *App. Prov.* 1. 71. One would nevertheless like to know why the vowel is long when it is short in ἄχυρα. Dindorf's conjecture is well worth recording.

1369 The transmitted text gives a split anapaest at the end of the second metron, for which one may consult Dover's note on *Clouds* 62, and the scansion of ποίαν as an iambus, accepted by White, *Verse*, 367, para. 801. But since there appears to be no better parallel than *Peace* 1111, which is a hexameter line, not an iambic, I feel that emendation has to be considered. (i) Elmsley tried ποίων cυμποτῶν, at first sight attractive, but if it is accepted 1371 seems inconsequential. (ii) Hermann's τὴν αὐλητρίδα is easy, but the cause of the corruption is far from obvious. (iii) The slightly less frequent expression πόθεν might have caused a scribe trouble, and I favour this suggestion by Dindorf.

1391 '... and four loaves besides' or something similar is the translation usually given. I find this rather weak. If she meant 'fourteen', why not say so? MacDowell is reduced to saying 'The reason for mentioning the four loaves separately is that they did not come to an exact number of obols.' This is not convincing, since there were coins for small fractions of an obol, and it is hardly conceivable that four loaves could not have been paid for by one or more pieces of small change. (I am grateful to Dr Henry Kim for his advice on this point.) I share Blaydes's doubts, which go back to Dobree, who did not make them explicit. I would hazard the guess that Myrtia was carrying a tray of loaves with a cover, and her claim that the latter was worth four obols is a comic exaggeration (like the figure ten?). ἐπιθήκη is less usual than ἐπίθημα, but as neither word is common it is rash to pontificate about their usage. One might even ask whether these words could have the meaning 'tray'.

1397 Kock is reported as having objected to the form θυγατέρος; Sommerstein and MacDowell accept it, the latter quoting Eur. *Or.* 751 as a parallel and alleging that the form is adopted here for metrical convenience, but there must be some doubt whether tragic usage can safely be invoked. Richards sensibly proposed γενομένης. For the intrusion of θυγάτηρ as a gloss cf. Soph. *OT* 1101.

1424 The variant τραύματος in B is striking and Blaydes wondered if it could be right. πρᾶγμα is such a common word and occurs at the end of 1426, that the notion is not absurd.

This variant runs counter to the notion that B reflects a later Triclinian recension than that seen in L; it is not the kind of change that one would normally ascribe to Triclinius, because he concentrated on the elimination of metrical faults, and now we know who the scribe of B was the case against that hypothesis is strengthened.

1443 Does B's variant here have any claim to be treated as the preservation of ancient tradition? If it is an emendation by the scribe of B, or as used to be suggested, by Triclinius, it goes rather further than might be expected. There was no obvious reason to alter the transmitted text. One cannot absolutely rule out the notion that the scribe had access to a good MS, now lost; but I am not aware of any other passage that could lend support to this hypothesis.

1507–8 The sequence of thought in these two lines makes it virtually certain that Badham was right to emend. The MSS have γε, which can be explained as either a careless repetition of the particle from earlier in the line or a misinterpretation of the letter gamma used as a numeral. To write the numerals in abbreviated form was not the normal practice in copies of Greek literary texts, but it was not unknown; see the valuable observations of E. G. Turner, *Greek Manuscripts of the Ancient World*, 2nd edn., rev. P. J. Parsons (London, 1987), 15.

1509 Sommerstein's note is an admirably clear statement of the puzzle in this line. Recently Thiercy 1128–9 has proposed to read ὄφις for ὀξίς, scanning the omicron as long. Though *Iliad* 12. 208 and Hipponax 28. 6W (39. 6D) are cited for this scansion, I very much doubt if it is possible in our author, and I observe that West in his edition accepts Bergk's emendation ὄπφιν.

1514 Hermann's objection to ὦζυρέ as an inappropriate repetition from 1504 has some point. The drawback of his proposal ἐπ' αὐτούς μοι. cὺ δὲ is that the enclitic μοι might be expected to occur earlier in the sentence.

Peace

6 There are three possible approaches to this line. (i) οὐ κατέφαγεν; means 'Didn't he eat it?' or 'Did he not eat it?', and is answered 'No, by Zeus, rather he . . .'. (ii) But Sommerstein does not print it as a question and renders 'He can't have eaten it.' Literally it is 'He hasn't eaten it', which is different in nuance. (iii) The negative implied in the response beginning μὰ τὸν Δία makes it attractive to assume an overtly sceptical question, as is obtained by Bentley's ἦ or Blaydes's μῶν. The negative appears more appropriate if there is a strong contrast between what the first speaker says and the reply from his colleague. The corruption is easily explained by the presence of the syllable ου at the beginning of l. 5, which could have provoked an error.

16 Olson points out that the late MSS PC have ἑτέρας τε, 'a typical majuscule error', i.e. TE for ΓE; but that explanation is not relevant here, as we are not dealing with a hyparchetype written in majuscule script. The particle might equally well have intruded from the following line. Triclinius inevitably corrected to γε. If that particle is needed, one might share Sommerstein's preference for placing it immediately after the verb, τρῖβέ γ'. Despite the absence of a parallel from Aristophanes for ἔθ' ἑτέρας, Dindorf's assumption of an error caused by haplography seems a good solution.

24 Richards' ὅςαπερ is ingenious, shifting the emphasis from the type of matter to its quantity (better 'totality' H.-S.). Defenders of the paradosis must rely on the following lines, in which preparation rather than quantity is in question.

ὡς ἄν 'however' is exemplified by LSJ s.v. ὡς A c 2 from Soph. *Aj.* 1369, Plat. *Symp.* 181 A, cf. Ap. Rhod. 3. 350. But they take l. 24 s.v.

ὥςπερ III 2 as meaning 'as soon as', citing no other example, and this is not very plausible. The Sophocles passage did not survive the scrutiny of the OCT editors, but the Platonic passage seems to be a sound parallel.

LSJ do not suggest that ὥςπερ ἄν is used in indefinite modal clauses, and the same impression is created by Cooper–Krüger ii. 1458–9 (§69. 64). H.-S. notes, however, ὅπηπερ ἄν in Plat. *Soph.* 251 A and *Tim.* 45 C, to which I can now add *Laws* 711 B.

41 The first part of this line may be a continuation of the preceding sentence, judging by the examples offered in Denniston, *GP* 338 and 585. If there were a change of speaker, as in Olson's text, I think it quite likely that different particles would have been used, e.g. οὐδ' αὖ.

42 Platnauer cites *Knights* 426 and 879–80 for instances of οὐκ ἔςθ' ὅπως followed by οὐ after one or more intervening words, and infers that Bentley's οὐκ ... τοῦ in place of τοῦτ' ... οὐ is not needed. As Platnauer and others have noted, Bentley's idea gains some support from V's reading τοῦ for οὐ. Does Platnauer's observation settle the matter? In the cases he cites οὐ still precedes the verb, which is not true of the transmitted reading. I suspect that this is the decisive criterion, and so believe that Bentley was right.

48 If the paradosis is to be retained and the reference is to Cleon, a verb in the past tense is required, as he was already dead. Hence the proposal ἔςθιεν by Palmerius, i.e. Jacques Le Paulmier (1587–1670), not the nineteenth-century scholar A. Palmer. The unaugmented imperfect might be acceptable as an Ionic form; Herodotus, apart from omitting the syllabic augment with frequentatives in -ςκω, sometimes omits the temporal augment (K–B ii. 19–21, §199. 6–7). Evidence for uncompounded ἐςθίω is incomplete; Herodotus does not use it in past tenses but has the imperfect κατήςθιον at 1. 78 and 8. 115. It is more attractive, however, to retain the present ἐςθίει and see in the adverb ἀναιδέως a mild corruption of ἐν Ἀΐδεω. The definite article is superfluous and on either view unmetrical. It could only be retained if κεῖνος were to be taken as referring to the beetle and Bentley's emendation ἀνέδην were accepted. But this makes the Ionian's utterance disjointed.

52 It is reasonable enough to accept B's reading as an intelligent conjecture.

83 The *Rhetorikai lexeis* published by Mark N. Naoumides (Athens, 1973) were compiled by a medieval reader who knew inter alia several of Aristophanes' plays; the variants he records need to be taken seriously. Sommerstein (2001: 274) does well to point out that the adjective seems more in accordance with the poet's usage than the adverb.

98 Dobree's φράζω may have been designed to restore the normal diaeresis in such a line. While that is not essential, it does seem to me that the injunction to the world at large comes better from Trygaeus than his slave. Dobree compared Soph. *Trach.* 468 and *Birds* 1085 (φράζομεν); but his preferred reading here was φράζειν, to be taken as the equivalent of an imperative.

107 Threatte ii. 534–5 deals with ἀναγορεύω (but not with the other compounds or with the uncompounded verb). He finds that the earliest example of the aorist in -cα in a place where ἀνεῖπον etc. would be normal is in an inventory of 325/4 BC. I do not see any means of determining whether this form was impossible in 421 BC in a literary text.

114 The scholia in R and V have ἦ ῥ' instead of ἆρ'. Dindorf (as quoted by Blaydes) noted that this usage is found in tragedy, but thought it had been introduced by scribal error both here and at *Thesm.* 260. In the latter passage he is obviously right; here, however, the context is paratragic, so there is a case for ἦ ῥ'. If the parody began with this formula, the stylistic register would be more elevated, but perhaps the poet did not take this opportunity, especially as Euripides was his target, and neither in fr. 17, which is the source here, nor elsewhere does Euripides appear to have used this interrogative formula.

125 Given that 124 and 126 are perfectly paratragic lines from the metrical point of view, and there is much more of the same in the immediate context, it would be perverse to leave uncorrected the offence against Porson's law that is so easily remedied, and I have therefore adopted Sharpley's τήνδε for ταύτην.

137 Olson accepts the form μέλε'; but though the trisyllabic adjective is to be expected in lyric and epic, it is not right for trimeters in comedy. And though it is two-termination in Eur. *Or.* 207, a lyric passage, I should not expect it to be so here; the required form would be ὦ μελέα. RV have μέλ' ἐάν, which Olson fails to report; this looks to me like false word-division arising from an exemplar which had *scriptio plena* of μέλε.

163, 185 It is worth noting that in these two passages, where a simple metrical correction was required, Triclinius appears not to have been able to make it; I find this particularly surprising in the second passage. Is it likely that L in both passages failed to reproduce his text correctly?

173–298, esp. 197 and 235 J. Irigoin in P. Thiercy and M. Menu (eds.), *Aristophane: la langue, la scène, la cité* (Bari, 1997), 17–41, accepts Holwerda's emendation of the Heliodoran metrical scholium (*Mnemosyne*[4], 17 (1964), 113–39, at 117–18) and places τί φῇς; between 197 and 198, with ἰή ἰή between 235 and 236. The result is a sequence of four units of text numbering 25, 38, 25 and 38 lines, i.e. 173–97, 198–235, 236–61, 262–98. Sommerstein originally did not mention the problem, but Mastromarco (p. 99) had followed Holwerda.

The MSS do offer an *extra metrum* insertion at 261a between the third and fourth of these blocks of text. It should be borne in mind that the scholium refers to 'some copies', and one of the numerals in it is corrupt, since it gives the figure of 51 instead of 25.

I wish someone could explain why an author should have chosen to compose a text in blocks of 25 and 38 lines; even those who believe in numerology as a valid tool for the exegesis of classical texts will not find it easy to demonstrate the significance of these two numbers. And who in the audience or among the reading public of later antiquity would have recognized the alleged symmetry? And if they had, what significance could have been attached to it?

Olson feels able to accept the scholium as it stands without emendation of the numeral; its transmitted reading gives us an *extra metrum* insertion after 223, and the minor emendation of φησί to φῇς was proposed already by von Bamberg, according to Dindorf. Holwerda did not consider this possibility. Sommerstein (2001: 274) is surely right to dismiss all this on the ground that εἰc ποῖον should follow directly εἰc ἄντρον βαθύ.

175 The MSS have cτροφεῖ. Cobet emended to cτρέφει, which is used in contexts of abdominal pain, as Olson's parallels show. But it is hard to see why cτρέφει should have been corrupted. Van Herwerden's approach seems preferable, invoking the principle *utrum in alterum*: the rarer word cτροβεῖ was more likely to have caused difficulty.

176 It is not immediately clear whether the verb should be in the middle, meaning 'to be on one's guard'. Olson dismisses the parallel for the active from *Wasps* 155 on the ground that it is a present imperative; but that fact does not weaken its validity as a parallel. It may be that the distinction between active and middle is to be upheld by taking 'keep guard' as the meaning in the *Wasps* passage, which is not susceptible of emendation.

243 Why is the comic numeral not formed with πολλα-, as is suggested by analogy? LSJ lists no formations in πολλο- from literary texts of the classical period; they offer nothing earlier than πολλοποιόc from Damascius, *De principiis* 34 etc.; see now the Budé edition by Westerink and Combès, ii (1989), 238 n. 3 and note that there is even a verb πολλοποιεῖν in this author.

253 For prodelision of ἕτεροc etc. Blaydes cites *Frogs* 64, *Ach*. 828, *Lys*. 736.

262 εἰ δὲ μή γε was printed by van Herwerden and van Leeuwen, although εἰ δὲ μή is the regular expression. Van Herwerden in his commentary notes Paley's objection to Meineke's 'γὼ κλαύcομαι: the emphasis on the pronoun is uncalled for and prodelision after a pause unlikely. Van Herwerden wondered if εἰ δὲ μή εἰμι should be tried. He dismissed Richter's κεκλαύcεται because μοι would be expected to go with it, and added 'pessime vero Raper κεκλαύcομαι, quod pro κλαύcομαι nemo dixit'. But if *Clouds* 1436 offers the impersonal use of the rare future perfect, why is a personal use excluded? Note also *Wasps* 930, where κεκλάγξομαι is accepted as a future perfect. A good survey of this tense is given by Cooper–Krüger i. 663–6 (§53. 9). The source of κεκλαύcομαι is Thomas Kidd's edition of Dawes's *Miscellanea* (London, 1827), 154 n. 58; the index reveals its author's name as Matthew Raper.

274 Dindorf's conjecture is worth a mention because of the rationale behind it: R is a very good MS and if it has a faulty text, it may nevertheless retain a hint of the true reading.

291 E. Degani, *Rivista di cultura classica e medievale*, 5 (1963), 286–7 = *Filologia e storia* (Spudasmata, 95; Hildesheim, 2004), 837–8, argued for acceptance of the Triclinian version of this line, in which the linguistic solecism is transferred to the end of the line. He has lately received support from Mastromarco in *Da AION a EIKASMOS* (Quaderni Bolognesi di Filologia Classica, Studi, 8; Bologna 2002), 40. They both attribute the reading in question to B and the Aldine, whereas it can now be traced a little further back. They would like to credit Datis with a rhetorically more effective line in which the important word occupies the most emphatic position; but the parallel adduced from *Plutus* 288 could in fact have provoked the variant, and the claim that τέρπομαι is a word of more elevated register than εὐφραίνομαι, which they regard as a gloss, seems to me doubtful.

300 Sommerstein obelizes, while Olson seems content to assume that ἁρπάcαι can be equated with ἑλκύcαι in the sense given by LSJ s.v. II. 4. Blaydes proposed ἑλκύcαι, and one can imagine the corruption being induced by λαβόντεc in the preceding line. Peter Jones ap. Sommerstein (2001: 275) suggests ἀναcπάcαι, which Sommerstein combines with νῦν γὰρ <οὖν>. This is a good idea, but a gentler form of this medicine had already been applied by van Herwerden. αὖ = 'once again' is discussed by Dunbar on *Birds* 226.

316, 326, 337 Sommerstein, who originally obelized at 316 and followed Blaydes at 326 and 337, has now changed his mind (2001: 275), arguing that the intrusion of καί three times in the space of twenty-odd lines is most unlikely. But he admits that emphatic use of the particle after a negative is not easy to parallel. I cannot explain the alleged corruption, but would remark that Byzantine *Kunstprosa* tends to exhibit use of the particle in contexts where a classical author would not have employed it, and a copyist brought up in that tradition would have been more likely to corrupt the text. Olson defended the paradosis at 316 by citing 326 and 337; but those lines both contain negative commands and are therefore different. It is conceivable that a scribe using a text already corrupt at 316 thought that there was a formula consisting of a negative plus τι καί and allowed his attention to wander. With considerable hesitation I have adopted Dobree's conjecture. Meineke's χαίρων has a superficial attraction, but my understanding of the idiom is that it is accompanied by a main verb in the future, and here we have ἔστιν. Could one consider εἶσιν? Or did the line begin νῦν γὰρ οὐκέτ'?

320 The MSS have ὡς followed by the third person imperative. Some editors assume an ellipse of ἴσθι, which seems to me very strained, because the alleged parallels all involve an emphatic assertion and are insufficiently similar. Blaydes suggested καί, which is palaeographically difficult; although the compendium for that word written like our capital S could have been mistaken for the compendium for ὡς, the use of such compendia in the period when the archetype was most probably written was relatively rare. A better approach in my view is to strengthen κυκάτω by making it a compound, e.g. συγκυκάτω, taking up the συν- of the preceding line; the word is used at *Ach.* 531 and *Plutus* 1108.

341 Olson says it is impossible to tell whether R and V have βινεῖν or κινεῖν. That is not so. The facsimile of R shows κινεῖν with no room for doubt. The reading of V is not quite so unambiguous, but I feel reasonably confident that it agrees with R.

364 Denniston, *GP* 438, notes 'the absence of a verb is remarkable' and 'Pl. *R.* 337 D is only superficially similar'. Olson says 'the sense is clear' and translates 'Yes, indeed', while Platnauer rendered 'Well' and Sommerstein 'Very well'. The diversity of opinion has led me to the conclusion that emendation is needed.

402 Most modern editors accept the Triclinian emendation of this line. Olson is the exception; he says it 'stands almost no chance of being what Ar. wrote', without giving a reason. Presumably he feels that Triclinius was simply resorting to the standard remedy of inserting his favourite particle, and it might also be objected that νῦν does not need emphasis in this context. Olson rejects Meineke's proposal because τὰ νῦν (or τανῦν) is not attested in Aristophanes, and in effect obelizes. Personally I doubt whether the expression should be disallowed, even if it would be unique in our author, and I am attracted by the possibility that here V preserves a trace of the true reading. Sommerstein (2001: 275) suggests γὰρ <οὖν>; Denniston, *GP* 446, notes that this is not common in comedy.

416–17 Olson retains the paradosis. He claims, reasonably enough, that a reference to Peace in τήνδε rather than to the ropes (Meineke's proposal τῶνδε) is in order. But his notion that ξύλλαβε 'help with' can take an accusative is dubious: his parallels are unsound, since he misconstrues *Eccl.* 861–2; fr. 626 is textually uncertain; Eur. *Or.* 1346 is quite different; the Xenophon passages offer an accusative of respect. The simple way to retain τήνδε is to accept Meineke's τε for καί, so that the pronoun becomes the object of the next verb. Other, more complex, solutions cannot be ruled out.

479 If van Leeuwen's suggestion is right, the corruption may be supposed to have occurred because a scribe thought of the other use of ἔχομαι which takes a genitive.

530 ὀπώρας is difficult and was obelized by Platnauer. Olson accepts it with the defence that 'the writing is somewhat loose'. But when that admission is taken in conjunction with the clumsy repetition of 524 as transmitted, one is led to the conclusion that emendation there is the simple and correct solution. Blaydes had an acceptable suggestion as an alternative to his emendation in 524. If a reference to Peace is to be made more explicit, a different pronoun might be in place; could the line have begun τηςδὶ δ', with Trygaeus pointing at her?

536 ἱπνόν, the v.l. in the scholium and a lexicon (but apparently with an incorrect smooth breathing), is the *difficilior lectio* and is preferred by Olson because 'it makes better sense in a context of rural festivity . . .'. I rather doubt if that is an objection to the traditional reading, which Sommerstein accepted, supported by two passages in Menander, *Dysc.* 557 and *Epitr.* 462, where the verb διατρέχειν means 'run an errand'; and he pointed to the errand indicated below at 1146. Brunck thought that εἰς ἀγρόν had intruded from 552, and the words occur again in the same position at the end of the line at 569. It also has to be asked how often Athenian women might have been found racing off to the country.

603 If coφώτατοι is right, Hermes must be complimenting the farmers on their devotion to the cause of peace. How do we then account for the variant provided by the indirect tradition? An interpolation of the very rare word could have occurred when a learned reader recalled either Archilochus fr. 109 or Cratinus 211 and perhaps made the dubious assumption that Aristophanes did not feel free to vary a well-known, semi-proverbial expression. If λιπερνῆτες is correct, the MSS of our play have been corrupted by an intrusive gloss; but normally glosses are fairly accurate explanations, which this would not be. I feel very uncertain here.

605 Sommerstein (2001: 276) was right to draw attention to the merit of Herington's suggestion ἧψατ' αὐτῆς, but in reviewing Henderson's Loeb, where it is adopted, he objected (*CR*² 50 (2000), 11) that the verb is less appropriate to Phidias than Pericles. One would like a reading which means 'started a commotion', which is achieved by H.-S.'s proposal.

612 ἄκους' 'unwilling' is just possible, but some reference to the fire would be more suitable, and Blaydes was not stupid to consider ἀφθεῖς'. One could get closer to the paradosis with αἴθους'; the question is whether this rare use of the intransitive active is to be attributed to Aristophanes; the available parallels are Pind. *Ol.* 7.48 and Soph. *Aj.* 286. In uncial script ἄκουσα and αἴθουσα would be fairly easy to confuse, especially if kappa was written in the 'Coptic' style, i.e. with a vertical stroke followed by a curved one that could resemble part of a theta.

613 Olson notes that the idea of πίθοι assaulting each other is odd. Doubts are not assuaged by what Taillardat, *Images*, 140, has to say; he cites Mazon, but only succeeds in proving that neither of them had thought hard about the passage. The sense is better if we have a verb meaning 'responded angrily with a noise'. Hence ἀντελάκησεν may be suggested, another compound of this rare verb being found at *Clouds* 410 (διαλακήσασα). If this proposal is right, the word is *lexicis addendum*. It may be argued that πληγείς justifies a form of λακτίζω. Yet it could equally well have induced corruption to the rather commoner verb. My suggestion coheres well with ἐψόφησεν.

680 The variant κρατύνει in Naoumides' rhetorical lexicon coincides with the brief scholium in R and is perhaps derived from it.

684 αὐτῷ is less forceful than Cobet's οὕτω and may have been imported from the following line.

730 φῶμεν, proposed by Meineke, is worth considering. Platnauer remarks that 'φάναι = κελεύειν is not well attested, though a case seems to occur in Lys. 16. 13'. A single sound attestation is valid evidence, and the passage in question runs ἐγὼ προcελθὼν ἔφην τῷ Ὀρθοβούλῳ ἐξαλεῖψαί με ἐκ τοῦ καταλόγου. The problem there is that ἔφην is the reading of MS C (Laur. 57. 4), whereas the Palatinus (Heidelberg gr. 88) has ἔτι, which was emended by Dobree to εἶπον. Thalheim's Teubner edition of 1901 accepts ἔφην but notes that Roehl kept ἔτι and proposed καταλόγου <ἐκέλευcα> while Weidner tried ἐκέλευον and Fuhr ἐδεόμην. Lamb's Loeb and Gernet's Budé editions follow Thalheim. Shuckburgh's Macmillan edition (p. 290), notes that Markland compared Xen. *Cyr.* 4. 6. 11 ἃ οἱ μάγοι ἔφαcαν τοῖc θεοῖc ἐξελεῖν. But there the Budé by M.Bizos adopts ἔφραcαν from MSS DW, while ἔφαcαν is in z (=HAG). So unfortunately the Lysias passage is not the clear parallel that we need, even though Dover on *Frogs* 133 finds the emendation in MS Laur. 57.4 plausible.

Support of a kind comes from a later source. Archimedes in the letter which serves as a preface to his treatise *Method* has φάμενοc εὑρίcκειν in the sense 'telling you to find': ed. Heiberg ii (Leipzig, 1913) 426. 5.

742–4 Olson's retention of the paradosis I find very strange. With that text the description of the stock figure of Herakles in 741 is fine, but it does not seem to be appropriately continued in 742, because attempts to escape, deceit, and beatings are less obviously part of that figure. In 744 ἐξῆγον is not the *vox propria*, though Paley's εἰcῆγον would easily restore it; and the feebleness of the second half of the line needs explanation—what is the point of the deictic τουδί? What is the meaning of καὶ τούτουc? Sommerstein is good on this passage, and Olson's objection to a complex chain of corruption is not decisive, especially if this is a case of an author's variants.

749 *Pace* Olson and Sommerstein (2001: 276), Blaydes (1899: 34) proposed 'malim ὑμῖν'.

758 One is used to Triclinius applying his standard remedy of inserting γε to repair the metre and is inclined to be condescending about any of his other attempts to deal with difficulty. Here it should be noted to his credit that he replaced the nonsensical καμίνου with καμήλου, doubtless remembering *Wasps* 1035.

831 Olson's note is a clear exposition, but I differ from him in one point. It seems to me that the scholium in V and Γ is correct in criticizing Didymus' acceptance of a word including the element -αυερι-, which is the reading of R and V; as the anonymous scholiast observed, the form αὐέρα is not found. -αυρι- 'swift' is very rare and easily corrupted.

847 Guy L. Cooper III, *TAPA* 103 (1972), 119 n. 24, favours the dual ταῦτα here and it may be that R and V are in error.

860 Parker, *Songs*, 280–1, says that in aeolic sequences one should not expect to find *brevis in longo* at line-end. So B's reading γέρων is probably right; but no scribe of the Byzantine or Renaissance period could have known that, and so we must treat it as the inadvertent substitution of one vowel for another which had the same phonetic value.

866 The correct reading in L is not simply a trivial metrical adjustment of the kind that Triclinius made so frequently. One wonders whether he made the improvement himself or found it in one of the MSS that he used; unfortunately he did not write a scholium here to enlighten us, and in any case his remarks about his sources do not give us the precise details that we would have liked.

882 The MSS give a text with αὐτούς, suggesting 'into your very midst'. This is open to objection, since Trygaeus can only take the woman as far as the front row. Seidler shifted the emphasis by reading αὐτός. Olson objects to an unwanted antithesis which implies 'since none of you can apparently be trusted'. I would rather see the implication that this is an important act which Trygaeus sees fit to perform himself.

886 What σκεύη can Theoria be supposed to carry? Sommerstein (2001: 276) refers to the scholiasts' explanation, that they are symbols of peace and agriculture. However, those belong to Opora. If Theoria can be taken as including not just visits to sporting events (cf. 894–906) but delegations to religious centres, then she might carry offerings that would be appropriate to pilgrims.

896 Sommerstein follows Rogers in deleting 896a as an author's variant. Another possibility is to suppose that the line is a parallel added in the margin by some learned reader in antiquity. Sommerstein rejects 896a because it does not have a clear reference to wrestling. This is probably right; but I do not feel entirely certain that πλαγίαν καταβάλλειν, if accompanied by a gesture, would leave the audience mystified.

916 Olson says that φήϲειϲ is easily explained as an intrusive marginal gloss, whereas τί δῆτ' is not. Is that true? A reader faced with φήϲειϲ might have been tempted to 'improve' or clarify the sense by the addition. The same reader faced with φήϲειϲ γ' was perhaps less likely to feel the need for any adjustment.

Triclinius obviously had knowledge of the variant as preserved in Athenaeus. Not that he is likely to have known of it directly from that source; the extant scholia do not have it either. Olson thinks that τί δῆτ' could be independent Triclinian conjecture. I find that a trifle unlikely but not impossible; it does in fact suit my notion of what a reader might have been tempted to do to the text.

Platnauer, Mastromarco, and Olson accept τί δῆτ' without a question mark, which I cannot understand. Parker, *Songs*, 283, rejects this reading because it requires the assumption that the chorus continue their utterance of 913–5, ignoring Trygaeus' intervention at 916, i.e. 917 is not a response to 916. Her point is made clearer if one adds that they had not ignored the intervention at 912.

929 It is an oversight on Olson's part to record δαί as the reading of R and V, which he does both in apparatus criticus and commentary. The facsimiles of these MSS show clearly that they have δή.

951 Parker, *Songs*, 286, insists that a syncopated iambic dimeter at this point in the sequence of the iambic lines destroys the metrical coherence of the passage. She obelizes, not mentioning Bentley's easy solution. One might also ask if a different supplement is possible, e.g.<νῦν> ἴδη.

961 Though Olson retains the MSS reading, I think τε is pleonastic and accept Enger's slight change.

972 If the chorus have stood in the same place while being sprinkled, as seems likely, ἰόντες is not the word one expects. Hense therefore wondered if ἑστᾶςιν ὄντες should be written. But that leaves εἰς without its proper function. Perhaps, as some editors assume, the chorus were drenched, and some took evasive action. The difficulty is to know how Trygaeus and the slave had enough water available for that, as Olson observes.

986 Although Olson says that R^{pc} has ἡμ*ς rather than ἡμᾶς, I am not at all sure after consulting the facsimile that the scribe intended to alter ἡμᾶς, which is still clearly visible. What looks like a stroke through the alpha, if it is contemporary—and I am not sure of that—may be the accidental result of touching the parchment with the pen.

1031 The compound ἐνημμένη is questionable, though apparently paralleled at Lysias 1. 14; that passage was emended by Stephanus. The compound in ἀν- would be normal, and Verrall's ingenious notion also deserves a mention.

1047 Denniston, *GP* 494, includes this line in his examples of γέ που, but gives no other occurrence from comedy. I rather incline to the view expressed by various commentators, that it would be part of a diffident statement, which is not suitable here. Some might defend που by reference to *Frogs* 565; there γέ που is the reading of V, whereas RAK have πω, which led Dobree to suggest πως, with some probability, as diffidence is not required in that context.

At pp. 550–1 Denniston shows that γέ τοι is a common idiom in Aristophanes and Plato and distinguishes three usages: 'giving a reason ... for accepting a proposition', 'restrictive', and contexts in which 'γε is emphatic or exclamatory, and τοι stands more apart'. One might consider the present passage to fall into the last category.

1071 The repetition may be deliberately ridiculous, but van Herwerden was not stupid to suggest that νύμφαι is an erroneous repetition from the preceding line, as a result of which the true reading was lost. H.-S. proposes an attractive possibility based on the same assumption.

1074 The addition of δ' to τοῖc could be explained as induced by the other demonstrative at the end of the sentence. There is no need for two demonstratives.

1077–9 Olson adopts the transmitted text, taking ὡc and τουτάκιc as correlatives, 'just as ..., so ...', and claiming support from LSJ. He did not notice that this support has been withdrawn in the *Supplement*, which deleted the relevant section of the entry. No parallel is forthcoming, and Olson admits that the meaning elicited is 'a bit incoherent'. Brunck's ἕωc is an easy change, and if χρῆν is the wrong tense, χρή would be equally easy; but I do not find the imperfect incongruous.

1078 There are serious difficulties here: what is the meaning of κώδων and is Ἀκαλανθίc to be taken as a bird or the name of a nymph? The critics' excursions into myth and ornithology have not provided convincing answers. Of the suggestions made so far the best may be that of Agar and Borthwick, to read κὠδίνων, which is economical palaeographically and involves the participle constructed with the genitive as in Homer, *Od.* 1. 309, *Il.* 19. 142, meaning 'to be eager for' (cf. Borthwick in CR^2 18 (1968), 137). The first of these parallels is not entirely secure since the participle is constructed with ὁδοῖο, which might be a genitive of aim or of space travelled over, as in τιταινόμενοι πεδίοιο; the second is better, though there too a genitive of aim cannot be excluded.

R. Renehan, *Glotta*, 77 (2001), 235, has removed one minor difficulty by pointing out that κώδων as a feminine noun is adequately attested, and has asked the pertinent question 'What is the likelihood that the unexpected (but correct!) collocation of ἡ κώδων got into the MSS by mere accident?' In fact there are many errors which provoke the same question because one cannot immediately see how they came about, but after some initial scepticism I have come round to the view that Renehan may well be right in not wishing to emend.

Can κώδων be the name of a bird? 'Trumpeter' would not be strange, but I can find no confirmation of it. And is a bird required in the context? A hasty birth is a notion in a proverb about dogs (Macarius 5. 32, Apostolius 10. 23; see V. Hinz, *Antike und Abendland*, 50 (2004), 124–48) and could also have a point in relation to Herakles; hence the ingenious idea of seeing a reference to the nymph Akalanthis. It was not, however, the nymph who was anxious to give birth, which is the result of having a participle referring to her own situation; it would have to mean 'eager for Alcmena to give birth', which is very strained. Still, as Sommerstein points out, the nymph was turned into a γαλῆ, and perhaps that animal is assimilated to the dog in the proverb. (If one read ἡ δὲ κύων here one would be hard pressed to explain why a relatively simple proverbial expression had been corrupted.)

It has not been noticed in connection with this puzzle that Akalanthis is the name of a courtesan in Alciphron 3. 64 Hercher = 3. 28 Schepers, Benner–Fobes. Alciphron exploited Attic Comedy, and I wonder if he got this name from a lost play. There is no other occurrence recorded in *LGPN*. My very tentative explanation of the line is that the prostitute Akalanthis was well known for her loud voice and had an unintended pregnancy which she did not wish to have prolonged. The allusion to the proverb about dogs adds complexity to the joke, since the word κύων was an abusive description known from *Wasps* 1402 and elsewhere since *Iliad* 6. 344. But this is probably one of those passages which we shall never be able to interpret to our satisfaction.

1142 Although Blaydes's conjecture is further from the MSS reading than Bentley's, if the latter is adopted a unique sense has to be attributed to the adverb.

1144 ἄφευε 'singe' is doubtless better than ἄφαυε 'dry'. Sommerstein (2001: 277) suggests 'scoop out'. Paley's ἀλλὰ φαῦζε relies on Hesychius φ 239 and Blaydes's ἀλλὰ φῶζε on Epicharmus 149 (but there the form is φῶγε).

1178 Sommerstein defends the paradosis by citing examples of long iota in λίνον from Soph. fr. 44 and Antiphanes 51; in the latter passage K.–A. accept the text but record conjectures. But neither he nor others address Platnauer's first objection to the paradosis, namely that the verb should be λινοπτεύω. However, P. Totaro, *Le seconde parabasi di Aristofane* (Stuttgart and Weimar 1999), 135, cites Suda λ 571 λινοπτωμένη and Hesychius λ 1067 λινοπτάζει· λινοπτᾷ, which do seem to protect the unusual formation. Totaro also draws attention, as Headlam had done (*CR* 27 (1913), 4), to the long vowel in the Latin and Gothic cognates.

1201 On the scansion of δραχμή see Gow on Machon 340, K.–A. on com. adesp. 1089. 5. The passages collected there do not explain the anomaly but are numerous enough to indicate that it was tolerated. In the Machon passage Gow was half inclined to emend, since normal prosody is restored by the transposition of the words at the end of the trimeter, and he might have been more inclined to do so had he noted that *vitium Byzantinum* would account for the word-order as transmitted.

1205 One possible factor inducing the change from -άναμεν to -αίνομεν is that alpha was sometimes written with an additional rising stroke so as to resemble alpha followed by iota.

1224 Is the formula τί δαί found in full-length sentences? Denniston, *GP* 262–3, while noting that the particle δαί is colloquial, raised no objection to its occurrence here and listed eight examples from Euripides, contrasting with its rarity in Aeschylus and Sophocles. By no means all of those eight passages have survived in Diggle's OCT, and his reference to Page's note on *Medea* 339 appears to be justified in its implied scepticism.

If δαί is right here, Aristophanes is perhaps making Euripides his target, if indeed any particular passage of tragedy was in his mind as he wrote these lines. It may be worth mentioning that δαί is not found in Index 4 of *TrGF* 2 (adespota). If δαί is doubtful here, we need to consider τί δ᾽ αὖ or τί δή. I have not found these proposals in the literature.

Birds

11 Though I have not accepted any emendation here, I am far from certain that the transmitted text is correct. The emphasis should probably be on ἐντεῦθεν, and Porson's γ' <ἄν> transposed to follow the adverb is attractive. For a discussion of Porson's view that γ' cannot immediately follow an oath such as νὴ Δία see Dunbar. She attributes the emendation to Reisig, but Bekker's edition of 1829 indicates otherwise, and Reisig's dissertation was not published until 1816. Dunbar finds Dindorf's ἔτι possible but not very natural in the context. My own view of it is more favourable: one may translate 'even Exekestides could no longer find his way back from here'.

23 The problem of attribution in this scene is hardly soluble. I have chosen to give Peisetaerus the major role with 27–48 and to make consequent adjustments. For a thoughtful discussion of this difficult question see H.-G. Nesselrath, *Museum Helveticum*, 53 (1996), 91–9.

56 The visitors want to attract attention by knocking loudly, and one of them encourages the other to pick up a stone for this purpose. λαβών makes sense, but might it not be better to say βαλών, 'throwing a stone'? This verb is regularly constructed with the dative λίθῳ. Rennie made a similar conjecture at *Ach.* 1168, which I thought worth recording.

63 Austin (ap. Dunbar) would delete this line. As he says (private communication of 27 Sept 1999) it 'is nonsense and the commentators fumble in the dark'. Blaydes here was uncharacteristically sparing with suggestions of his own. Nevertheless one would like to find an explanation for the presence of the line in our text. It does not look like a gloss or a parallel added in the margin of some earlier copy. Before giving up all hope of finding a solution one should ask whether there is anything that Peisetaerus might reasonably say at this point in reply to the Hoopoe's expression of horror. Possibilities are (i) 'Why say such shocking things when you have not even been threatened?' Or (ii) 'Why insult people who are not in any way to blame?' Van Herwerden's οὐδὲν αἰτίουc results from this approach. A very speculative rewriting of the line would be οὗτοc, τί δεινῶc οὐδὲν αἰτίουc ψέγειc; For ψέγω see above on *Clouds* 528. H.-S. points out a possibility that had not occurred to me: is the line part of a longer sentence, the beginning of which has been lost?

90 I have treated the metrical question here in the same way as at *Clouds* 214 and 1192. It is often easy to remove a split resolution in the anapaest, and Bentley proposed to do so here. There is a change of speaker in all these cases, and I have preferred to assume that the actor was allowed to complete his utterance, which would otherwise have suffered elision of the last word, incidentally requiring the other actor to be extremely precise in the timing of his reply. But I do not feel entirely confident about this: at *Peace* 41 and in some passages in tragedy my suggestion is not possible. One must therefore assume that some actors at least had great skill. On ἀντιλαβή see W. Köhler, *Die Versbrechung bei den griechischen Tragikern* (Darmstadt, 1913); elision in such cases is much commoner in Euripides than in Sophocles.

115 Blaydes's proposal has the merit of introducing a conjunction to follow πρῶτα and an imperfect to match the tenses in 114 and 116.

134 Dunbar argues in favour of Gelenius' simple emendation, and she may be right. She does not adduce the legitimate suggestion that the particle γε was interpolated from the following line. If the scholium is correct in saying that the line is a proverb and is quoting it accurately, her view has much to be said for it. But the proverb is not found elsewhere; was it a figment of some scholiast's imagination? The consideration that τότε γ' appears to be confined to epic seems to me to have little force. Are we really to believe that it was not possible to emphasize this adverb with γε? Cobet favoured the *Suda*'s reading ποτ', which also makes good sense.

Birds

150 Dunbar's complex note suggests that ὅϲα μή is idiomatic in contexts similar to the present, and there is one example of ὅϲ' οὐ in Euripides, where, however, as she says the presence of πλήν and the position of the phrase after instead of before the main verb make the parallel less precise. Her citation of ὅϲον μή from Soph. *Trach.* 1214 and *OT* 346–8 also seems wide of the mark. She is probably right when at the end of her note she allows for the possibility that corruption here is more extensive. Fraenkel, *Philologus*, 104 (1960), 11 = *Kleine Beiträge*, i. 429, obelized.

It may be worth making one more suggestion about the meaning of the original text: could it have been 'having merely seen him'? If so, one might wonder if Blaydes was nearer the mark with ὅϲον γ', one of a number of suggestions Dunbar does not consider.

323 μήπω has to be understood as indicating that fear is not yet necessary. But πω could have intruded through the influence of πῶϲ at the beginning of the line, and Blaydes's suggestions μηδέν and μή μοι/μου have a very good chance of being confirmed one day by a papyrus.

326 Here too it is tempting to follow Blaydes and insert γ', 'Yes, as surely as I am here among you'. But Denniston, *GP* 131, notes that where a word is echoed in agreement, normally δῆτα or μέντοι is the particle used. Here one pronoun may be said to echo the other. In these circumstances I feel that Blaydes's suggestion is plausible rather than essential.

336–7 ὕϲτεροϲ in 336 makes part of a neat antithesis with 337 if we accept Dobree's νῦν for τήν. Though one could understand the reading of the MSS as 'the (appropriate) penalty', I feel that Dobree was right.

338 Dunbar's deletion of the line, restoring a two-line exhortation such as would be expected in the context, has much to commend it. Admittedly the texts of comedy were not subject to the manipulation by actors or producers that affected tragedy; but on balance I think her decision is right.

346 Despite Dunbar's note I have accepted Reisig's emendation to avoid hiatus after παντᾷ (cf. Parker, *Songs*, 307). ἐπι- could easily have been introduced as a result of its triple occurrence in 344. H.-S. noticed that it is possible to arrange the anapaests more naturally (though tripodies may remain in some places; see Parker, *Songs*, 60).

377 Two features of this line invite attention, the vague τοῦθ' and the divergence between R, which reads εὐθύc, and the other MSS, supported by the *Suda*, which have αὐτόc. The divergence is odd, as Blaydes noted; it should be recorded that in several other passages (*Knights* 701, *Wasps* 255, 715, *Peace* 1176) he proposed to write εὐθύc for αὐτόc. One may also compare *Lys.* 673 and *Plutus* 209. Not dissimilar is *Birds* 788 οὗτοc MSS: εὐθύc Blaydes.

Dunbar's αὐτίκ' is ingenious as a way of accounting for the variants; the repetition of the word in its other sense in the next line may seem inelegant to modern taste, but we should be wary of declaring it unacceptable to the ancients. Bentley's αὐτό c', even though palaeographically close, seems rather forced.

Tentatively I offer the following alternative solution: for τοῦθ' we should read αὖθ' and then accept εὐθύc, supposing that αὐτό was in a scribe's mind as he approached the end of the line and as a result he wrote αὐτόc.

433 Here and at 1390 below I prefer to treat the verb form as an aorist and accentuate accordingly. At *Frogs* 1173–4 = Aesch. *Ch.* 5 Dover considered doing the same but decided against; West in his edition of Aeschylus follows Wilamowitz in accepting the aorist form.

484 As Dunbar says, the paradosis must be wrong with πρῶτον, since the required sense is 'was the first of all to rule the Persians, *before* Darius and Megabazus'. Her preferred solution, Bergk's πρῶτοc, involves a superlative with πάντων followed by two examples in apposition, for which the only parallel she finds is Theognis 173–4, where, however, the two examples receive clarification and extra emphasis from καί ... καί. And in fact the text as printed in her edition does not contain any element that can be translated 'before', while her assertion that the actor could pause perceptibly after Περcῶν is speculative. Most editors follow Haupt in converting Darius and Megabazus into the plural. But, as Dunbar says, it is unlikely that such plurals would have been corrupted into the singular, especially if the preceding word in the text was the plural πάντων. This is a drawback to another solution, which would be to combine the proposals of Haupt and Hirschig by reading πρότερος πάντων Δαρείων καὶ Μεγαβάζων. At the cost of making a more drastic emendation I have preferred to make the text say 'long before', πρότερον πολλῷ.

516 I am not convinced that Apollo should be described as a servant, nor that it would be natural to imagine a servant holding a bird on his forearm in the manner of a medieval falconer. Unless drastic emendation is to be undertaken the only other meaning to be extracted is that Apollo has a hawk as his servant. Was there a connection between this bird and the god? There is a little evidence, far from decisive, assembled by Dunbar. One may add that in Aelian, *NA* 1. 47–8, cited by Blaydes, Apollo's θεράπων and ἀκόλουθος is the κόραξ, and Sommerstein notes that *NA* 12. 4 gives the θεράπων as περδικοθήρας καὶ ὠκύπτερος. Blaydes proposed but did not print θεράπονθ', and referred to a similar view held by Meineke. In the light of the available evidence I feel that this is the solution to be preferred. It may be worth adding that I have not traced any proverb which would help to explain the line.

An alternative has recently been put forward by M. Griffin, *CQ*[2] 54 (2004), 610–13. He proposes ὡς θεραπεύων, making explicit Apollo's role as a healer and alluding to a plausibly inferred public discussion or controversy about the high fees charged by the medical profession. The loss of a syllable from θεραπεύων is of course easy; it is not quite so easy to assume that some scholar in antiquity or a Byzantine earlier than Triclinius would have noted the need to repair the metrical damage. But one would not go so far as to say that that this is an impossible assumption. The use of the participle as equivalent to the noun at Plat. *Polit.* 293 c which Griffin cites is facilitated by the occurrence of the word ἰατροί earlier in the same sentence, and the same is true in Thuc. 2. 47. 4. H.-S. notes that Griffin's proposal involves an anticipation of 584.

The idea that various types of ἱέραξ were associated with individual gods is of uncertain date; if it was current in 414 BC it does not seem to me to rule out Blaydes's view.

524 Modern editors seem unconcerned by the hyperbaton in the text as transmitted. But van Herwerden in *Mnemosyne*², 24 (1896), 308 and *Vindiciae Aristophaneae* (1906) 66, preferred to make the simple transposition ἤδη δ' ὥσπερ. This has the advantage that ἤδη gives a better reinforcement of the preceding νῦν.

531 Objections to the transmitted text have been cogently urged by several scholars. Dunbar adopts as the simplest correction κοὐ μόνον. She does not mention that οὐ μόνον is part of the wording of the scholium. It is not easy to say whether this is the preservation of the true text or an attempt to extract suitable meaning from a puzzling sentence. Blaydes made a good point in his addenda (p. 463 of his edition), which has been neglected: 'sed vereor nonnihil ne parum hic conveniat εἴπερ (if indeed). Qu. κοὐδ' εἰ γ' αὐτοῖς etc.'. Not only are there objections to the transmitted κοὐδ' οὖν at the beginning of the line, as Dunbar says; the following 'if indeed/in fact' provides an emphasis that is not required. Van Herwerden, *Vindiciae Aristophaneae*, 67, was uneasy and wondered if the poet wrote κοὐδ' οὖν, εἰ ταῦτα δοκεῖ, φαύλως, whereas in *Hermes*, 24 (1889), 617, he had tried κοὐδ' οὖν μόνον, deleting δρᾶν, and in *Mnemosyne*², 24 (1896), 308, οὕτως for ὑμᾶς in 532. Sommerstein translates 'granted that . . .', which seems to me not to reflect the nuance of the Greek, whereas Thiercy has 'si'. The sense might be better with 'if they really must do this . . .', but parenthetical εἴπερ cannot be made to fit in here. (*Clouds* 227 does not help, and one should note Dover's remark ad loc. on the nuance.) I have given consideration to C. Bevegni's ᾗπερ, 'in whichever way they decide . . .', but now prefer οἵσπερ 'the people who decide . . .', noting from Denniston, *GP* 490, that περ with relatives and relative conjunctions often has little force.

535–8 Sommerstein (2001: 288) proposes to retain γλυκὺ καί, which leaves 536 as an anapaestic line open to the objection raised by Dunbar, p. 366.

544 Blaydes objected to μοι followed by ἐμοί and substituted που, also suggesting καί. Van Herwerden's τοι is closer to the paradosis. Dunbar defends μοι by a comparison with 465; but there the repetition is of an enclitic or unemphatic word, whereas here in 545 the second occurrence of the pronoun is not enclitic. Perhaps the transmitted text can be accepted in view of the distance between the two pronouns; but van Herwerden may well have been right.

553 Kebriones is not necessarily the right name, for reasons expounded by Dunbar, and it is distinctly odd that the vocative inflection of a name known from Homer should be incorrectly transmitted in the MSS. Dunbar's apparatus mentions a conjecture by Schroeder that is not dealt with in her commentary, namely <Ἀ>λεκτρυόνα; Alektryon, the young friend of Ares, was metamorphosed into a bird (cf. Lucian, *Gallus* 3). This at first sight is very far removed from the paradosis; but the similarity of beta and kappa in pure minuscule script is well known as a source of confusion, and once prodelision had taken place the next stages of corruption would follow easily. But the attempt to justify the conjecture by citing as a parallel Pindar fr. 81 Γαρυόνα fails; as H.-S. notes, the Attic form of that name is Γηρυόνης.

577 Sommerstein rejects the attribution to the coryphaeus and the emendation ἡμᾶc because he takes δ' οὖν as 'anyway', returning to the main theme after a digression. But Denniston, *GP* 465, listed this passage in his section on εἰ δ' οὖν, 'but if, in reality . . .' Dunbar correctly quotes this, while suggesting that δ' οὖν has also resumptive force here. Is it likely to do double duty?

586 Dunbar is right to follow van Herwerden and Blaydes in feeling that βίον is inappropriate here and a reference to Zeus is required. But I agree with Sommerstein, *CR*² 48 (1998), 9–10 (cf. 2001: 288), that there was no need to make the additional transposition. The lack of the usual diaeresis is not a decisive objection to the simplified version of her solution; see l. 600 and parallels cited in her note there.

599 Dunbar is probably right to prefer the adverbial phrase; it could so easily have been altered by the process of assimilation.

602 For γαῦλον Lenting proposed to substitute τὴν ναῦν, feeling that an article is needed; cf. Sommerstein's translation 'I'm selling that cargo-boat'. Blaydes noted 'breviloquentia excusanda est, praesertim in anapaestis'. I am not sure that he was right. Dunbar does not comment, although she has previously stated that Aristophanes uses the article in anapaests wherever it would be used in trimeters or prose (479 n., 489 n.).

641 I am not convinced by Dunbar's assertion that 'γε underlines the unusual nature of the invitation'. Sommerstein accepts Reiske's τε, and I follow suit.

652 δή τι is the only example of this use of δή in Aristophanes noted by Denniston, *GP* 213. As he was able to cite a few examples from Plato, the text can probably stand; note, however, that he found no parallel in the orators and only one in Thucydides.

663 I find it difficult to accept Dunbar's translation of αὐτοῦ as 'from where you are', since 'from' seems an alien addition to the usual adverbial meaning and not justified by the other passage she cites. The meaning is 'there' or, assuming dependence on ἐκ- in the verb, 'from it', i.e. ἐκ τοῦ βουτόμου, and one understands why more than one scholar has felt uncertain about the text. αὐτοῦ could easily be a corruption arising from the presence of ἐκ τοῦ in the line above and αὐτὴν just after. Blaydes considered ὦ τᾶν or ὅδε, while Meineke applied more substantial surgery with αὐτὴν δῆτα πρὸς θεῶν (accepted by Sommerstein), on which Blaydes produced the variation αὐτὴν δεῦρο πρὸς θεῶν, which seems better. Could αὐτίκα be a less drastic solution?

724 Is Μούcαιc adjectival? Sommerstein translates 'musical prophets'. μουcόμαντιc at 276 is perhaps a hint of what Aristophanes wanted to say here. Was he constrained by metre?

725 The Athenians may have invoked the Horai, but I doubt if Dunbar's evidence about the Aurai is enough to suggest that these too were goddesses to the average member of the public. So I follow Blaydes here; perhaps the corruption was induced by the next word.

755, 757 In 755 some of the MSS have the variant word-order γάρ ἐcτιν ἐνθάδ'. Dunbar gives reasons for rejecting it. One factor she does not take into account is Wackernagel's Law about the position of enclitics and other unstressed words, which would favour the variant. But on balance she may be right.

κρατούμενα is a problem. The parallels cited by Dunbar perhaps justify the word; if it is corrupt, the cause of the mistake is not immediately obvious. A very late parallel needs to be mentioned: in a passage referring to national customs governed by local laws Gregory of Nyssa, *De fato*, ed. M. Bandini (Florence, 2003) xx.1 = Migne, *Patrologia graeca* 45.169 CD, says τίνι λόγῳ διαφεύγει τὴν ἐκ τῶν ἄςτρων ἀνάγκην τὰ νόμοιϲ τιϲὶ κεκρατημένα παρὰ πολλοῖϲ τῶν ἐθνῶν; But I have thought it worth while to mention conjectures other than Blaydes's replacement of the article by καί.

Another approach is worth considering. The chorus are making a deliberately outrageous proposal. It is a common enough complaint in Greek literature that the laws are being trodden underfoot as a result of criminal or immoral acts that go unpunished (cf. e.g. Aesch. *Cho.* 644, *Eum.* 110, Soph. *Ant.* 745, fr. 683, and in comedy *Wasps* 377). Could it be that the chorus here turn the complaint on its head and say that misdemeanours are trodden underfoot by the application of the law? πατούμενα would then be a possibility.

763 I am inclined to think ἐνθάδ' here would be slovenly writing, and the word might easily intrude after its occurrences in 755 and 757.

771 Should βοάν be written to match the form in 776? It is the form adopted by Dunbar in the lemma to her note but not in her text. Or is there a minor inconsistency on the part of the poet?

777 Hermann's transposition is generally accepted, but it leaves τε with nothing to do, and in my opinion the justification of the syntax given by Dunbar is special pleading. Bentley's idea may well be better, despite Dunbar's objection to the presence of a definite article in lyric and to the altered balance in the word-order of this and the following clause. In these two clauses I do not see any necessity for the noun and the verb to be adjacent in chiastic order.

792, 796 Perhaps I am being too logical, but at the risk of falling into the trap of trying to improve the classics I am inclined to follow van Leeuwen here. καθέζετο is most natural in 792, but is transmitted only in 796, where it creates a difficulty of syntax which Dunbar is willing to accept and Sommerstein is not. Given the frequency of similar verb forms at the ends of the lines in this passage I think the confusion postulated by van Leeuwen entirely plausible.

823–5 I do not share the confidence of modern editors in Bentley's λῷον for λῷϲτον. His proposal is based on the scholium, which may be no better than a desperate attempt to wring syntax out of corruption. A corrective clause where the initial concept is modified by καί is a rarity; the only parallel given by Denniston, *GP* 479, is Aesch. *Pers.* 1032, where the sense is 'even more than παπαῖ', whereas at *GP* 325 in his discussion of the present passage he had accepted καὶ λῷcτον as meaning 'No, best of all'. That seems to me ill-suited to the context. Here καὶ λῷον is elliptical, as Sommerstein rightly remarks.

However, starting from the sense required one might make a fresh suggestion: 'No, they preferred/chose the Plain of Phlegra . . .'. One word that would fit is κατέχουcιν 'occupy'. Another, a little closer palaeographically, is κατέλαβον. The origin of the corruption remains unclear.

836 is puzzling, as Dunbar says. I therefore feel it advisable to record Fritzsche's conjecture πῶc for ὡc. This has the merit of indicating an alternative way of understanding the line. But the resulting question does not receive an answer, which is odd.

866–7 The correct dative forms are difficult to establish. Dunbar notes that until *c.*420 the form after epsilon, iota, and rho was predominantly -αcι. She then quotes Menander, *Kolax* 1. 4, cited by Athenaeus 659 D. Two questions arise: (i) Why quote Menander? Presumably to make the point that this termination continued to be in use long afterwards, at least in some words, perhaps confined to religious formulae, which may be expected to preserve an archaic form. (ii) Was there an alternative to the predominant form? The use of the alternative here by Aristophanes at a date slightly after 420 seems possible; yet Wade-Gery, *JHS* 51 (1931), 78–82, noted that dissyllabic forms disappear 'with great suddenness round about the year 420'. Similarly Threatte ii. 96–101.

The MSS cannot be taken as evidence for the distinction between -ηcι and -ηcι, given that scribes in antiquity and the middle ages were so erratic in their treatment of the subscript/adscript iota.

899 The transmitted text is objectionable on two counts. It involves split resolution in an iambic metron, which if not impossible is certainly inelegant (cf. Parker, *Songs*, 34, 323). Syntactically the change of direction is abrupt; Dunbar accepts it, as does Sommerstein, the latter employing a device of punctuation to indicate broken syntax.

Blaydes with his customary ingenuity reinterpreted the paradosis by writing μάκαρά c'. The change of subject, with unstressed pronoun, is not attractive.

But another simple solution is available: the metre can be healed and the syntax normalized by reading ἕνα μὲν οὖν τιν', 'no, just one', which restores a well-attested usage of particles and is not in palaeographical terms a violent change.

974 There is a certain attraction in Dunbar's argument in favour of accepting the form βυβλίον in this scene, while recognizing that in 1024 and the *Frogs* the alternative form βιβλίον attested by the older MSS may reflect its growing use in everyday language. But her hypothesis is very far from certain: see D. Obbink, *Philodemus On Piety I* (Oxford, 1996), 301, who notes that the Herculaneum papyri of Epicurus Περὶ φύϲεωϲ have the form with iota, whereas works by Philodemus and Demetrius Lacon exhibit the form with upsilon.

On one small point I take a different view: she notes that 'later [i.e. Christian] copyists were used to τὰ βιβλία', and implies that they changed the spelling accordingly. βιβλίον of course became standard, but more often than not the Byzantines referred to the Bible as ἡ (θεία) γραφή.

994 I am inclined to agree with Sommerstein that Coulon's punctuation, followed by Dunbar, which results in one question being sandwiched inside the other, is 'a linguistic monstrosity'. That being so, one needs to adjudicate between the claims of Sommerstein's own tentative conjecture τῆϲ κοθορνωτῆϲ, a word properly formed but not otherwise attested, and emendations which introduce a different concept. Sommerstein posits the corruption of a rare word and the change of a few letters; this is well within the limits of plausibility. A recollection of *Frogs* 47 τίϲ ὁ νοῦϲ; τίϲ ὁ κόθορνοϲ τῆϲ ὁδοῦ; may also have affected the process of copying.

Blaydes followed up an idea of van Eldik τίϲ ποτ' ὄρνιϲ ...; 'What is the omen that prompted your journey? He produced a suggestion which has greater palaeographical plausibility, τίϲ ποθ' οὔρνιϲ ...; If that is correct, the corruption is to be explained as an ingenious attempt to restore the passage after a first stage of corruption had occurred, again with a memory of *Frogs* 47 probably playing its part. Blaydes's own ingenuity is further shown in his citation of Lucian,

Menippus 2 τίc ἡ ἐπίνοιά cου τῆc καθόδου ἐγένετο, τίc δ' ὁ τῆc πορείαc ἡγεμών; which may be derived from this passage. It would appear that Lucian did not have κόθορνοc in his text.

1012–13 Sommerstein and Dunbar accept Elmsley's correction 'They are banishing aliens', which is possible. But might it not be better for Peisetaerus to identify himself completely with the new city and use the first person? Hence I prefer Dindorf's proposal. Blaydes noted that Meton's question in 1014 is in the second person plural, which is suggestive. He also wondered if ξενηλατεῖται should be considered, comparing 1160.

With regard to the next verb, one needs to ask if κινεῖν is appropriate with πληγαί. I have some doubts, even if this is alleged to be an instance of παρὰ προcδοκίαν. *Frogs* 796, cited by Dunbar, does not seem to me to be a precise parallel. cυχναί in apposition to τινεc also strikes me as a bit odd. Once again a suggestion by Blaydes leads to a more elegant text; was he improving his author?

1040 Though the Inspector had brought κάδω with him as insignia of office, it is much less obvious that the Decree-Seller could have been carrying specimens of weights, measures and decrees, all to be fished out of a bag and displayed, which is the implication of the transmitted reading τοîcδε τοîc. With some hesitation I accept Boissonade's emendation.

1046 ff. The attribution of parts is difficult. Dunbar may be right to follow Wilamowitz. But she translates 1048 'Are *you* still here?', with the emphasis not supported by any particle in the Greek. So I would think it better to follow Sommerstein, who italicizes *still*. It may be a little more effective to have the earlier intruder make his return at 1046, with the Decree-seller then speaking very much in character.

1052 Brunck suspected the text and proposed γράφομαι. The middle verb was also recommended by Blaydes in his addenda (p. 471). Of the various remedies the simplest is to read γράψομαί τε for καὶ γράψω cε. This use of τε seems to have a parallel in *Ach.* 1062.

1066 Sommerstein, Dunbar, and P. Totaro, *Le seconde parabasi di Aristofane* (Stuttgart and Weimar, 1999), 149–51, adopt Dobree's ἐφημένα. Dunbar and Totaro also mention Hermann's ἐφημμένον, adopted by Kakridis, which refers to the fruit hanging on the trees. A consideration which they do not advance seems to me important. With Dobree's ἐφημένα the meaning is that various creatures perch on trees to consume the fruit. But the speaker is a bird, and it is chiefly birds that sit on trees and enjoy the fruit; Aristophanes was hardly thinking of squirrels or monkeys. So the chorus is made to say something quite inappropriate.

1072–5 Is there a difficulty in this passage? Dunbar notes that the Athenians were very sensitive on certain religious questions and presumably hostile to Diagoras, so that this part of the period is spoken in earnest. If she is right in saying that the remark about the (long-)-dead tyrants contains 'mockery of an absurdity', there is an abrupt change of tone. Reiske saw this, according to Blaydes, and proposed in 1075 πεφευγότων or προϲηκόντων (the latter occurs in the scholia). But the considerations adduced by Dunbar may be a sufficient defence of the transmitted text.

1087 The present παλεύετε in RVEMA creates a mixed conditional sentence. Dunbar cites some parallels, but as H.-S. observes the apodosis in those case is short and pithy; it describes immediate and/or drastic consequences. I do not know if anyone has taken the present as an imperative as in 1114. But there the word stands first in its clause, which is much easier.

1172 'One of the gods, those who come from Zeus ...' is intelligible, but it is not very elegant, and Blaydes's conjectures (1899: 48) seem worth a mention. He could also have tried περὶ τὸν Δία, since περί and παρά are frequently confused.

1229 The reasons for doubting τοι may well be sound, but Dunbar's proposed solution ἔτυμον is perhaps too ingenious. Though it introduces the high style it produces an anapaest that somewhat conflicts with paratragedy. Bentley's solution δή is fairly close to the paradosis and yields a sentence akin to the 'surprised, or emphatic and crucial questions' exemplified by Denniston, *GP* 259. Perhaps τοι came in from 1225 above.

1233 The case for Harpocration's variant ἀγυιάϲ may be a little stronger than appears from Dunbar's discussion. Material collected by J. Diggle, *Studies on the Text of Euripides* (Oxford, 1981), 34, suggests that the altar and statue of Apollo Aguieus were regularly to be seen on the Athenian stage. If the plural is felt to be out of place here, could Ἀγυιᾶ be right?

1255 Blaydes's supplement <c'> ὅπως is not a bad idea, but it can no longer be supported by his quotation from Kuster's edition of the *Suda* s.v. τριέμβολον, where he claimed to find θαυμάζεις in place of the infinitive.

1267 In the discussions of this line I miss a reference to the position of βροτῶν. The translation 'no mortal' implies that βροτῶν depends on τιν', but the two words are very far apart. Would it be any clearer if one read βροτόν? I suppose this may have been what influenced J. M. Stahl, *Kritisch-historische Syntax des griechischen Verbums der klassischen Zeit* (Heidelberg, 1907), 64 n. 2, when he suggested <ἕν'> ἔτι. As Dunbar says, the neuter <ἕν> 'a single precinct' would be better.

1289 Sommerstein (2001: 290), refers to Soph. fr. 144 and C. Catenacci, *QUCC* 62 (1999), 49–61, in support of ἀπενέμοντ' in the sense of 'read'. But the text of the Sophoclean fragment is very uncertain. Catenacci starts from Pind. *I.* 2. 43–8; the point of the verb here would be a play on the meanings 'feed on' and 'read'. But W. J. Slater, *Lexicon to Pindar* (Berlin, 1969) s.v., suggests the meaning 'impart' and *DGE* has 'dar noticias, referir'.

1297 Although ἐκεῖ is followed at 1304 by τἀκεῖθεν, at this point in the narrative it seems rather flat, as Blaydes noted. Sommerstein concurred, accepting his suggestion δέ γε, which is suitable as the introduction of the last item in a list.

1321–2 Are the Doric features of this song confined to 1313 and 1316, or should they be extended to the rest of the strophe? The exalted tone of the strophe, noted by Parker, *Songs*, 338, is a factor to be taken into account; on the other hand, perhaps the elevated tone was not intended by the author to be maintained throughout.

1338 Dunbar wonders if ὑπὲρ ἀτρυγέτου can be taken absolutely = 'above the sea'. This could well be right; the adjective is then a kenning, though not recognised by I. Wærn, *Γῆc ὀcτέα: The Kenning in Pre-Christian Greek Poetry* (Uppsala, 1951).

1343b looks like a paraphrase of 1344–5, or conceivably a parallel originally added in the margin. I think that the view of this passage taken by Kakridis and Sommerstein is best.

1363 I think it worth while to note that the occurrence of γάρ in conjunction with an imperative seems odd. Denniston does not refer to this passage.

1395 R. Campagner, *Lessico agonistico di Aristofane* (Rome and Pisa, 2001), 63–4, defends ἁλάδρομον as meaning 'hurdling', derived from ἅλλομαι. I have doubts about the formation of the compound: is alpha in the second syllable correct? I would expect ἁλμο- or ἀλλο-.

1441 Sommerstein and Dobree accept Dobree's τῶν μειρακίων, on the reasonable assumption that the dative offered by the MSS is an error of assimilation caused by the following words τοῖcι κουρείοιc. The alternative is to suppose that the dative is correct and that the noun has been corrupted under the influence of τὸ μειράκιον in the next line, i.e. the scribe of the archetype allowed his eye to wander for a moment and made a mistake. In that case we may consider such possibilities as τοῖc φυλέταιc, τοῖc ξυγγενέcιν, τοῖc δημόταιc.

1496 G. Agosti, *AION*. 9–10 (1987–8), 37–41, defends the *hapax legomenon* cυγκαλυμμόc against the conjectures of Dawes and Zanetto (οὐγκαλυμμόc and οὐγκαλύψαc respectively). He usefully points out that the compound verb in cυγ- with the meaning 'cover the head' is found in Xenophon, as had been noted by D'Orville on Chariton in 1750. So a noun based on the same compound is not in itself objectionable, and it suits the context.

1609 κύψαντεc is not very clear; perhaps, as Dunbar and Sommerstein say, the perjurer looks down to avoid eye contact. Dunbar cites *Knights* 1239 κλέπτων ἐπιορκεῖν καὶ βλέπειν ἐναντίον. She does not point out that the parallel could equally well favour this interpretation or van Herwerden's emendation κλέψαντεc.

1628 Blaydes wondered if còν κάρα was the Greek implied by the Triballian's utterance, an attractive idea were it not for the fact that κάρα is a poetic word not likely to figure in the vocabulary of a barbarian. νάκη of human skin, as Dunbar says, appears to be a unique usage; one would expect a more obvious word to be recognizable under the disguise of the Triballian's speech.

1717 With regard to the position of δ' in the MSS here, it may be noted that the same practice is found at *Frogs* 298 and *Eccl.* 351–2. In L of Sophocles (MS Laur. 32. 9) there are nine instances; see G. Zuntz, *An Inquiry into the Transmission of the Plays of Euripides* (Cambridge, 1965), 232.

Lysistrata

Hypothesis I 29–30 ἀναμνήcαcα is the reading of R, *pace* Hangard, who indicates that it has the infinitive in -αcθαι; but the theta is not there and what he took to be an iota is the flourish added to an alpha.

34 Wilamowitz's deletion of ἄρξαντοc is commended by Kassel, *Rh. Mus.*² 137 (1994), 34. Though this has much to be said for it, one does not know the date at which the argument was drafted and whether the author was capable of elegant Greek; but the comparison with Hypothesis I c of *Frogs* probably tips the balance.

Hypothesis II In the last line Rutherford's ἐξεώρταcαν introduces a word not known to LSJ or its *Supplement*, which he did not see fit to justify. Henderson adopts instead O. Montanari's ἐξήραcαν. This proposal in *Museum criticum*, 5–7 (1970–2), 140 I do not understand; the author cites αἴρωcιν from l. 4, but αἴρω cannot provide the form she posits, and if ἐξαράομαι existed in the active it would still not provide a short penultimate syllable in the form required here. Perhaps Brunck's solution is best here; his ἐξορίζω is a common word and part of the corruption assumed is simply iotacism.

Text 45 I feel very uneasy about the syntax. It is too slovenly to be plausible. Although Henderson and Sommerstein do not comment, earlier editors were justified in seeing a problem here. Bentley's τί ... περιβαρίδεc; has some merit. Van Leeuwen declared it necessary to supply φοροῦcαι, which Blaydes had thought unacceptable. Wilamowitz punctuated with a comma at the end of 44, noting 'Die Nomina stehen in der Luft. Also wird sie von Lysistrata unterbrochen.'

Although Lysistrata herself has been interrupted just above at 33 and 35, it is not clear, as H.-S. notes, why it should be so appropriate here. A further point is that Lysistrata in her reply lists five specific means for the women to achieve their aim, and of these five only the first and third correspond precisely to Kalonike's remark. It is worth considering the possibility that the reply corresponded a bit more closely to what her companion had said. If one then takes into account the syntax it seems best to follow H.-S.'s suggestion of a lacuna.

49 The plural μηδένας is rare, but Meineke's restoration of it was accepted without comment by Wilamowitz and van Leeuwen. As Blaydes noted, a plural sits much more easily with ἀλλήλοιςι in the following line. The plural οὐδένες is attested at Plat. *Euthyd.* 303 c 1 and Dem. 5. 5; it is also convincingly restored at Dem. 18. 304. These forms were advocated by Cobet, *Miscellanea critica* (Leiden, 1876), 460, 485.

64 If ἀκάτειον is correct, the form can be justified as an adjective to go with ἱςτίον. R's error of orthography is trivial. I agree with Sommerstein that the pun of ἄκατος/ἀκάτιον 'cup' derives no support from the context or what we know of Theogenes; so with this reading the point of the line will be a reference to him as a ship-owner. In fact most editors believe that there is a reference here to the reserve sail carried by warships. To hoist this sail indicated a desire to escape from a dangerous situation or to exploit the wind better by adding an extra sail. The former is not appropriate for Theogenes' wife here, *pace* J. S. Morrison and R. T Williams, *Greek Oared Ships 900–322 B.C.* (Cambridge, 1968), 298–9, who interpret the expression as 'take to flight'; the latter might be, but if so it reads a bit oddly in a passage which complains of the non-arrival of the women. The semi-proverbial advice of Epicurus (fr. 163 U. = 89 A.) (cf. Plut. *Mor.* 15 D, 1094 D) is quoted in such a way as to suggest that the dominant concept remained the need to escape. On this sail see L. Casson, *Ships and Seamanship in the Ancient World*, rev. edn. (Baltimore, 1995), 236–7, 241–2 n. 72, where he expresses the opinion that the present passage may have nothing to do with sails. The matter is not discussed in J. S. Morrison, *Greek and Roman Oared Warships* (Oxford, 1996).

Faced with this uncertainty one must consider the alternative: one of the scholia is clearly based on a text which read Ἑκατεῖον, and the Suda (ε 361) goes so far as to say that Θεαγένουc Ἑκατεῖον was proverbial and that this man always asked permission of the goddess before going out. Part of this entry is repeated at θ 80. It could all be a scholiast's invention, nothing more than inference from the text; but why should he say that there was a proverbial expression? That looks more like an additional detail, not extracted from the text. On balance I incline to the view that Wilamowitz was right to prefer the indirect tradition here; and it should be borne in mind that the *Suda* is for practical purposes a twin of the Ravenna MS.

66 αὖτε seems not to be part of colloquial usage. It occurs in Cratinus 182; but that passage consists of anapaestic dimeters, and *Wasps* 1015 is an anapaestic tetrameter. Bergk's proposal is essentially the transposition of two syllables.

79 Either ὦ or cου could easily have been inserted. I follow Blaydes and Wilamowitz; the enclitic following a vocative is not objectionable.

83 One could delete τῶν with Kuster to mend the metre, but it is fair to assume according to the principle *utrum in alterum* that the rare τιτθός, attested at *Thesm.* 640 and Lysias 1. 10, has been ousted by the commoner word. H.-S. notes that the diminutive detracted from the pompous grandeur of the line or indeed the fullness of Lampito's figure.

87 Bothe's νὴ Δί' ὡc is close to the paradosis and gives the usage of ὡc seen at Soph. *OT* 1078 and various passages in Thucydides. Henderson adopts this reading; most editors prefer Meineke's ναὶ μὰ Δία. It is difficult to choose with confidence.

118 There are uncertainties here. If R is essentially right with ὅπα, perhaps it should have an iota added or be accented perispomenon, but one can hardly be sure. Henderson claims that 'where' = 'if there' and quotes M. Lejeune, *Les Adverbes grecs en -θεν* (Bordeaux, 1939), 262–3, but I do not find the material there helpful. He also adduces Soph. *Ant.* 666 for this type of relative clause, with K–G. ii. 429. The Sophoclean line is no parallel to our passage; the meaning is 'whoever'; we need an analogy with a conjunction, not a relative. Wilamowitz made the slight change to ὅπω 'whence', which is attractive; C. D. Buck, *The Greek Dialects*, 2nd edn. (Chicago, 1955), 103, attests this form for literary Doric. Some editors make more substantial alterations in order to obtain a conditional; hence Blaydes ἔλcοιμι κ', αἰ and Meineke ὅροc αἰ. One might also wish to treat the clause as final; C. D. Buck, loc. cit., reports ὅπαι used as a final conjunction in Cretan. H.-S. notes that if one reads ὅπω the image will be one of descrying peace at a distance from the vantage-point of Taygeton. Seeing is hardly enough, as Henderson inadvertently admits in comparing Trygaeus' flight on the dung-beetle, which was to fetch Peace, not merely to see her; one might have expected λαβῆν.

I would not exclude the possibility that if there is a slight oddity or imprecision in the expression of this line, it is due to Aristophanes' incomplete mastery of a different dialect.

124 Though Bentley transposed the verb and the pronoun he appears also to have written ἐcτὶν ἧμιν with a short iota in the unstressed pronoun. Brunck and Bergk accepted this form of the pronoun and as a result saw no need for transposition. Did Bentley perhaps feel that ἐcτίν had a right to be closer to the gerund? Probert 150 refers to unstressed forms as occurring in poetry; the colloquial register of l. 124 should perhaps discourage us from accepting one here.

125 The form μοιμνᾶτε was preferred by L. Dindorf on the basis of Pollux 2. 90 and Hesychius μ 1547. Pollux records a similar word μοιμυλλᾶν, which perhaps speaks in favour of Dindorf's view.

Editors assert with confidence that R reads μοι μνᾶτε as two words. They do not realise that word-division in MSS of that date was still not rigidly enforced, and in fact the scribe may have thought he was writing a single word. On the other hand the lemma of Suda μ 1367 is μνᾶτε and it is well known that R and the Suda offer almost identical texts. The Oxford scholia have the lemma μοιμνᾶτε according to Hangard's edition; but after inspection of the MS I was not quite sure what the scribe intended. Frisk prefers μνᾶτε, noting Hesychius μ 1771 μνᾶτε. cκαρδαμύττετε. He wonders if μοιμνάω is 'aus der Ar.-Stelle erschlossen' but notes the existence of μοιμύλλω/ μύλλω.

143 Wilamowitz said that the lengthening of the first syllable of ὑπνῶν was quite likely in Laconian. Certainly it occurred in literary Doric, e.g. Theocr. 11.22. ὕπνος in Pindar occurs at P. 9. 25, where the first syllable is long, and again at I. 4. 23. H.-S. notes that Aristophanes may have had Laconian acquaintances and observed this feature in their speech.

144 As Denniston, *GP* 96, remarks, the word-order is curious. He refers to a parallel in Alexis 150. 6 (cf. also 165. 1). One may still wonder whether this freedom of word-order should be accepted in a text as early as 411. Emendations should at least be mentioned. I am not sure how much weight to give to Blaydes's observation that ὅμως γε μήν without a verb is hard to parallel. If that is thought to matter, one can follow Dawes and punctuate after δεῖ rather than before, with his further emendation of μέλει at the end of the line; if not, the alteration of a single letter will remove the anomaly of the word-order: read δεῖται (or perhaps its Doric equivalent). The middle, though not common, seems adequately attested.

149 At *Frogs* 919 Dover accepts as the optative καθῆτο, the reading of EUVs1 (though without the iota subscript). He notes *Lys.* 149 but regards the choice between the forms as uncertain; Plat. *Theag.* 130 E has καθοίμην, while there are variants at Xen. *Cyr.* 5. 1. 8. Threatte ii. 627 is unable to provide epigraphic documentation.

153 The discovery of the Cologne papyrus reveals that the paradosis is not unanimous. So one may doubt whether προcίοιμεν 'approach' is necessarily right against προcίδοιμεν 'glance at them'; the occurrence of παρίοιμεν two lines above could have influenced a scribe. Equally good sense is obtained with Halbertsma's conjecture, which restores the rarer word προcείμεθ' 'receive their advances' (the aorist was adjusted by Coulon to the present in order to match the other verb in the line, and his parallel from *Birds* 946 seems to have stood the test of time; see Dunbar ad loc. for the scansion of iota in compounds of ἵημι as short).

180 Despite Wilamowitz, who is followed by recent editors, I find the brachylogy of the transmitted text unacceptable. If a concept occurs twice, it may be possible to omit the second occurrence, but hardly the first. Wilamowitz's scornful remark 'Verse sind doch dazu da, gesprochen zu werden' seems to me to point in the opposite direction to the one he intended. For what it is worth I mention that the scholiast repeats καλῶϲ, which could mean that he had εὖ in his text.

183 ὁμιώμεθα with ιω < εο is quite possibly right; see V. Schmidt, *ZPE* 30 (1978), 14, who cites the form μετριώμεναι from the Heraclean Tables and ἐμίω (= ἐμέο) from Rhinthon (10 K.–A.). Colvin 156, 215 is unaware of this observation.

187 The Cologne papyrus has some lines in the wrong order: 182–7, 197, 199, 198, 188, omitting 189–96. Henrichs and Koenen, *ZPE* 1 (1967), 117–20, saw in this a 'Kurzfassung eines Regisseurs', a view repeated in the publication as P. Köln 14 by B. Kramer. Dover, *ICS* 2 (1977), 154, wondered about two authorial versions. But (i) not enough of the codex survives for us to be certain that the scribe remained unaware of the muddle he had created; (ii) it is rash to assume that there were further productions of this play, *pace* O. Taplin, *Comic Angels* (Oxford, 1993), 94 ff.

It is incidentally worrying that the papyrus agrees with R in what appears to be an impossible variant reading; many corruptions in our texts go back to an early stage in the tradition and Alexandrian editors appear not to have eliminated them.

277–8 Parker, *Songs*, 362–3, declares the metrical problem insoluble, and I share her scepticism about the efforts of previous editors. Hence a bolder proposal: perhaps we have here further examples of choriambs substituted for iambic metra as discussed by Parker at pp. 78 ff. So by transposing ἐμοί and omitting πάνυ we get ᾤχετ' ἐμοὶ θὤπλα παραδοὺϲ | ϲμικρὸν ἔχων τριβώνιον. This does admittedly lead to one split resolution, on which see Parker 34–5; so the proposal can only be very tentative.

306 ἕκατι is poetic in tone, as noted by van Leeuwen. It is found again in Teleclides 44. 4. Prose usage is supposed to have been ἕκητι, and this passage is relatively prosaic. One wonders if Γ is right in offering that form.

307 ff. Should we accept anacolouthon here? Wilamowitz did so in his commentary (1927), whereas a few years earlier (1921) in *GV* 483 he had applauded Blaydes's dissatisfaction with οὔκουν but felt that with τί δῆτ' too great an alteration was being made. So he suggested τί οὖν, not noticing that Blaydes had offered this as an alternative. Neither suggested any reason for the corruption; conceivably οὐ at the beginning of 301 distracted a copyist. Perhaps the question to be decided here is whether the speaker is so excited that he loses control of his syntax.

But we should also note that οὔκουν normally introduces very emphatic questions designed to serve as orders to others. K–G ii. 165–7 cite a milder type of sentence with ἄν from Soph. *Aj.* 1051. Here we seem to have a different usage, if the old men are meant to be addressing themselves in mild tones.

One may feel that neither this nor the anacolouthon is above suspicion. If the tone is wrong τί οὖν becomes attractive. If syntax is to be adjusted, could one not consider writing ἄψαιμεν for ἄψαντες? As is well known, assimilation of terminations is probably the commonest of all types of error.

316 Henderson and Sommerstein favour Blaydes's πρώτιστ' for πρῶτον or πρῶτος of the MSS. Despite what they say I do not find it wholly convincing to make the invocation end with the concept of the lighted torch as the first stage of the assault, and they do not notice that πρώτιστ' as a superlative seems too emphatic. Bothe's πρώτῳ γ' is the kind of change Triclinius would have made if he had read the play. It confers unwanted emphasis. Thiercy 1215 proposes to read ὅπως ἐμοὶ πρώτῳ ϲυνοίϲειϲ, but has failed to notice that this is metrically impossible.

The comically high-flown invocation to the bucket is a request to provide a lighted torch. The provider can be the bucket or, if one wishes to be pedantic, the coals. In the latter case one accepts with Wilamowitz a third-person verb (προϲοίϲει) and his emendation παρών, which agrees with ἄνθραξ. As he said himself, the emendation is not easy, but the word would be suitable. However, I think that Reisig, *Coniectaneorum in Aristophanem libri duo* (Leipzig, 1816), 125, was on the right track with πρόφρων 'graciously', for which he did not adduce any support. This grand word is in fact found in the parody of Pindar at *Birds* 930.

324 Oeri's ὑπό τ' ἀνέμων has enjoyed general favour. It was queried by G. Paduano, *La Lisistrata* (Milan, 1980), 95: 'con molte riserve accetto l'emendamento di Oeri ... il cui maggiore merito è la coerenza semantica e figurale con περιφυcήτω. Forse però la corruzione del testo è più estesa, e un segnale potrebbe essere la struttura sintattica coordinante ὑπό τ' /ὑπό τε che suona faticosa, più che ricercata'. I am not sure that this objection, which seems to be based purely on grounds of euphony, carries much weight. V. Tammaro, *Museum criticum*, 25–8 (1990–3), 138, rejected Paduano's view, insisting that the allusion to *Iliad* 13. 795 is important. But that allusion does not have to be made verbatim; indeed, quite the reverse, if one believes that ancient authors and readers appreciated *variatio* in topoi; poets were free to alter phrasing, and in CQ^2 50 (2000), 597 I pointed out that the change of one letter is more economical than the change of three: read ὑπό τε νότων.

As a curiosity I mention the proposal to restore *Notus* in a Latin text where the usual reading *locus* is not entirely easy. See G. Giardina, *Museum criticum*, 19–20 (1984–5), 201–2 = *Contributi di critica testuale* (Rome, 2003), 27–9 on Horace, *Epp*. 1. 11. 25–7.

330 It is odd that the MSS have the form δούληcιν. Perhaps it is no more than absent-minded conversion to a form familiar to readers of Homer and Herodotus. Threatte ii. 95–101 says that on inscriptions the change from -ηcι(ν) and –αcι(ν) takes place *c.*420. The forms in -η(ι)cι are not characteristic of choral lyric, and so this one would not add to the effect created by ὑcτερόπουc, κνεφαία, and πατάγου. Could it simply be that women in some contexts used slightly old-fashioned language? For further guidance on this complex matter see Barrett on Eur. *Hipp.* 101 and M. L. West's edition of Aeschylus (Leipzig, 1990), p. xxxvi. I note that Willi 162, while not referring to this passage, reports the view suggested by Sommerstein and others that women 'prominently furthered linguistic innovation in Attic' (which I suspect is exaggerated) and at p. 241 states a general preference for forms in -αιcι(ν).

338 Most modern solutions of the metrical problem seem to me to involve implausible suppositions; cf. Parker, *Songs*, 369. I mention in the apparatus the two possibilities that have some chance of being right.

350 J. Wackernagel, *Beiträge zur Lehre vom griechischen Akzent*

Lysistrata 139

(Basel, 1893) 29 n. 1 = *Kleine Schriften* ii. 1098 n. 1, recommended writing πονωπόνηροι as one word here and at *Wasps* 466, where RE have that form, while VΓ divide it into two words. Here only B has the recommended form. It is supported by Hesychius and Photius. Wackernagel reasonably enough asked how πόνῳ as a separate word could be understood.

384 ἀναβλαστάνῃc in the MSS raises difficulties. (i) The lack of ἄν in a final clause is a mark of later Greek. Wilamowitz was willing to accept it as the first instance of what in due course became normal. Dobree's ἀναβλαστανεῖc looks easy, but is the form possible? (ii) The prosody of short alpha before the combination of beta and lambda, though unusual, can be defended by Autocrates 3 and *Wasps* 570. Wilamowitz must have assumed that it was impossible and followed Reisig with ἀμβλαστάνῃc, saying that the apocope of prepositions in comedy needed no exemplification. (iii) Is ἀνα- 'again' necessary? Despite the majority view of editors I think not; 'I'm watering you to make you grow' is a good enough joke, addressed as it were to a tender young plant.

421 Lenting was worried by the position of the particle and wondered if it would be preferable to read ὅτ' ὦν γ' or ὅτ' ὦν. Denniston, *GP*, does not mention the passage.

433 N. Gonis informs me *per litteras* that the papyrus is not correctly reported by Sommerstein and Henderson; its reading is uncertain. He thinks van Leeuwen's ποῦ 'cτι has a good chance of being right.

435–6 Sommerstein's note on the punctuation and interpretation is excellent. I would only add that if one accepts the rendering 'if he, public slave that he is, dares to touch me, I'll make him howl' and punctuates after ὦν (which Henderson does), the emphatic pronoun ἐμοί, found in MSS other than R, becomes appropriate.

449 Wilamowitz thought ὁ τοξότης was a collective like ἡ ἵππος. Perhaps, but in 462 τὸ τοξικόν is used. Henderson translates 'the archer (I need) . . .', which also seems possible. Dobree's conjecture is not in my opinion as far-fetched as it may seem at first sight.

507 To the many suggestions for putting this verse right may now be added that of Thiercy 1215: ἡμεῖс τὸν μὲν πρότερον τοῦ πολέμου χρόνον ἠνειχόμεθ' ὑμῶν. It suffers from the lack of diaeresis after the second metron.

Blaydes on p. 319 of his edition anticipated Sommerstein in taking a lead from Reisig but preferring the imperfect to the aorist.

526 ποῖ in the sense of 'how long?' or 'to what end?' appears to be protected by Soph. *El.* 958. The scholiast's gloss πότε is not helpful, though Henderson's note might be taken to imply otherwise.

528 Kuster's minimal change produces two balanced infinitives and avoids a switch from aorist to present subjunctive.

542 Jackson's transposition is likely to be right, though other solutions cannot be entirely ruled out. Sommerstein follows Hermann's approach, with the difference that he accepts the adjective καματηφόροс from the scholium in R. This word is not specifically offered as a variant reading by the scholiast. It seems not to be attested elsewhere; one wonders whether it could have been invented by the scholiast on the analogy of θανατηφόροс.

583 B has ὑμῖν, which matches the second person in 572 and 580; the main MSS have ἡμῖν, which is accepted by van Leeuwen, Wilamowitz, and Henderson, who do not even bother to record the variant. It is probably the scribe's conjecture, and an easy one with a good chance of being right; Sommerstein argues correctly.

583–4 The repetition of κάταγμα is not entirely easy, and I record a conjecture which Paul Maas would have termed diagnostic.

589 We may as well keep γε, since it goes well with καὶ μήν. Though there are a few parallels for scanning the first syllable of διπλοῦν as long, perhaps it is better not to add to the list when another easy solution is at hand.

629 The proverb λύκοс ἔχανεν in Diogenian 6. 20, on which see Jacques's note on Menander, *Aspis* 381, seems to have been used of the ravening animal that had failed to catch its prey. Here that can hardly be the implication, as it would suggest that the threat was actually less grave than it appeared.

644–5 Sommerstein follows Sourvinou-Inwood in punctuating after

Lysistrata 141

ἀλετρὶς ἦ. The resulting asyndeton seems to me harsh. He also reverses the positions of τἀρχηγέτι and Βραυρωνίοις, because he claims that the epithet in its transmitted position is obscure before Brauron has been mentioned. Stinton, CQ^2 26 (1976), 11–13, did not like the asyndeton and argued strongly in favour of a simple emendation: καὶ χέουσα. He emphasised that ἀρχηγέτις is a well-attested title for Athena, with one pretty certain example from the mid-fifth century (IG i^3. 252). Sommerstein takes a different view, but I do not share his scepticism.

654 Modern editors defend the misplaced εἶτα. Wilamowitz admitted that the word-order was 'sehr kühn'. But as the word occurred at the beginning of 644 I have preferred to suppose that a distracted scribe repeated it here at the expense of an unusual compound verb.

673 αὗται seems otiose after ταῖσδε. Van Herwerden's αὖθις has the best chance of being right. One should note also that forms of αὐτός have in a few places been plausibly replaced by εὐθύς (cf. Birds 377 n., Peace 1176, Wasps 255, 715), and 'immediately' would not be bad in the context.

678 One can see that the particle δ' as transmitted is not wanted as the introduction to an example of what has just been stated. But Dindorf's deletion, popular with modern editors, is not necessarily right. Lenting proposed γ', and this would fit in the category described by Denniston, GP 145, as 'the opening of a statement forecast by the preceding words'.

696 ἐμοί seems to put the emphasis on the wrong word; Lampito and the other women have pride of place in this clause. Blaydes was right to try ἤν γε. The particle is suitable; see Denniston, GP 142.

742 Threatte i. 342–4 records nine different spellings of Eileithuia in Attic texts. On vases the normal spelling is Ἰλείθυα with no trace of the form in -θυια. The latter is the regular termination in Roman times. R is closer than other MSS to the truth.

749 ἀλλ' ἤ is not easy; see the discussion in Denniston, GP 24–7. R reads ἀλλά, which Wilamowitz preferred. It may be a scribal simplification. Chadwick 129, did not include this passage in his discussion.

763 The oddity of the singular verb is defended by Henderson, who quotes *Eccl.* 504 ff. as a parallel. However, in that passage both Ussher and Sommerstein are aware of a difficulty and willing to suppose that the line may be parody of tragedy, which led to the insertion of a singular verb in 508 in a series of plurals. Even if such an explanation is plausible there, I doubt whether it justifies the anomaly in 763.

776 I have ventured to prefer a *difficilior lectio* in the form of the comic adjective here. Schwyzer i. 535 states that the comparative termination -ίcτεροc was used in words for unflattering characteristics and particularly in comedy. Most of the forms in question derive from words which are not exactly comparable, but he cites ἀλαζονίcτεροc, which is. LSJ quote the superlative from Plat. *Phil.* 65 c 5, where it is given by MSS B and W, Athenaeus and Eustathius, whereas T, Stobaeus, and Eusebius have the more obvious -έcτατον. *DGE* adds Dio Chr. 55. 20, where von Arnim records -ίcτατον from M (Leidensis 67 = B.P.G. 2C, a late but apparently important codex of the 16th century), -έcτατον from all the other witnesses. Though the attestation of this word is not very strong, on balance I incline to accept the evidence in favour of it and to use it as justification of the reading of *Γ* and **p** in 776.

779 The deictic τουτογί has no obvious point of reference. Van Leeuwen refers to his own note on *Frogs* 965, which does not help to explain the present passage.

803 Coulon wrote ἐπᾴccειν for ἅπαcιν. His citation of *Iliad* 13. 483 seems to me *nihil ad rem*, and his advocacy of the conjecture in *REG* 43 (1930), 41 no better. Instead I have thought it just worth while noting Meineke's suggestion ἀπαντῶν, since he cited the proverbial expression μή τευ μελαμπύγου τύχῃc (Archilochus fr. 178 W., cf. Zenobius 5. 10 and App. Prov. 3. 62) and Eustathius 863. 31 οὔπω μελαμπύγῳ ἐνέτυχεc.

816/18 The syntax here is odd. Hangard notes on the scholium, which reads ὡc εἰ ἡμεῖc ὑμᾶc 'fort. dividendum (ut R[u]t[herford] fecit). Tum ὡc εἰ ἡμεῖc ad οὕτω pertinet, ὑμᾶc autem v.l. ad ὑμῶν esse putaverim'. An acute observation, which may well be right as far as the scholium is concerned.

Henderson adopts what he reports as Bergk's proposal ἡμῖν, with alleged support from the scholium. This seems a tenuous argument. In fact Bergk's preface in the 1892 printing (p. ix) says ἡμῶν, fort. ἡμῖν, id est ἡμῖν ὁμοίως'. So it was a tentative conjecture. My feeling is that the resulting Greek is unsatisfactory.

834 If the transmitted text is to be believed, an invocation to Aphrodite is followed by an instruction to the man approaching. This will hardly do. Even if we prefer to see an exclamation here rather than an invocation, the resulting sequence is still disjointed.

839 Jackson, *MS* 101–2, argued against Dobree's conjecture by pointing out that it would be strange for a copyist to mistake ἤδη for εἴη. But in speaking of a scribe's eye he made the assumption that the error must have been visual. If instead we are prepared to think of it as the result of 'dictation interne', the two vowels are identical to a medieval scribe, and in his haste he has simply omitted the consonant of ἤδη. Jackson's solution cannot be ruled out, however; for him ἔργον would be an intrusive gloss. Fraenkel's εἶα is also attractive, since it would give credit to R for preserving a trace of the correct reading.

865 Does γε emphasize the right word? Denniston, *GP* 143, accepts it in the category ὡς ... γε 'in which γε often retains little force'. He quotes from this play 1029, 1241, and 1246; but in those passages the particle is next to a word that could bear emphasis; so I think a slight doubt remains. Blaydes contemplated ἔχω τι τοῦ βίου (the genitive was a suggestion by Hermann), but printed Cobet's ἐγᾦδα, which is conceivable.

895 The MSS have the form διατιθεῖς, accepted by van Leeuwen, Wilamowitz and Sommerstein. Henderson corrects it to -τιθῇς, following Maire (1624) (cf. *HSCP* 82 (1978), 87–119), and referring to K–B ii. 193, who indicate that there is an uncertainty. Could the paradosis be interpreted as διατιθεῖς', with elision because the speaker is interrupted?

898 Although Wilamowitz and Henderson accepted the paradosis, the absence of an adversative particle, which can so easily be introduced, seems unlikely. Cobet placed it after the goddess's name, Hall–Geldart after the definite article, which would also be possible.

901–2 ἄν is the form of the conjunction found in these two lines in the MSS. Threatte ii. 672–4 states that Ionic ἤν probably does not occur at all in Attic inscriptions (there is one dubious exception, dated c.430); but ἄν is found sporadically in inscriptions of the fifth and fourth century. It is odd that it should be attested here and on balance I suspect that Dindorf was right to make the adjustment; but he was not followed by Wilamowitz or Henderson. Hoffmann–Debrunner i. 116 take the view that ἤν is normal in Thucydides and Aristophanes, and 'Die Inschriften beweisen nichts weiter, als daß die Orthographie der Kanzlei ἐάν war und blieb.' Although I have in general accepted epigraphic evidence in orthographical matters, cases like this provoke some doubt. Denniston, *GP*, pp. lxiii f., remarked that 'it is probably true that a word will run in a writer's head at a particular time', and he quoted examples from various writers of a short-lived linguistic habit.

937 Wilamowitz did not even bother to record van Herwerden's introduction of the deictic τουτογί. The transmitted text can be understood, but given the presence of the deictic in 942 there is a good case for making the slight change.

944 *Pace* Wilamowitz, who said that the Rhodian perfume is unknown, it is mentioned by e.g. Apollonius the Herophilean ap. Athenaeus 688 E. But ῥόδινον is common, and Bergk may have been right.

945 Blaydes' ἀγαθόν <γ'> is likely to be right. The situation is not wholly unlike the category given by Denniston, *GP* 132, 'affirmative answers contradicting a denial', and may be thought still closer to another category, ibid. 137–8, 'In drama the speech of one character is sometimes completed by a second, who either (*a*) interrupts or (*b*) carries on a sentence which is already complete in itself, often giving a new and malicious turn to the thought.'

962 With much hesitation I adopt Meineke's solution. νέφρος seems not to be found in tragedy, but the preferred remedy of modern editors involves acceptance of it with tragic prosody νεφ'ρός. Jackson, *MS* 200, avoided that with κἄν, which seems to me not very natural. One would ideally like to explain the intrusion of ἤ into the tradition; how could it have been a variant, as Wilamowitz supposed?

One might rather wonder whether ἂν ἢ is the residue of a scribe's mistaken beginning ποῖοc γὰρ ἀνὴρ ... It might also be suggested that the sequence would work very well without νέφροc, especially as Sommerstein has cast doubt on the common view that the word is a euphemism for ὄρχειc. So perhaps ποῖοc γὰρ ἀνὴρ ἔτ' ἂν κτλ.

969 The accentuation of the adjectives is problematic. Chandler, *GA* 155 (§542), says that παμβδελυρόc and παμμυcαρόc at 969 'are singular, but seem to be so accented in MSS.' He notes ibid. παμμίαροc at *Frogs* 466 as proparoxytone. Blaydes in his edition (1880) states a preference for not adopting oxytone accents on the two adjectives here but does not act accordingly in his text. He cited some compound adjectives in παν- which are proparoxytone and later gave another list (1899: 64).

975 The MSS here and at *Thesm.* 61 have verb forms ending in -ίcαc. Cobet, *Variae lectiones*, 2nd edn. (Leiden, 1873), 375–6, extracted from Hesychius the form ξυγγογγύλαc. He argued from the analogy of verbs formed from adjectives in -λοc, e.g. ποικίλλω κωτίλλω cτωμύλλομαι.

γογγυλίζω is cited by *DGE* from the scholium on *Peace* 28, which seems to be a phantom, and Suda γ 361, where Adler was unable to cite any other source. But the *Lex. byz. gr.* proves that it is well attested in later Greek, which perhaps accounts for the MSS readings; note also that R at *Thesm.* 56 has γογγυλίζει, corrected by Porson.

980 The form γερωχία looks anomalous, since the internal aspiration characteristic of Laconian is rendered differently in other passages, e.g. 1001 and 1296. But the spelling with chi may well represent Aristophanes' intention: ἁγερωχία i.e. ἁ ἀγερωχία, 'arrogance'. The following words ἢ τοὶ πρυτάνιεc then force the audience to revise their analysis of the preceding phrase as ἁ γερωχία. See A. C. Cassio, *Seminari romani*, 1 (1998), 73–8. Wilamowitz defended the paradosis, taking the word to be a derivative of *γεραοῦχοι > γερῶχοι. Colvin 236 says that this is unconvincing, but adds no explanation.

981 The correct form of the infinitive given by B is probably to be treated as a lucky accident, not preservation of genuine tradition or conscious and well-informed emendation by the intelligent scribe of this MS.

988 The intrusive rhotacism, a feature of much later Laconian, in RΓ^{pc} and Hesychius is odd. It suggests that some ancient scholar tried to improve the text. An interest in dialect is attested for grammarians from the time of Philitas onwards.

993 Why do almost all editors follow Porson in giving the emphatic form of the first person pronoun? Emphasis is quite out of place here. Bergk was right.

996 Hesitantly I adopt the slight emendation by J. Taillardat in *Mélanges Chantraine* (Paris, 1972), 255–61. Παλλάνας has the advantage of a double entendre: it (i) alludes to a territorial claim to an Athenian colony which the Spartans had been unable to take during the Archidamian War, and (ii) is a personal name that could easily have been borne by a hetaera, of the same type as Cyrene at *Thesm.* 98, *Frogs* 1328 (other examples are known).

1037 I find the expression μὴ ὥρας' rather puzzling, as at 391, where the syntax appears to be different. From Sandbach's note on Menander, *Perikeiromene* 321 I infer that Bothe's reading is probably right, but that one cannot exclude from consideration Bentley's insertion of εἰς.

1053 Coulon is unlikely to have been right in suggesting that the scholium gives support for the deletion of πολλά. R simply has ἔcω ἡμῖν ἐcτιν.

1062 The discrepancy between R's ἔχεcθ' and the other MSS' γενέcθ' is puzzling, and I would not rule out Reisig's proposal to read κρέ' ἔδεcθ'. I agree with Sommerstein that γεύομαι is not suitable here, as it requires a genitive.

1078 I have come to the conclusion that Dobree was right to suggest ἤδ' ⟨ἤ⟩. Van Leeuwen dissented, saying 'tragicam dictionem dux chori imitatur; cf. *Ach.* 454'. But is the language here tragic? βαβαί hardly creates that impression; the rest of the vocabulary does not obviously support the notion, and Porson's Law is not observed in 1079.

1099 Having consulted Hangard's edition of the scholia I am unable to understand why Henderson records -φλας- in his apparatus as the correct reading derived from that source; Sommerstein's note is similar. Meineke deserves the credit for the correction.

1120 As van Leeuwen saw, if the text is right, καί must be taken with τούτουc. If so, the pronoun cύ occupies a position which can perhaps be deemed to accord with Wackernagel's Law, but the collocation with καί seems unusual, if not positively misleading, as if someone else were required to take the Athenians across the stage. Van Herwerden's drastic emendation is diagnostic. But ἴθι δή would be easier; cf. Denniston, *GP* 218.

1133–4 I do not feel sure that recent discussions have settled the textual question here. The transmitted text, accepted by van Leeuwen, is acceptable if one believes that cτρατεύματι can be taken as 'by your campaigning' or adopts the very slight adjustment proposed by Reiske, cτρατεύμαcιν. Wilamowitz and others accept Blaydes's βαρβάρῳ, which is certainly an easy change and only presupposes a scribal mistake of assimilation, probably the commonest of all faults. I have taken the slight risk of following them, while noting that Blaydes did not venture to print his own conjecture.

1165 Cobet's proposal is worth a mention, on the assumption that a scribe's eye wandered down the page to 1175 where δράcετε stands at the end of the line.

1172 As Blaydes noted (p. 322 of his edition), a singular verb follows ἐᾶτε, which is suspicious. At 945 above, which he did not cite, there is a parallel for his proposal.

1176 With van Leeuwen and Sommerstein I prefer the articulation of the sentence which results from punctuating after βουλεύcαcθε, not before.

1218 Though modern editors accept χωρίον on the strength of Thuc. 1. 97 and Eupolis 108, where it looks as if it may have been a term used in early rhetorical theory (see now I. C. Storey, *Eupolis* (Oxford, 2003), 124–5), their translations betray a difficulty ('procédé' van Daele and Thiercy, 'routine' Sommerstein). Blaydes's emendation could be right.

1224 Threatte ii. 483 discusses εὐωχέω and says 'the augment to ηὐ- is unattested in MSS, even of classical writers, cf. LSJ s.v.' and he refers forward to p. 499. He does not consider the possible case at Plat. *Gorg.* 522 A, where editors print ηὐώχουν without any note in the apparatus. The Clarkianus (B) at that point has εὐ- (fo. 402ʳ).

1257 The form ἥνϲει offered by the MSS is problematic because it fails to provide the expected cretic. How do Blaydes with ἄνϲει and Sommerstein with ἄνϲη interpret the metre? Colvin 138, 145, takes ἥνϲει to be bad dialect. One drawback to ἥνϲεεν = ἀνέθει is that sweat or foam normally runs downwards, which is not what the prefix would imply. Coulon, *Essai*, 122, defended the word by reference to Soph. *Trach.* 767 ἱδρὼϲ ἀνῄει χρωτί.

1289 Sommerstein makes an interesting case for retaining the transmitted adjective μεγαλόφρονοϲ, citing Pindar, *P.* 8. 1–2 and fr. 109. He could be right. But Aristophanes is not Pindar and is not exploring civic ideology in the same way as in the passages cited; so it is hard to be sure.

1299 The choice here is between Ἀϲάναν and ἄναϲϲαν, the latter being a γράφεται variant in R's scholium. The last notable editor to accept ἄναϲϲαν was Wilamowitz, who did not discuss it. Van Leeuwen had claimed that χαλκίοικοϲ is a name and implied that Ἀϲάναν would therefore be an inappropriate addition. But the fact that in 1320 τὰν Χαλκίοικον stands by itself simply indicates that the adjective was a sufficient description. Blaydes followed the basic rule of textual criticism by stating that the unusual form Ἀϲάναν was likely to be corrupted to the simpler ἄναϲϲαν. How can one imagine the reverse corruption from ἄναϲϲαν to Ἀϲάναν? The first stage would have been a gloss Ἀθηνᾶν; then someone made an unnecessary display of his knowledge of dialect by correcting it to Ἀϲάναν. Stranger things have happened, but the balance of probability is much in favour of the other view.

Thesmophoriazusae

5 Sommerstein's ὅϲ <γ'> seems worth a mention because the particle creates a useful link between what has been heard and what will be seen.

12 Sommerstein's objections to this line are well formulated. He conjectures that it may possibly be part of an early draft, mistakenly left in the author's copy that was the starting-point of our tradition. Whether or not this is so, it is better deleted. Thiercy retains it and gives it all to Euripides, but I do not follow his rendering, and I suspect that he has interpreted τοῦ . . . ὁρᾶν as two notions when in fact they are one. Austin & Olson retain the line as a funny garbled version of what Euripides is saying. They do not, however, offer a translation, and I confess to finding the syntax so odd that I do not see how to get an amusing line out if it.

34 Denniston, GP 543–4, shows that οὔτοι is sometimes accompanied by γε. So Kaibel's removal of the particle and transposition can hardly be thought obligatory. But the repetition of γε may seem inelegant; or is it just colloquial?

60 κατά is written above the line in R. Austin, *Dodone*, 16 (1987), 71, argued that since it is not found in Mu2, the copy of R, nor in the *editio princeps*, it must be a modern conjecture. But on looking at the facsimile I am inclined to think that the script is of the same date as the text hand. The kappa is a genuine minuscule letter, i.e. a form less likely to be in use after the Renaissance. Inspection of the original might reveal whether the ink is the same or not; in the facsimile it does not look different. If I am right, this is an extremely puzzling detail; one would not expect the interlinear correction to be missed by both the copyist of Mu2 and the printer. If this is a modern addition, one wonders who made it and when.

80 On balance I slightly prefer Sommerstein's view to the alternative and so Nauck's conjecture is to be accepted. At first sight the corruption is hard to account for; but this becomes less of a problem if one avoids the assumption that it can only be explained palaeographically. What presumably happened is that a scribe knew of the Thesmophoria as a festival lasting three days and allowed the numeral to influence what he wrote. If the festival held at Halimous on the 10th is included in the reckoning, as the scholiast suggests, the festival becomes a four-day event, and 'the middle day' is not a very precise locution.

87 V. Tammaro, *Eikasmos*, 13 (2002), 93–6, favours keeping the transmitted ἐκ ταύτης and understanding the pronoun as a reference to Agathon's house. But is that a normal way of referring to an οἰκία?

99 δή as proposed by Sykutris and supported by Austin (1974) seems to me the best particle to substitute for ἄν. Confusion of delta with alpha and of eta with nu in uncial script could explain the error. Andreas Divus translated *utique*; might this imply that he too favoured δή? Austin–Olson now prefer γάρ (Burges); this and Austin's alternative suggestion ἤν (1987) are also very suitable.

101 ff. The idea of dancing as a privilege of full, freeborn citizens participating in the city's ritual is strongly suggested in this passage; cf. LSJ s.v. χορεύω. For that reason it seems to me that Hermann's conjecture is worth recording and I prefer the sense given by Wecklein's ingenious proposal. The textual criticism of the song is made almost impossibly difficult by our inability to gauge the extent of the parody of what was obviously an eccentric style.

113 The meaning of προφέρων is uncertain; Sommerstein proposes 'winning before others', a sense not otherwise attested, and I would not deny that this could be right. Austin–Olson take the obscurity to be deliberate parody of Agathon's style, which is certainly possible. But I should also like to suggest the minimal emendation προφέρω 'I offer'.

124–5 Though Austin–Olson say that ὕμνων on its own is rather

Thesmophoriazusae 151

pointless, on 124 they had correctly observed that ματέρ' ὕμνων is a kenning, which seems not quite consistent.

142 The reading of R has often been reported as cπέοc, which I doubt, because the ligature of sigma and pi is incorrectly formed. I think the scribe wrote pi and inadvertently added an extra loop under the horizontal stroke.

The *Suda*'s addition of the definite article spoils the paratragic rhythm.

148 ἅμα <τῇ> γνώμῃ was proposed by Meineke. This seems to me out of court not merely because, as Austin remarks, *Dodone*, 16 (1987), 75, the article is normally omitted in phrases with γνώμῃ, but because it would introduce a resolution in a speech which otherwise conforms to the metrical rules for tragedy, as is appropriate for Agathon.

217 The ellipsis is not entirely easy and it is worth mentioning Hamaker's adjustment. There are occasions when the compendium for ὡc looks rather like an eta, but whether it figured in the script of a lost antecedent of R must remain uncertain. At the period in question, to judge from surviving manuscripts, the use of compendia was sporadic in the texts (as opposed to the marginalia).

225 After reading Austin–Olson and previous discussions cited there I think the decision whether or not to follow Porson is very finely balanced.

232 αὖ requires the assumption of a complex ellipsis as suggested by H.-S. ap. Austin–Olson. Rather than that I prefer οὖν as proposed by von Velsen and accepted by Coulon. Cf. *Clouds* 791 τί οὖν δῆθ' ὁ κακοδαίμων πείcομαι; in a somewhat similar context of anticipated trouble.

261 The superfluous accent in R's reading τουτί may simply be the result of the scribe first thinking that he had to write the definite article τοῦ and then not deleting the accent he had written. Bergk's ποῦ; forming a question by Euripides, though attractive, is not therefore strongly supported by the palaeographical detail of R's reading. λάμβαν' in R and the *Suda* may be a faulty anticipation of the verb in 262.

288 ἔχουϲαν is translated by Sommerstein 'ample possessions' (similarly Austin–Olson), which is fine; but I have wondered if this could be a case of the usage given at LSJ s.v. B IV 2, indicating continuous or regular action.

289 In case anyone has been puzzled by Hall–Geldart's apparatus entry 'τὴν θυγατέρα(ν) R', the position is that the scribe originally wrote the termination -αν, familiar to him from contemporary usage, and then erased the nu.

295 Austin–Olson mention the interesting scholium on *Knights* 941 which notes that there were many prose passages in Eupolis (fr. 401). It may be added that the scholium on the present passage says that comic poets use prose for a prayer or a decree, but does not add any detail, probably because it has been severely abbreviated.

320 As Austin–Olson report, the scribe of R wrote a horizontal stroke after παῖ. I have to admit that I do not know what he intended by this.

327–9 Most editors seem to accept Blaydes's δέ for τε in 327; in 1899 (p. 75) he hesitantly proposed the opposite change in 329. It seems to me quite likely that a scribe accidentally inverted the order of the two particles.

373 P50 (Satyrus) had the name Archicleia, recorded in *LGPN* ii as occurring only in *IG* ii^2. 1529. 15 (iv BC). This turns out to be a list of donors and the garments they donated at Brauron. It seems likely that this name, much rarer than Timocles/-eia, is the truth. If so, this might be another case of the poet mentioning the name of an acquaintance. See above on *Ach.* 46 ff. and *Wasps* 230–4.

392 Sommerstein accepted Bothe's μοιχοτύπαϲ, which was supported by citing Hesychius μ 1560 μοιχοτύπη. ἡ ὑπὸ μοιχῶν τυπτομένη. But this is not enough to guarantee that the word came from the present context, and Bothe himself said 'nihil temere mutandum est'. Daubuz' -τρόφουϲ is ingenious and apt, especially if μοιχόϲ is normally used of men. One may also wonder whether -τροποϲ follows a noun in compound adjectives at this date.

472 Valckenaer's ἐκφορά could be right. ἔκφοροϲ is defended by reference to Plat. *Laches* 201 A, but in that passage not all editors accept emendation of the transmitted reading ἔκφορος λόγος to ἔκφορος λόγου.

480 The form of the verb is in doubt. R has διεκόρευcεν, supported by MSS FS of Pollux 3. 42, whereas MS A of Pollux has -ηcεν. It may be that the form in –έω is earlier. Lucian, *Dial. Meretr.* 11. 2, also apparently has the form in -εύω, but elsewhere seems to have used -έω.

489 κῦβδα with properispomenon accent was printed by Meineke in his 1860 edition (he makes this point in the apparatus without stating his authority). Chandler, who may not have known this, does not follow his example, but Coulon and Sommerstein have.

490 It is tempting to follow Dawes and read ὁρᾷς as in 496 and 556. But perhaps the interjection could be used in the singular or plural.

511 Hirschig's τὸ κηρίον assumes that τοῦ παιδίου is a gloss, and τὸ δ' then has to refer back to the child, which does not seem to me to be as difficult as Austin–Olson suggest.

514 The formation αὐτέκμαγμα may be compared with the description of Herakles as τῷ Διὸς αὐτόπαιδι at Soph. *Trach.* 826.

554 Hirschig may well have been right to adjust the verb form, but I share Dover's view as expressed in his note on *Clouds* 329 that the transmitted form could be early evidence of morphological change in Attic. This consideration should be borne in mind when dealing with other similar problems.

557 Austin–Olson accept Kuster's emendation οἶνον for cῖτον, take the strigils to be made from reeds, as is attested for Sparta (Plut. *Mor.* 239 B), and state that a cίφων was shaped like an inverted U. They note Aristotle's remark that strigils could at a pinch be used for drawing off liquid (*Top.* 145ᵃ23). I suppose this means that a hollow reed, cut and bent for this purpose, was used and called a strigil because of its similar curvature (but see below). It could further be argued on the principle of *utrum in alterum* that cῖτον is a corruption induced by the identical first syllable of cιφωνίζομεν.

But there are difficulties in this view of the passage. It seems to me that cίφων does not automatically mean what we call a siphon. It may do so at Hipponax 56 W (= 58 D), but even there I can imagine that the object in question might have resembled what we would call a drinking-straw. At Aeneas Tacticus 18. 10 the word pretty clearly refers to a straight pipe; perhaps the most useful illustration of that very difficult passage is in D. Barends, *Lexicon Aeneium* (Assen, 1955), diagram 3/V on p.166. And Hero, *Pneumatica* 1. 1, seems to allow the same inference from his phrase τῶν καμπύλων cιφώνων, suggesting that others might be straight. As to the strigil made from a reed, that is attested for Sparta rather than Athens, and one cannot altogether dismiss the feeling that it was regarded as an eccentricity, something primitive or second-best, typical of Spartan austerity. The Aristotle passage is very puzzling, because one does not see why a reed shaped like a siphon was not called a siphon. It has occurred to me to wonder—but this may be too bizarre a suggestion to be taken seriously—whether an ordinary strigil was occasionally used for scooping viscous liquids such as some forms of honey. Another possible source of support for the emendation, though not exploited by Kuster, is Pollux 6. 19, who cites the infinitive cιφωνίζειν from Aristophanes without naming the play or adding any other word from the context; but as it is clear enough that the preceding sentences are concerned with liquids, it is generally thought that he read οἶνον. Here however the principle of *utrum in alterum* can be invoked in the opposite sense; Pollux or an earlier scribe may have assumed that, because the verb was normally used for liquids, it necessarily implied οἶνον in this context as well and an adjustment of the text was to be made accordingly.

Sommerstein here takes the view expressed by the scholiast, that the verb is used metaphorically. It does not figure in the index to Taillardat, *Images*.

567 δή is not common as a strengthener of negatives, but Denniston, *GP* 222, accepts it here. Most editors prefer Lenting's τοι, which is acceptable but less close to the paradosis.

570 On this aorist form of the verb χέζειν see my remark in the preface to the OCT, p. vii.

596 R's deictic form ταυτί at first sight seems a strange error, but it is explained by the presence of τουτί in the following line.

603 ff. P. Maas, *Rh. Mus.*² 68 (1913), 358–9 = *Kleine Schriften* (Munich, 1973), 57–8, queried the sequence of the lines. Despite the defence of the paradosis by Austin–Olson I feel that on balance he was right to observe that the comic effect is not improved by having 604 in its transmitted position, interrupting the progress of Cleisthenes' inquiries. He transposed 604 before 603 and so made it the beginning of the search.

In this new sequence ζητητέαι does not pick up the words of the previous speaker in the way that one might expect. Although he did not make that observation, Maas claimed that ζητεῖν does not mean 'investigate' (a view which one may doubt after consulting LSJ s.v.) and wondered if one should read ζητητέον τἄρ' ἐστί.

Is there any other possibility? In 607 the speaker invites Cleisthenes to investigate the other women. ζητητέαι would fit in naturally there, and γάρ does not then need to be altered. So transpose 604 after 607. I imagine that Cleisthenes addresses the other women; but one might consider substituting εἰcί for ἐcτέ.

642 Thiercy 1239 reverts to the reading of R νῦν. τότε δή. But since it does not scan we must make some change. Mu2 made the minimal correction τότε δέ, which leaves νῦν rather abrupt and staccato, though it is accepted by Austin–Olson. Van Leeuwen's νυνδὴ δέ, though further from the MS reading, seems preferable; τότε may be an intrusive gloss.

664 It has sometimes been suggested (cf. Sommerstein, p. 147 of his edition, Parker, *Songs*, 419) that τόποις is the reading of R², whereas R originally wrote τούτοις I doubt this. There is very little in the facsimile of R to suggest a correction, and what might conceivably be taken to be the residue of an original reading could instead be ink showing through from the other side of the parchment. The form of pi is admittedly not the one used in pure minuscule script, but this scribe does sometimes employ the alternative form.

667 The corruption is not easy to explain. My tentative suggestion would be that μὴ λάθῃ was part of a paraphrase used by a schoolteacher to explain the sentence.

710–11 I agree with Parker, *Songs*, 426, that the alleged parallel Soph. *OC* 273 ἡκόμην ἵν' ἡκόμην is not really support for the transmitted reading of R and the *Suda* ἧκεις γ' ὅθεν ἧκεις, and that Reisig's proposal places οὐ in a more natural position, with metrical responsion as an added advantage. I am also quite willing to accept the evidence of the scholium as affording some support, while recognizing that frequently scholiasts are wide of the mark.

716 ξύν is not the word expected with ἀδίκοις ἔργοις. Austin–Olson cite as a parallel 104, but there outré parody of Agathon's style perhaps creates a difference. Has the preposition been inserted here under the influence of cύμμαχος in the previous line? Meineke's τοῖς is worth a mention, though it gives a rare form of dochmiac.

720 ff. With Burges's transposition ἀθέοις γὰρ ἔργοις, which avoids the need for the supplements of ἐπ' by Enger and καί by Hermann, the chorus are made to threaten impious deeds of retaliation. I find it hard to say whether it is right for them to condemn themselves out of their own mouth in this way. Parker, *Songs*, 427, finds it implausible rather than comic. If, as I believe—see my remarks in *GRBS* 23 (1982), 157–61—the audience was largely or entirely male, would such an ill-conceived threat have appealed to their prejudices? Parker also has a metrical objection, though it is not strong enough to be decisive. On balance I follow her view, but with some hesitation. H.-S. asks whether anyone in Greek drama, comic or tragic, says 'I shall act godlessly'? Not even Medea goes that far, and she is a soul in torment. It sounds more like the Chinese drama, in which the villain obligingly tells you that that is what he is.

736 ὑμεῖς seems not to have been queried, but its position is odd and it seems rather weak; one might expect the speaker to allege that women are always seeking every opportunity for a drink. Could ἀεί have been the original reading?

777 Austin–Olson treat the hiatus after the transmitted χρή as parody of a Euripidean mannerism, and perhaps they are right, but the present instance is in the middle of a line rather than a question of synaphea.

809 Thiercy 1249 rejects Maas's emendation Ἄνυτος (*Rh, Mus.*[2] 68

(1913), 360 = *Kleine Schriften*, 58); Coulon accepted it and Sommerstein does not discuss it, nor do Austin–Olson beyond saying that it is clever but a shot in the dark. The first problem is the verb. φήϲειϲ in R, accepted by Sommerstein, involves a direct address of a member of the council, presumably seated in the area reserved for that body. As Thiercy, who also accepts this, says, it is 'inhabituel' for the chorus to do this in a parabasis, and he cites no example. Besides, how could the poet be sure that the offending person would be present?

Can αὐτόϲ refer back to τιϲ? I share Sommerstein's view that τιϲ indicates someone not named but easily identified. If that is acceptable, the text needs no further alteration. But it has to be admitted that Maas's idea is very attractive. And there is a puzzling palaeographical detail that was noticed by von Velsen but has been lost sight of since: in R τίϲ is written with the accent. If that is accepted, αὐτόϲ cannot easily be understood with the verb in either person, and so Maas's conjecture provides the solution.

811 Though Greek word-order is a dangerous subject on which to dogmatize, I find it very hard to believe that the position of ζεύγει as transmitted, dislocating the participial phrase, can be justified. Austin–Olson cite *Plutus* 205 for unusual order, but the text there has been questioned, and the stylistic register seems to me a bit different.

813 R has αὖτ' ἀπε-, which can be understood, but the syntax is irregular and the change easy.

819 Denniston, *GP* 396–7, suggests writing δή που as two words, since δή is more closely linked with μέν than with που.

843 The repetition of τόκον, though possible, is not elegant, and Blaydes may well have been right with ἔτι or ποτέ. As the same word ends l. 845, the corruption would have been very easy. Note also the mistake in R at the end of 833 *ante correctionem* (ποτέ for τινί).

878 The Ionic form πεπλώκαμεν needs to be explained, since in the corresponding line *Helen* 461 πεπλεύκαμεν is transmitted. Hoffmann–Debrunner i. 130 (§202) took it to be an allusion to *Helen* 532, where the Ionic form is transmitted; but 530–40 were deleted by Willink, followed by Diggle, and in any case some justification of the Ionic form of an otherwise common verb is desirable.

Kannicht on *Helen* 455 conjectures that forms from other dialects were used to make the stylistic register higher and cites 878 as his example. He repeats the notion in his note on *Helen* 461, citing archaisms and dialect from elsewhere in that play (159, 500, 532, 605, 1010). I record this explanation without feeling fully convinced; Colvin and Willi appear not to comment.

887 Thiercy revives van Leeuwen's κάκιcτ' ἄρ', which its author did not justify in detail; one may conjecture that he wished to reduce the frequency of γ' in these lines. Though at first I was not attracted, and the confusion of gamma and tau in their uncial forms is notoriously frequent, this alternative proposal is well worth recording, since it too presumes a scribal error involving only one letter. It has now been adopted by Austin–Olson. κακῶc γάρ is conceivable, but see Denniston, *GP* 94–5. γ' ἄρ' has a parallel at Eur. *Cycl.* 261 if one accepts Kirchhoff's minor adjustment there.

909 R has Ἑλένηc', the mark of elision being quite clear. So the scribe did not intend to write the genitive -ηc; he merely neglected, as often, the iota adscript.

910 This extremely difficult passage has been discussed several times in recent years; Sommerstein accepted Austin's arguments of 1990 as convincing but nevertheless obelized ἰφύων. If that is the right reading, as Austin–Olson now suggest, R's ἀφύων is the product of scribal distraction when confronted with a very rare word. But I am not at all sure that it is correct. To speak of lavender or some other flowering plant is not the best way to describe Euripides' appearance if he came on draped in seaweed; Sommerstein pointed out that the alleged allusion to Euripides' mother's activities as market gardener is strained, because she dealt more in vegetables than other plants (cf. Austin 1990, 27 n. 1). Also, if the parody respects the original production of the *Helen*, the figure of 'Menelaus' will be in rags. Austin (1990: 27) dismissed Gannon's suggestion τιφύων, rightly in my opinion, as it is unattested. But it has occurred to me to wonder if Gannon was right to think that the text indicated recognition of some part of the anatomy, e.g. ἐκ τῶν ἰcχίων. This type of solution might be better if one could find a word with sexual connotations. Austin went on to take l. 935 to be the key to the puzzle and suggested either ἰcτίων or Grégoire's ἀμφίων, expressing a slight preference for the latter, which he described as a word 'de couleur populaire' and a comic equivalent of the grand language of *Helen* 423. He and Olson now regard ἀμφίων as flat; Thiercy 1252 was also sceptical about it, observing that it is not found in Euripides and that as many Euripidean heroes were shown in rags, this was no distinguishing mark, which is true enough but perhaps the kind of point that a theatre audience would not have time to appreciate. As to the word, it is rare; the only contemporary instance is from an unidentified context in a Sophoclean satyr-play (fr. 420) and so we can hardly be sure of its connotations. Later it occurs in Callimachus fr. 177. 31, and is used as a term for ragged clothing by the scholiast on Aratus, *Phaenomena* 1073. This last instance cannot be dated at all precisely, but it is obviously much later and one does not know what stylistic register the word then belonged to. With great hesitation I have opted for Grégoire's conjecture, assuming that the rare word was simplified by the scribe of R and more seriously corrupted in the *Suda* to a word which someone was then willing to comment on. This train of events is not as implausible as it may seem to those who have little experience of dealing with MSS. H.-S. wonders if ὀcφύων might be a possibility.

952 Zanetti's μέλcιν, matching Divus' *curae esse*, means that Pauson is praying to have such concerns as celebrating a festival frequently, year in and year out. I do not follow Sommerstein's objection that this implies a mental disposition foreign to classical Greek thought processes.

987 My doubts here stem from the feeling that ὧδε = δεῦρο seems not to be what we want.

990 Enger's εὗιε ὧ Διός κτλ. creates a hiatus of a kind which seems dubious. Dr Parker kindly informs me (private communication of 7 January 2002) that she too has doubts; she refers to the treatment of hiatus in drama by W. von Christ, *Metrik der Griechen und Römer*, 2nd edn. (Leipzig, 1879), 39–41, which gives no support to Enger.

995 R reads cυὶ, emended by Divus and Zanetti to cοί. Wilamowitz, GV 476, remarked 'cυὶ κτυπεῖται wird schlecht als cοί κτλ. genommen'. I suspect he was right; cοί was not very likely to be corrupted into ϲυι, and it is easier to suppose that a scribe was puzzled by the rare compound ϲυγκτυπεῖται, which apparently is not otherwise attested until the post-classical period. Ole Thomsen, *Classica et Mediaevalia, Diss.* IX (1973), 27–46 (at 41–2) objects to Wilamowitz's emendation on the ground that it removes the second-person address so often repeated in prayers.

1001 Sommerstein argues that the ekkuklema was not used here to bring In-law back on stage, because this would impede access to the door through which the Archer must later pass four times. This does not seem to me conclusive. If the ekkuklema was a kind of trolley, why could it not have been wheeled a little further forward, towards the front of the stage, leaving enough room for an actor to go in and out of the stage-building unimpeded?

1014 There are various proposals for dealing with the problem here. I merely remark that there is no feature in the diacritics in R at this point which can point towards a solution.

1026 ff. are difficult because more than one view can be taken of the metrical requirements. Austin's recent suggestions are very acceptable. He had also proposed the similar ἐφέϲτηκε ⟨καί μ'⟩ ὀλοόν (ap. F. Lourenço, *Euphrosyne*, 28 (2000), 322). He noted there that the epic correption of πάλαι resulting from the word-order in R does not appear to be authentically Euripidean, and also gave alternative views of the metre in 1036–8 and 1039–40. It is hard to adjudicate in questions of lyric metre. The objection to a lecythion at 1037 is perhaps to be countered by noting that there is one at 1049.

1105 Austin–Olson record R's rendering of the word παρθένον, which is παρνον with a theta written above. In the OCT apparatus I have not bothered to include this because the scribe has simply employed an abbreviation belonging to the class of *nomina sacra*; see L. Traube, *Nomina sacra* (Munich, 1907), 126–7, who noted that in the case of this word the horizontal stroke between the theta and the letters in the line is commonly omitted. As happens from time to time, these abbreviations designed for use in theological texts and covering various key concepts of Christian theology were employed by scribes elsewhere (and so emendations in classical texts which presuppose the misinterpretation of *nomina sacra* are entirely legitimate).

1115 Sommerstein gives κόρης as the reading of Mu2 and κόρ followed by two suprascript dots as the reading of R. But I am inclined to think that the two marks in R were intended by the scribe to serve as the compendium for ης. It would be a variant of the usual form of this abbreviation, since the use of two curved strokes looking like our letter s normally signified εις; but G. F. Tsereteli, *Sokrashcheniya v grecheskikh rukopisyakh*, 2nd edn. (St Petersburg, 1904), 63, noted an example from a tenth-century MS and correctly suggested that the identical pronunciation of εις and ης at this date led to confusion.

1125 The entry in Austin–Olson's apparatus criticus suggests that R intended μαςτιγῶ ς' to be taken as two separate words. This cannot be regarded as certain, because the scribe is erratic in the matter of word-division.

1173 A word of clarification about the reading ἔφραζον: the scribe of R corrected his initial mistake by adding the missing syllable above the line; the alpha is represented by a horizontal stroke, which is not unusual at this date for a scribe willing to use the full range of abbreviations.

1175 Austin–Olson print the vocative of the girl's name in -όν on the strength of a variant attested by some but not all of the MSS in the *Suda* quotation and refer to West's edition of *Anacreontea* 10. 2, where the Palatine MS has the vocative χελιδόν. This may be right, but the MSS are hardly decisive authority when the difference is merely that between omicron and omega (identically pronounced in Byzantine times). Threatte ii. 125–6 suggests that a vocative in -ών is not excluded. In Sappho fr. 135 χελίδων is accepted by Voigt in her edition, though she mentions I. Voss' proposal χελιδόν.

1181 If ἄνωθεν means 'from the top', can φέρε mean 'pull'? Or is this a colloquialism, with the main verb to be understood from the context? Willems ii. 578–9 translated *trade, porrige mihi*, claiming support from 1115, 1196, *Knights* 118, *Clouds* 1297, *Peace* 15 and twenty other passages. In those passages the meaning is 'bring' or 'hand over', and I suspect that the movement in question is less complex than pulling a garment over one's head, gripping it at the top. Austin–Olson cite Plat. *Rep.* 449 B; that does not actually involve removal of a garment. Maas, *Kleine Schriften*, 180, made a useful diagnostic conjecture.

Frogs

The title of the play is the subject of a stimulating article by M. Matteuzzi, *Futurantico*, 1 (2003), 265–80, who argues that the frog was understood to be a symbol of the renewal of life. The key text in support of this view is Pliny, *NH* 9. 159: *Mirumque, semestri vita resolvuntur in limum nullo cernente, et rursus vernis aquis renascuntur quae fuere natae, perinde occulta ratione, cum omnibus annis id eveniat*. Some other evidence is assembled. Such a belief could not be without significance in the context of a play which dealt with the afterlife and had a chorus of initiates, since they were convinced that they had secured the assurance of life after death.

Is a simpler explanation in order? The play is about the underworld, and the marsh or lake at the approach to Hades is prominent not only in the play (137, cf. 211) but in the generally accepted vision of Hades, as suggested by Eur. *Alc.* 443, Soph. fr. 523. 2 and perhaps Aesch. fr. 273. The frogs as the natural inhabitants of the marsh or lake do not need to be invested with any special significance.

14–16 have been a source of difficulty to many editors. As Kassel says, *Rh. Mus.*² 137 (1994), 35, if 15 is deleted εἴωθε ποιεῖν seems bald, as one is not told what was done on stage in plays by the other poets; but it might be argued that the audience could easily infer what was meant. If it is retained it creates asyndeton unless emended. Though Dover accepted the asyndeton, Kassel doubted whether his parallels were adequate, and I am inclined to agree. The asyndeton can be removed in two ways. Sommerstein punctuates after ποιεῖν, which is certainly neat. I prefer this gentler medicine to the alternative, which is to follow Porson and Fritzsche in supplying <οἵ> (anticipated, as it turns out, by the late MSS G, Marc. gr. 475 of the late fifteenth century and Np1, Naples II F 22 of the late fourteenth century) and adopting cκευοφοροῦc', attested only by M^ac and Θ^pc among the more important MSS. Dover objected that this looks like an attempt to restore the metre, and Kassel replied that the same could be said of the reading involving the form cκεύη-. I wonder if Blaydes had a point when he remarked 'exspectabam ἐν ταῖc κωμῳδίαιc'. However, perhaps *Plut.* 423 defends the text here.

27 The *difficilior lectio* οὖνοc is transmitted in several important MSS. I find Sommerstein's discussion of the textual problem convincing; it is a refutation of Radermacher's note in favour of ὄνοc (p. 147 of his commentary). Dover says nothing.

31 Denniston, *GP* 467, fits this instance of δ' οὖν into a sparsely represented category 'all right then, if . . .'; i.e. a concession is made, followed by a fresh suggestion, as in *Wasps* 764 and *Birds* 56. So I have taken the view that Blaydes' νῦν οὖν and van Herwerden's οὔκουν do not need to be recorded in the apparatus.

55 Threatte i. 507–8 shows that cμ- is the normal form of the adjective, but there are a few instances of μ- in late fifth-century inventories.

57 There is uncertainty about the form of Dionysus' exclamation. Dover's advocacy of Fritzsche's ἀπ- seems reasonable. If RV were right with ἀππ-, or most of the other *veteres* with ἀττ-, one might delete τῷ, as Blaydes tentatively suggested. That eliminates the definite article, which Fraenkel, *BzA* 132, found objectionable; he preferred the enclitic τῳ. He has not been followed; yet it seems to me that there may have been something in his feeling that the definite article is not wanted here. Is πωc conceivable? 'Did you by any chance . . .?' may have been the idea. Less attractive palaeographically is γάρ.

If the exclamation indicates disgust, Heracles is to be understood as suggesting a further possibility. If instead it indicates pain or disappointment, Heracles assumes that the sexual partner was unsatisfactory and identifies the obvious culprit.

84 Though the variant τοῖc coφοῖc is not at all well attested, it has to be given consideration (on questions raised by variants that are not well attested see my paper in *Revue d'histoire des textes*, 17 (1987 [1989]), 1–13). Blaydes notes that it is easy to see how τοῖc coφοῖc could have been altered to τοῖc φίλοιc, whereas the change in other direction is less likely. Though Dover accepts the possibility that coφοῖc is a variant, not just an explanation—it would certainly not be a good one—he does not consider its merits. Blaydes followed Dobree and put it in his text, as does Del Corno. Sommerstein remarks that τοῖc φίλοιc 'is redolent of epitaphs', without noting that this is another factor potentially leading to corruption. If one accepts this reading, it has to be on the ground that there is point in the notion of some of Agathon's friends being more than friends.

90 Even if Herakles is something of a buffoon and speaking in very colloquial style, μύρια in agreement with μειρακύλλια seems to result in an extreme exaggeration; it might be better for him to say that the glibness of these youths resulted in innumerable plays; hence Dindorf's μυρίαc could well be right.

Ancient grammarians believed that there was a distinction between μύριοι 'ten thousand' and μυρίοι 'countless'. Chandler 116 (§§375, 377) accepted this; LSJ casts doubt on it and Schwyzer i. 593 says 'der Akzentunterschied muß sekundär sein'. The MSS exhibit some variation, and the position is complicated by the fact that when πλεῖν ἢ μύριοι occurred at the end of a trimeter the Byzantine scribes were exposed to the temptation of writing μυρίοι so as to create a line that conformed to their rules for versification by having an accent on the penultimate syllable. For convenience I have adopted the policy of treating πλεῖν ἢ μύριοι as meaning 'more than ten thousand' with proparoxytone accent (cf. *Birds* 1305, *Plutus* 1184); but in other contexts I have left μυρία if transmitted, as it is e.g. by R at *Thesm.* 475 (Austin–Olson do not comment). As Holzinger on *Plutus* 1184 observed, it is impossible to imagine how a classical author could have indicated to a reader which accentuation he had in mind. On this puzzling question see the paper by P. Probert in J. H. W. Penney (ed.), *Perspectives in Indo-European Languages* (Oxford, 2004), 277–91.

113 V's addition of καπηλίδαc after ὁδούc puzzles Dover, who does not see a word on which it might have been a gloss 'with the possible exception of ἀρτοπώλια'. That is an oversight: πανδοκευτρίαc seems to me close enough in meaning to have attracted the gloss καπηλίδας. I feel fairly certain that the word is a gloss even though it does not occupy the normal position of a gloss as it stands in V.

132f. See above on *Peace* 730, which if correct would suggest that φῶςιν here could mean 'order', despite the doubts of Dover. But Sommerstein is probably right to argue that the runners' initial spring is compared to the suicide's fatal leap, which justifies Seidler's emendation.

168 This line was deleted by Hamaker, followed van Leeuwen and Willems, not all agreeing on the reason. As H.-S. points out, it takes the edge off the ensuing joke. As transmitted, though Dover accepts it without concern, it seems unacceptable. Bergk's ingenious minor adjustment at first sight seems to be satisfactory and is accepted by Sommerstein. However, he translates 'to the same destination', whereas I would have thought the natural meaning is 'for the same purpose', which in the context will not do.

177 Cobet urged that the optative should have the form -βιοίην. Threatte does not appear to have evidence to settle the point.

186 It seems to me that Sommerstein's discussion of the textual difficulty settles the question in favour of the indirect tradition, and so I have not mentioned emendations in the apparatus.

188–9 The staccato exchange is favoured by recent editors. The alternative is to give Dionysus 188b–189a; he is thus made to ask about the destination ἐς κόρακας because it is less specifically geographic than the others named by Charon. V. Tammaro, *Museum criticum*, 21–2 (1986–7), 179–80, notes that ὄντως is not found elsewhere as a single-word utterance, and Kassel, *Rh. Mus.*[2] 137 (1994), 40, feels that it is unacceptable.

ποῖ and ποῦ are easily interchanged. One might be tempted to prefer ποῖ as the *difficilior lectio*; if ποῦ were the original reading, would Byzantine readers have wished to alter it to ποῖ, which is found in MSS EUPar20? Conceivably some of them would have been capable of restoring a refinement of Attic usage. I do not follow Sommerstein's remark about these two interrogatives.

Radermacher's enclitic που, taken as part of Charon's order 'Take your place somewhere, quickly', with cχήcειν... ὄντωc; given to Dionysus, is perhaps too ingenious.

193 is difficult. Sommerstein and Dover both print τρέχων and the latter cites the somewhat similar passages Soph. *Phil.* 55 ὡc λόγοιcιν ἐκκλέψῃc λέγων and *Ach.* 177 φεύγοντ᾽ ἐκφυγεῖν. The first passage looks close, whereas in the second the emphasis is probably on the preposition ἐκ-, i.e. 'I must escape', and here there is no corresponding preposition. If τρέχων is right here, perhaps the repetitive element reflects a common feature of colloquial language. *Pace* Dover, I do not find it hard to imagine a glossator adding τρέχων to κύκλῳ. I feel very uncertain on this question and have wondered if it would be better to read δρόμῳ.

209 ff. Henry Wansbrough's observation of frogs in a pool near Jerusalem (*JHS* 113 (1993), 162) is important; he noticed that there were two groups, who had different chants, one βρεκεκεκέξ, the other κοὰξ κοάξ. Producers might like to take note of this when the play is revived.

238 D. Iordanoglou, *Eranos*, 97 (1999), 62–7, proposes ἐκκτυπῶν for the transmitted ἐγκύψαc/ἐκκύψαc. He shows that the objections to the reading of the MSS which have been made occasionally in the past need to be taken seriously, and that there is room for doubt about the distribution of parts. The passage deserves attention; one might ask if it is possible to find a suitable aorist participle—a present seems less idiomatic—that is palaeographically closer to the paradosis. My suggestion would be ἐκρήξαc 'bursting out', as at Ar. *Meteor.* 366ᵇ32 of a wind. Since Dionysus is seated, his πρωκτόc is not very likely to become visible.

300 Recent editors accept Dindorf's τοῦτ᾽ ἔθ᾽. The chief MSS offer τοῦτό γ᾽ (RVKL) or τοῦτό γ᾽ ἔcθ᾽ (A and the lemma of the scholium in E). While Dindorf could argue with some degree of plausibility that ἔcθ᾽ is a corruption of ἔθ᾽, it is not clear that γ᾽ should be sacrificed. I do not regard the resulting split anapaest as a decisive objection. In Bekker's London edition of 1829, v. 394 I find γ᾽ ἔθ᾽ recorded as the preferred reading of Bentley and reported by Brunck as the reading of 'membr. Et C [etiam Borg.]'. Blaydes gives γ᾽ ἔθ᾽ as the reading of DBorg. schol. His D is 'Paris (C. B. 2)'.

312–15 Kassel, *Rh. Mus.*² 137 (1994), 42, follows van Leeuwen and Fraenkel against Dover and Sommerstein. The decision is finely balanced. I personally feel that despite the analogies from other scenes of eavesdropping cited by Sommerstein, it can hardly be a cast-iron rule that the suggestion to eavesdrop continues something else said by the same speaker; and so with slight hesitation I follow Kasssel, who draws attention to the difference between the slave's respectful behaviour at 301 and 318 and his later contempt for his master at 479 ff.

320 Sommerstein argues that δι' ἀγορᾶc is wrong because ἐν ἀγορᾷ would be needed. But if the procession went through the Agora, I find the expression only slightly elliptical. *Pace* R. Janko, *ZPE* 118 (1997), 88 n. 234, I think Dover is right to say that a joke is not what we expect here.

340 Kassel, *Rh. Mus.*² 137 (1994), 43, is right to note that τινάccων here may be a faulty repetition deriving from 328. Sommerstein appears to have a point when he says that the facts reported in 344 ff. imply that 340 is a statement, not an imperative. If 341 is a genuine vocative, not just a ritual cry, a second person verb is called for, and I have ventured to adopt Sommerstein's conjecture.

350 φέγγων is palaeographically easy to accept in place of the unmetrical φλέγων, but it is not the only possibility. The wrong word might have been introduced under the influence of l. 343; so Blaydes's πέμπων is worth a mention.

353 In this song the MSS exhibit few signs of Doric vocalization apart from ἦβαν, which appears to be the reading of all witnesses so far reported. As H.-S. observes, consistency requires the Attic form. If the song has anything to do with Athenian mystery religion, Doric is hardly in place.

365 For Blaydes' Ἑκατείων see above on *Wasps* 804.

369 Dover's defence of the transmitted text against Richards's emendation is to take the words between αὐδῶ and ἐξίcταcθαι as parenthetical. I find this very awkward, as it creates a poor climax to a powerfully expressed catalogue of misdemeanours.

389 Blaydes reported, and Dr Natalie Tchernetska of Trinity College

Cambridge kindly confirmed, that two late MSS in Cambridge (University Library Nn 3. 15. 1, 2) have the variant γελοῖ᾽ ἄμ᾽ for γελοιά μ᾽. The diacritics are clear enough to indicate the intended word-division. Since the scribes of the MSS have not been identified in *RGK* i, one cannot offer a provisional identification of the scholar responsible for this suggestion.

422 Sommerstein is right to draw attention to the difficulty of translating τὸν Κλεισθένους as 'the son of Cleisthenes', which entails an unacceptable absence of the definite article with πρωκτόν, whereas it is found with τὰς γνάθους. Blaydes had already seen the problem and proposed ἐν ταῖς ταφαῖς τὸν ὄρρον.

464 R. J. Clark, *PCPS* 47 (2001), 106–11, supports the view that Aeacus rather than his servant appears. He combines the functions of *ianitor Orci* and assessor to the judges of the underworld.

478 Sommerstein notes on this line 'further anticlimax' and approves of David Barrett's translation 'just wait there a moment while I go and fetch them'. I think that is mistaken; Dover cites Eur. fr. 495. 3–4 πάλιν ὑποστρέψας πόδα/χωρεῖ δρομαῖον. This is still tragic language, even if not as overblown as what preceded.

483/528 The variation of accent in προσθοῦ and κατάθου is in accordance with a rule given in *Et. Magn.* 688. 38–44, which Lentz printed in revised form in his Herodian i. 468. 12–14. This oddity is accepted by Probert 47 (§93), who is perhaps basing herself on Schwyzer i. 390–1, where, however, the position is outlined rather than explained. H.-S. finds the anomaly very odd, and I agree. Cf. the variant ἀπόδου at l. 1235, and προσθοῦ *Birds* 361.

506–7 It is just possible that V has preserved a trace of the truth by adding τ᾽ after βοῦν in 506. Even without this palaeographical hint there is a strong case for Blaydes's insertion of the particle in the next line.

516 Dover's apparatus records τἄρτι as the reading of Herodian (not listed in his apparatus fontium). This turns out to be the text printed by Lentz ii. 494. 1–5, which comes from *Et. Magn.* 283. 45–51. But Gaisford does not record such a variant, nor does De Stefani in his *Et. Gud.* 375. 11. So do we have here an emendation by Lentz? Or a misprint? If it were a genuine variant, one might ask whether it could conceivably be taken as lending support to Lenting's γ', ἄρτι.

526 Denniston, *GP* lxiii, 492, accepted the reading of VK τί που on the ground that Xanthias is cheekily mocking the language of his master in 522. Denniston here noted the frequency of repetition, whether intentional or not, in Greek texts, thereby anticipating in part John Jackson's famous discussion in *MS* 200–2.

546 αὐτόc as in VAK (om. R) gives the wrong emphasis 'himself'; Meineke's καὐτόc 'he too' is far superior. The scholium in R reads ὁ δὲ Ξανθίας γνούς, ἅτε καὶ αὐτὸς πρότεροc τὰ αὐτὰ ποιῶν, ἐπάταξεν ἄν με, which perhaps lends support to his proposal. Palmer thought the slave's keen sight should be explained and suggested Ἄργοc (transposed to follow πανοῦργοc).

554 Though ὀβολόc became the standard spelling of the word for the coin, it appears that for the half-obol the form ἡμιωβέλιον was the usual spelling, and the derivative in -βελιαῖοc is cited from P. Cair. Zen. 59019. 5 of the third century BC. Threatte i. 215 refers to M. N. Tod, *Numismatic Chronicle*⁶, 7 (1947), 1–27; see esp. pp. 5 and 22.

565 An expression of diffidence seems out of place and the indefinite location wrong when the next words specify where the speaker and her companion went. Denniston, *GP* 491, aware of the poor attestation of the particle, nevertheless accepts it, translating 'I believe we ran up' and adding 'she was so frightened at the time that she hardly remembered afterwards exactly what happened'. πω has more claim to be considered the paradosis than που, which is found in V alone of the important MSS. Though που is accepted by some editors, they have to go to some lengths to justify it. Alternative solutions should at least be considered. Dobree's πωc is said by Blaydes to be the reading of his S (= G, Marc. gr. 475) and Laur. 31. 16; to my surprise no confirmation or denial of this is to be had from C. N. Eberline, *Studies in the MS Tradition of the Ranae of Aristophanes* (Meisenheim am Glan, 1980). But 'somehow we leapt up' is not implausible, and if one is willing to depart a little further from the transmitted reading ὅμωc 'still', i.e. despite their fright, would also make good sense.

573 μου is the reading of R and V, and von Velsen, in his very accurate edition (Leipzig, 1881) does not indicate any variant in other MSS. So I do not see why Dover and Sommerstein print μοι, even though it is obviously idiomatic. Once again Eberline, op. cit. on 565, fails to throw any further light on this minor puzzle.

599b Blaydes' ὅδε for ὅτι is commended by the fact that in the previous sentence the subject is emphatically indicated as someone different from the subject of the verb in the present sentence; in other words, the transmitted text is less clear than it might be. Dobree saw the same difficulty and proposed ὅδε at the end of the sentence, but as Blaydes remarked εὖ οἶδ' ὅτι is a regular phrase which one would prefer not to alter. Blaydes's proposal received the support of van Herwerden, and now has that of Parker and Sommerstein (2001: 313).

639 Blaydes preferred the order ἡγοῦ ... εἶναι and I think he was right. An unstressed form of the verb 'to be' occupying first position in its clause is unexpected. Dover's note refers to the possibility of a semantic reason for the transmitted word-order; I do not understand this. The alternative is an aesthetic reason, which he does not formulate, and I am unable to do so.

649 As H.-S. notes, one expects the exclamation to be in the same form when used and when quoted. Hall–Geldart followed Thiersch to achieve this. The alternative is ἰατταταῖ repeated without change of speaker.

673 The editors prefer the emphatic form ἐμέ (RMd1Vb3) to με (cett.). Dover says 'the contrast between 'your thinking' and 'my suffering'. . . is more effective'. Such a contrast requires both pronouns to be emphatic, yet ϲε is not printed with an accent by editors. And anyway the contrast is between the thought and the suffering, not the pronouns. Emphatic ἐμέ does not correspond to the intonation which I infer from Sommerstein's rendering.

691 τὰϲ προτέραϲ ἁμαρτίαϲ in EUVb3Vs1 is an example of the very common error of assimilation, and as it is found in none of the leading MSS I did not think it necessary to include it in the apparatus of an OCT.

704 The word-order is not above suspicion. The only other example of καὶ ταῦτα postponed appears to be Diodorus comicus fr. 3. 5, cited by Fraenkel, *BzA* 151–2. He there noted and accepted the emendation μετά for καί, which he ascribed to Meineke. K. -A. ad loc. trace it back to Stephanus, *Comicorum graecorum sententiae* (Paris, 1565), 424 and report Bothe's proposal of 1844 κατὰ ταῦτα. They retain the transmitted text and cite l. 704 as parallel. Some doubt is justified, however, both on the ground that Diodorus is of the third century and the sense given by the transmitted text would certainly be improved by Bothe's adjustment. In 704 ταῦτ' could be intrusive, as a result of its occurrence in the preceding line. Confusion of this word with πάντα is found elsewhere; 'the city and all our affairs' would make sense. Cf. *Clouds* 588, 697.

747–1530 are printed, with some omissions, among the testimonia for the judgements passed on Aeschylus in S. L. Radt, *Tragicorum graecorum fragmenta*, iii (Göttingen, 1985), 73–94. The material collected there is very helpful.

786 The dual form αὐτοῖν found in V is adopted by many editors. They may be right; Blaydes notes the dual form of a verb in 806. It is to be remarked, however, that Byzantine authors show a great liking for the dual and were keen to display their knowledge of it, while literate readers of that period may also have been tempted to insert it where possible into their copies of the ancient texts.

788 I doubt if it is possible to solve this puzzle, and with some hesitation adopt the view of Naber, *Mnemosyne*^{2}, 11 (1883), 35–6; cf. J. Fettes, *LCM* 15 (1990), 132–8.

797 Beare's cταθήcεται could well be right. But see Taillardat, *Images*, 454 (§781), and R. Renehan, *Greek lexicographical notes*, ii (Göttingen, 1982), 127.

815 Editors now tend to accept περ ἴδῃ and with it the complex syntax outlined in Dover's note. It does seem rather clumsy; one wishes a verb of perception taking a genitive could be found, so as to yield a more normal construction.

Dover may well be right to say that in this type of writing περ has no particular meaning and simply intensifies the epic tone of the song. If one is not satisfied by that, V's παρίδη would be acceptable if it meant 'catch sight of'; but this sense is not unequivocally attested. One might consider προcίδῃ, though it is less close palaeographically.

818–19 Borthwick, *CQ*² 49 (1999), 623–4, prefers ἱππολόφων because of the allusion to *Iliad* 2. 1 with its compound ἱπποκορυcτήc. But it can be urged that ὑψίλοφοc has Pindaric precedent (*O*. 13. 111), even if not in the sense seen here, and Homeric reminiscences could all too easily intrude upon scribal consciousness. So perhaps the rare word is to be preferred, despite its relatively poor support in the tradition.

Borthwick's suggestion for the second half of 819 is to introduce a reference to light shields, the word γέρρων having a nearly anagrammatic resemblance to ἔργων. This is very ingenious, but brings with it a difficulty: if cμιλεύματα γέρρων is accepted we are left with asyndeton between the second and third items of a list, which is unattractive, and his preferred cμίλευμά τε γέρρων suffers from a drawback he seems not to notice, namely the change from plural to singular where a plural noun is vastly more suitable.

One might wonder if some rare word other than γέρρων is concealed by ἔργων. I have thought of ὄζων, since Ar. *Rhet.* 1414ᵇ18 cites ὄζοc as a technical term used by the fifth-century rhetorician Licymnius. Blass, *Attische Beredsamkeit* (1868–70), i. 85 n. 8, cites the scholia for an explanation of ὄζοι as τὰ ἄκρα, ἤτοι προοίμια καὶ ἐπιλόγουc, but admits that the term is obscure. I should have thought it was a way of referring to the sub-divisions of a subject; the resulting word-play is satisfying. One could account for the corruption by supposing that ἔργων was introduced under the influence of λόγων above.

In 819 Dover records cχινδαλμῶν, but R and V have cκ- (contrary to the rule suggested by Moeris s.v.); at *Clouds* 130 he kept cκ-.

841 At one stage in the preparation of this edition I inclined to the view that 'You indeed say that of *me*...' best catches the tone of this remark, and I still think it possible that Sommerstein was right to follow Meineke's accentuation of the second pronoun.

857 It is hard to see why θέμιc, the reading of EUVs1, should have been substituted for πρέπει. Being a rarer word, it does not look very like a gloss. Dover points out that θέμις in *Clouds* 140 and *Peace* 1018 occurs in contexts with a religious flavour. If that is a guide to the usage of the word, it may nevertheless be special pleading to note that the speaker here is a god. The alternative explanation that an ancient reader made a suggestion for the 'improvement' of the text is perhaps better. On this topic see my remarks in *Revue d'histoire des textes*, 17 (1987), 1–13.

866 ἐβουλόμην without ἄν is perfectly in order; examples are cited by Cooper-Krüger i. 625 (§53. 2. 7D), and 'the more courteous form of these statements involving ἄν' is dealt with at §54. 3. 10. Here the insertion of the particle would result in a second metron of the form ⏑ / ⏑ / – ⏑ –.

867 The minor correction ἀγών attributed by Dover to Dindorf is found already in Dawes, *Miscellanea critica* (p. 238 in the Oxford edn. of 1781).

888 The variously disturbed word-order in the papyrus and in R has induced von Velsen, Blaydes and modern editors to follow Fritzsche's transposition λιβανωτὸν καὶ cὺ δὴ λαβών. Blaydes noted that λιβανωτόν thus occupies the same position in the line as at 871 and *Wasps* 96. Dover quoted postponed καὶ cὺ δή from Plato, *Epist.* 13. 362 D, a text of disputed authenticity, and noted Xen. *Cyr.* 1. 5. 6 καὶ οὗτοι δή, but was on firmer ground when he suggested that in the present context καὶ cὺ δή may be superior to καὶ δή. Mistakes in word-order occur at all stages of the tradition; so it is difficult to claim that the papyrus here has much greater authority because of its antiquity.

909 Dover in his apparatus notes 'fort. οἴουc R'. After consulting the facsimile I feel sceptical.

911 I have recorded Vs reading as τινάν. At first sight it looks as if the accent is impossibly placed over the nu (cf. Dover's apparatus), but elsewhere on the same page the scribe is evidently much inclined to misplace his accents in a way that a better calligrapher would have avoided.

As to the form of the verb, Threatte ii. 474 appears to give support to Wackernagel, *Sprachliche Untersuchungen zu Homer* (Göttingen, 1916), 64 n. 1, who in turn cited the authority of Jensen.

914 ἐρείδω in this context is not easy. Taillardat 461 (§790) cites the scholium on *Peace* 25, according to which the verb was used in Attic for any vigorous action. Perhaps this is true. It is odd that γ' is absent from all the leading MSS. Blaydes's ξυνεῖρεν may be worth considering.

919 Threatte ii. 627 does not have enough evidence about forms of κάθημαι to help us decide which form is to be adopted here.

935 H. Kronasser, *Die Sprache*, 6 (1960), 173–4, defends κολοκτρυόνα, as being R's reading and exemplifying the use of κολο- as an intensive prefix. He notes the attestation of the word in the scholia, Hesychius (κ 3366), and the *Suda*. (He fails to realize that the *Suda* entry depends on the scholium and so is not additional evidence.) The form has to be explained as a haplology. Other compounds of this kind are κολόκυμα and κολοcυρτός. Schwyzer throws no light on this, and Dover's note rightly draws attention to the difficulty of accepting the scholiast's translation 'locusts'; probably we should assume that the scholiast was in error.

936 ποῖ' ἄττ' as in VL may well be the right reading, but Dover's assertion 'Corruption of ποῖ' ἄττ' to ποῖά γ' (RAEKMNp1U) is considerably more likely than the reverse' does not entirely convince. ἄττ' could be a faulty anticipation of the almost identical word later in the line. While ποῖά γ' has no great merits, Tucker's ποῖ' ἄρ' is conceivable (cf. Denniston, *GP* 39–40).

948 Lenting's οὐδένα is a good idea—it is the characters who are not left idle—and Blaydes achieved an equally plausible result by assuming that the word-order was wrongly altered.

950 Richards saw that the master does not belong in the list of persons of inferior status, and recent editors have not even bothered to note his remark, let alone try to refute it.

956 D. Kovacs, *Museum criticum*, 29 (1994), 172, considers the possibility that κανόνες are to be understood in the literal sense of carpenters' rulers, like γωνιαcμοί at the end of the line. His emendation λεπτῶν τε κανόναc εἰcβολῶν 'I taught them to draw their subtle proems with a straight line' seems to me an improvement. It is based on the simple assumption that two inflections were inverted.

957 Sommerstein accepts ἕδραν, Ussher's conjecture (in fact, as Dr B. Henry kindly informs me, it was anticipated by Bergk, *Poetae lyrici graeci*, 4th edn. (Leipzig, 1878), i. 266, in his note on Pindar, *N*. 4. 23), meaning 'twisting the hip'. But every other item in this list refers to intellectual processes rather than physical actions. Though consistency is not an invariable feature of Aristophanic lists, it is worth trying to find a suitable term. cτρέφειν may be analogous in its use here to *Ach*. 385, even though the latter is perhaps in the middle, not the active. What I suspect we need is φύρειν 'confuse the argument', as at 945 above and Plat. *Phaed*. 97 B, 101 E. The long vowel in that verb means that we must transpose two words, as Lobeck, *Aglaophamus* (Königsberg, 1829), 1309, did for his proposal. We may note also the existence of the other verb from the same root, φυράω, originally used to describe processes of cooking, but then extended metaphorically, as at *Clouds* 979, where Sommerstein translates 'water down (his voice)'. An attractive example is found in a text which is too late to serve as a secure parallel: Cicero, *ad Atticum* 6. 4. 3, 6. 5. 1 πεφυρακέναι τὰc ψήφουc, 'to cook the accounts'.

991 The spelling Μελητίδηc is not well attested; Dover records it only from Par20[ac]. But J.-M. Jacques on Menander, *Aspis* 275, where metre requires a long second syllable, brings some further support for it. Evidence from later writers of the Second Sophistic period is hard to assess because by their time the gradual loss of distinction between various vowels had begun, and so their grasp of the finer points of classical Attic orthography will have been limited.

1001 Dover may well be right in his defence of ἄξειc, and various conjectures such ἄξειc (Thiersch and/or Fritzsche), οἴξειc (Bergk), ἕξει (von Velsen) are not convincing. Perhaps it is worth considering whether some part of ἵημι 'set in motion' is called for; it could be transitive or intransitive.

1005 Alone of modern editors Dover judiciously remarks that the variant κλῆρον, which he cites only from the lemma of the scholium in V, is not to be rejected out of hand. In fact it is better attested than he supposed, since it is found in the *Vita Aeschyli* 2, again as a variant. In Radt, *TrGF* iii. 32 we are told that it occurs in a majority of

Frogs 177

the witnesses, but not in M (Laur. 32. 9); more specific information is given by C. J. Herington, *The Older Scholia on the Prometheus Bound* (Leiden, 1972), 59; it is there recorded as the reading of nine of the ten witnesses other than M, the exception being D (Milan, Ambrosianus G 56 sup.). I find λῆρον too strong a term of contempt to be applied to what were no doubt primitive beginnings of an art form. And can one bring adornment to something which is translated as 'balderdash' by Sommerstein and 'nonsense, drivel' by Dover? I also note that if πυργώcαc ῥήματα cεμνά is intended to be complimentary, λῆρον changes the tone in a way which I find most inappropriate. It can of course be argued that if λῆρον is wrong, the corruption is odd, despite being the loss of only one letter. For what it is worth I would point to the occurrence of λῆρον at 809, in a somewhat different context. To adopt Radermacher's ληρόν from an entry in Hesychius (λ 895) is an alternative, but the rarity of the word gives one pause and, as Dover says, the usages of κοcμεῖν do not provide obvious support.

1009 Blaydes noted the highly unusual position of τε; Denniston, *GP* 517, includes it in a list of instances of postponement. But this, as H.-S. notes, is much more extreme than others and creates an expectation that another good service performed by poets will be mentioned. The expectation is not fulfilled and there is no reason to think that the speaker is interrupted in mid-sentence.

1018 Blaydes notes the word-order at *Clouds* 906 and *Wasps* 1483, which are identical expressions, and proposes tentatively to bring this passage into line by transposing τουτί in front of the particles.

1028 There are numerous conjectures here. Some presuppose that Aristophanes was referring to a different version of the *Persae* or remembered it incorrectly. While such views cannot be entirely ruled out, I should prefer to think that that the reference is to the text as we have it. Sommerstein may well be right to press the point that this line should express a fact which leads logically to 1029. If we follow this train of thought, Tyrrell's suggestion ἐκώκυcαc, παῖ, modified by Coulon to ἐκώκυcαc περί, may be worth considering. If one is to retain instead the notion of hearing, Dover's ἐπήκοοc ἦ τοῦ is ingenious, as the unusual wording could easily have been corrupted.

The principal MSS offer no variants. Blaydes reports ἀπηγγέλθη from his D, S (= G, Marc. gr. 475), and Δ (Laur. 31. 16) but says that this reading is a 'merum grammatici alicuius commentum'. That is probably right, although it has the unusual merit of meeting the requirements of metre. S. P. Peppink, *Mnemosyne*², 60 (1933), 382, confirmed its presence in G.

παρά for περί, recommended by Bothe and Welcker, was adopted by Richards with the minimal further alteration ἡνίκα γ' ἤκουσαν.

1042 αὑτόν is in B and L. In the latter at least the rough breathing is not an accident, since a gloss above reads ἑαυτόν. Many scribes had difficulty in understanding the distinction between the breathings.

1046 The question of word-order is delicate. Denniston, *GP* 548–9, without discussion accepts Dindorf's transposition ἐπί τοι coί, which may accord better with Wackernagel's law. The transmitted ἐπὶ coί τοι is printed by most editors other than Radt.

1047 Dover's note implies an element of doubt about the legitimacy of tmesis in a sentence of this kind. Denniston, however, *GP* 430, interpreted this oddity as a parody of the Euripidean fondness for tmesis. It is perhaps worth noting that on the evidence of L Triclinius had doubts too, but his remedy is not right; it appears to be a correct version of the reading reported from M by von Velsen: κάτω ἐνέβαλε.

1057 Sommerstein is more sympathetic than Dover to Bentley's conjecture. The material in my note on *Ach.* 348 may justify the conclusion that Bentley's idea was essentially right, but did not require both his adjustments of the spelling, since Parnes could be written with one or two sigmas.

1058 ὃν χρή = 'whose duty it is . . .' The MSS reading is accepted by Dover and appears to give good sense. Fritzsche's ὃν χρῆν 'whose duty it was, who should have . . .' is preferred by Radt and Sommerstein. Though Radermacher thought the form ἐχρῆν necessary, Kassel pointed to χρῆν at *Knights* 535; see also Jacques on Menander, *Aspis* 94. Other conjectures worth mention are οὐ χρή Blaydes, ἀχρῆν Platt.

Frogs

1102 Sommerstein renders 'able to wheel round and make a sharp counter-thrust'. This is good, and despite the unanimity of the MSS in favour of ἐπερείδεcθαι I think Blaydes was right to wish to find in the Greek a clear indication of the opposition about to be provided by Euripides in the agon; hence his κἀντερείδεcθαι.

1112 As the long sequence of dual forms is broken here, Blaydes was justified in wondering whether a simple adjustment should be made in order to maintain uniformity.

1130 At first sight the word-order in R looks attractive, so that γ' emphasizes πάντα. But that results in the sequence οὐδὲ ταῦτα, which is not an improvement. Probably πάντα ταῦτα is to be taken as one notion, which receives emphasis from the particle.

1157 Though the MSS all give ἥκειν, this infinitive introduces a pointless imprecision into what ought to be a strictly logical riposte. Perhaps the error is to be explained as due to the presence of an infinitive at the beginning of 1163.

1180 Sommerstein's apparatus gives one to understand that the *Suda* has the particles in the usual order οὐ γὰρ ἄλλα, which was recommended by Blaydes. But I am not quite sure that this is the position. After the lemma, which essentially agrees with the MSS, the entry continues τὸ τέλειον, οὐ γὰρ ἄλλα μοι κτλ. , and probably this just means 'In full, the wording is...' with μοι written in full without crasis. One would like to know whether the dislocation of the normal order is to be accepted; Denniston, *GP* 31, while not citing an exact parallel, raised no objection, and Dover does not go into the question.

1185 Dover rejects van Leeuwen's notion that πρὶν καὶ γεγονέναι could be a puzzled question by Dionysus, and I think he is probably right. But he argues from the absence of any hint in the MSS of a change of speaker, which is dubious, since the MSS are not authoritative in this matter.

1203 M. Chantry, *Scholia vetera in Aristophanis Ranas* (Groningen, 1999), 139, has an ingenious note suggesting that the scholiast probably did not read θύλακον. This may well be right.

1228 Kock's ἔτι is tempting, since the use of τὸ τί; here is abnormal. But it was noticed by Blaydes (1899: 94) that *Birds* 1039 is a possible parallel to this passage, and I agree with Dover in finding it enough.

1235 ἀπόδος is problematic. Kassel, *Rh. Mus.*[2] 137 (1994), 51, cited Eupolis 260. 22 as the best parallel. That verse is identical except for the word πιθοῦ in place of ἀπόδος. This difference, however, is not a minor detail. We still need evidence of ἀποδοῦναι in the sense 'pay'. Blaydes and others cite 270 ἀπόδος τὸν ναῦλον; but that means 'give me your fare/coin'. Sommerstein explains the sequence of corruption implied by Hamaker's conjecture: πρίω > ἀποπρίω (cf. 1427) > ἀπόδος (an adjustment by someone with a little knowledge of metre).

ἀπόδου 'sell' would have to be addressed to Aeschylus, which is not satisfactory; this variant may be an attempt to deal with the difficulty of the active imperative.

1240 The curious variant πολύβοτρυν in R's scholium and Par20 is explained by Dover as the work of 'a copyist καπηλεῖον cκοπῶν'. Not impossible; one may also note that the name Oeneus could easily induce error even in a scribe who was not an alcoholic.

Since Par20 is a Triclinian MS and he is not thought to have had access to R, one is reminded that some channels of transmission are imperfectly understood.

A further point in this line is that Dover records the variant word-order cτάχυν λαβών in E^pcU. Normally one might not pay much attention to this, but it should be remembered that *vitium Byzantinum* would have led to the reading found in the majority of MSS, and so one cannot exclude the possibility that E^pcU have somehow preserved the truth.

1248 The reading τράπου (paroxytone) in RV is reported by Dover and mentioned by Chandler 221 (§783) among a few exceptions to the rule that would lead one to expect a perispomenon accent. Chandler refers to Phavorinus (Camers) 1144. 10 and 1152. 17; this enormous Renaissance compilation does not specify its sources, and so one does not know how much weight, if any, to attach to any rules it suggests. Some information about its sources is given by K. Alpers, *Das attizistische Lexikon des Oros* (Berlin, 1981), 42–4. In l. 1248 *vitium Byzantinum* may have operated, which was the case at 483 and 528 above.

Frogs 181

1278 Dover, noting that *Clouds* 2 is a very similar line, remarks 'This could fairly be called self-parody'. I venture to suggest that it is just a case of a standard colloquialism reappearing.

1281 Does the syntax require Elmsley's supplement (in his note on *Ach.* 176) of ἄν? Dover and Sommerstein do not think so; Dover notes that ἄν is sometimes omitted in poetry. But there is also evidence for πρίν with subjunctive and no particle in prose, especially Thucydides; see Cooper-Krüger i. 761–2 (§54. 17. 3).

1298 N. O'Sullivan, *CQ*² 50 (2000), 297–8, revives Tyrrell's proposal of κάλω for καλοῦ (*CR* 1 (1887), 128–32). It may be that the absence of a parallel casts doubt on Denniston's view, reported by Dover, that we have a colloquial or semi-proverbial expression here; but even if that view is not upheld I still think that one may take ἐκ τοῦ καλοῦ as defiant insistence on the part of Aeschylus that his sources were good.

1301 I find μέν here dubious, even though Dover accepts it; the contrast is oddly put, and it is not a case of 'the contrasted idea is not expressed in a following co-ordinated clause', as Denniston, *GP* 377 puts it, because that has already been indicated in 1298 ff. Palmer's μέλι is 'an impossible compliment to Euripides' (Dover) or a sarcasm, as suggested by Sommerstein. He now (2001: 317) has expressed doubts about this and tried οὗτος δέ <γ'> ἀπὸ πάντων φέρει. Meineke's μεταφέρει seems a better option.

1307 Blaydes in his text accepted the singular ἐπιτήδειον as suggested by R^ac, and then took μέλη to be a gloss which had replaced ταδί. He later (1902) preferred to read τάδε γ', as proposed by Hermann, who was followed by von Velsen.

Dover and Sommerstein accept from Θ ταῦτ', omitting ἔστ', which is found in RVAK. The assumption is that ἔστ' is a gloss. Radermacher tried ἐπιτήδεα τάδ' ἔστ'. If ταῦτ' or τάδ' is right, do we need an article? Blaydes thought so; I have accepted the usual text, but with some unease.

1308 The linguistic difficulties in this line are indicated by Dover. From conjectures listed by Blaydes I note Hermann's (ap. Fritzsche) πόθ'. . .; ποῦ; I have wondered whether ποθ' (enclitic) . . . που (ironical, 'I suppose') might be considered. Though I have printed the traditional text, I have some doubts.

1322 A. Bagordo (forthcoming article) makes the point that the aorist περίβαλ' is to be expected if we follow Attic usage of the fifth and fourth centuries; cf. Eur. *Ba.* 1021, *Birds* 344, *Thesm.* 913, Com. Adesp. 1017. 26. He did not find counter-examples. In the present passage the aorist is the reading of K as well as Triclinius. I incline to the view that the joke is not based on two different meanings of the word πούc, one metrical and the other literal (Sommerstein), but on Aeschylus' wildly exaggerated movements (Dover).

1329 Scaliger proposed coι. I suppose this is addressed to Dionysus. The idea is not bad.

1330 Only R of the principal MSS has τρόπον; why should the others have corrupted it into πόνον? Fritzsche was surely right to raise the question; he suggested τόνον 'metre'.

1354 Dover and Sommerstein print δ' rather than τ', and Blaydes emended to δάκρυα δὲ δάκρυα, apparently without support from MSS.

1368–9 'To weigh poets' art like cheese' is generally accepted, but the definite article with τέχνην might have been expected. Hence Blaydes tried τυροπωλεῖν τὴν τέχνην. He states that the Aldine edition has the aorist infinitive with τὴν, which is of course unmetrical.

1374–5 Blaydes and others do their best to rescue the text by translating ἐπιτυχόντων as 'bystanders'. That I believe is indeed the meaning required, but the participle transmitted so often has a different meaning that I am fairly confident in adjusting the preposition in the compound verb. Note that the following word begins with ἐπι- and could have induced an error.

Sommerstein is right to observe that Blaydes's proposal, οὐκ for οὐδ', fails because it implies that they would have believed a reliable informant; I am less convinced by his suggestion that we follow Tucker in supposing that there is a gibe at the Athenians' willingness to believe anything they are told.

1389 is given to Euripides by modern editors. Dover notes that two

MSS make Dionysus continue, which is possible. Reiske thought it better coming from Aeschylus. There would then be a note of condescension after his initial success, as if to say 'Let him have another chance'. I prefer that.

1406 If we retain οὕc there reference is to only two corpses, and it is hardly funny to say that (numerous) Egyptians could not lift them.

1410 Fritzsche posited a lacuna because (i) 1411ff. are the words of someone replying to Pluto, (ii) 1414 is so abrupt that Pluto must have said something previously. His supplement *exempli gratia* is worth recording:

ὑμῖν μὲν ἤδη πᾶν τετόξευται βέλος,
ἥκω δ' ἀκοῦcαι, πῶc ἀγὼν κριθήcεται,

comparing Aesch. *Eum*. 676–7. Though Sommerstein defends the transmitted text, I feel that Fritzsche's argument has force.

1431, 1435 ff. The debate on this passage shows no signs of ending, as is clear from Sommerstein (2001: 317–18). I have no new contribution to offer, and think it best to provide a text which is intelligible and may reflect accurately the redrafting that the author appears to have undertaken. So I follow Sommerstein, admittedly with a little hesitation. His view presupposes two dislocations of the text at an early stage of the tradition. A more complex sequence of events obviously cannot be ruled out.

F. Cannatà in R. Nicolai (ed.), *ΡΥΣΜΟΣ: Studi di poesia, metrica e musica greca offerti dagli allievi a Luigi Enrico Rossi per i suoi settant'anni* (Rome, 2003), 271–82, has continued discussion, with copious bibliography, of this difficulty. At 1431a he gives three verses to Aeschylus, obtaining symmetry; he feels that 1431a and b do not constitute alternatives which one has to choose between because they are mutually inconsistent. Verse a may be a quotation from Aeschylus or a reference to a proverb; verse b makes an adjustment to it, necessary because 'cub' is not the way to refer to Alcibiades. Insofar as there is repetition, he suggests that this is not pleonastic, but characteristic of the oracular style, which is suitable in the context. Though his view has the advantage of achieving symmetry of length in the responses given by the two poets, I still feel that the transition from one verse to the other is anything but smooth.

1448 The longer form of the optative is not accepted by many editors, but Sommerstein quotes it from other verbs at Eur. *Cycl.* 132, *Ion* 943, and *Helen* 1010.

1470 Is the enclitic μ' correct? Paley read ἔμ' ἄξειν. The corruption presupposed could have occurred, yet there is no obvious reason. Dover may be on the right lines in his paraphrase of what Euripides says when he prints 'you *swore*' with italics; in other words, the emphasis is on the verb rather than the pronoun. Blaydes wondered if the singular τὸν φίλον would be preferable.

1497 Mras on Eusebius, *Praep. Ev.* 14. 5. 4 accepted in that passage Dindorf's reading cκαριφηθμοῖc and insisted that this spelling be adopted also here in l. 1497; he compared the formation seen in μυκηθμός, κηληθμός, ἑλκηθμός. The MSS of Eusebius offer cκαρφηθμοῖc. The passage is Numenius fr. 24. 46 des Places. But Schwyzer i. 492–3 seems to indicate that -θμός is Homeric and Ionic and that it was 'aufgenommen in jüngerer Epik und Kunstprosa', e.g. βληκηθμόc in Aelian, ὀγκηθμόc in Lucian, whereas Attic uses the formation in -cμόc. So Mras's view seems to be wrong.

1501 With regard to the conjecture that is credited by some editors to Scaliger, my copy of the 1670 edition with notes on pp. 917–35 gives the siglum 'Vet.' after the emendation τὴν ὑμετέραν, and this refers to a 'vetus editio', not necessarily anything to do with Scaliger. This latter ascription goes back at least as far as von Velsen's edition of 1881 and Blaydes' of 1889.

1517–18 'In case I ever come back here' translates Sommerstein. But is 'back' in the Greek as it stands? Von Velsen had doubts and considered αὖθις ἐγώ for ἄρ' ἐγώ ποτε, while van Leeuwen tried ἐπανέλθω.

Ecclesiazusae

Hypothesis II In l. 4 the phrasing is much improved by E. Degani's reinterpretation of the transmitted letters οὖν as the result of crasis of οἱ ἐν (*QUCC* 21 (1976), 143–4 = *Filologia e storia* (Hildesheim, 2004), ii. 872–3).

Text 2 If the variant ἐν εὐσκόποισιν can mean 'in a prominent position', one might be tempted to adopt the reading of Vb1 ἐξηρτημένον 'hanging', and assume that Praxagora is approaching her lamp with a view to lighting it. Presumably she would then have to be indoors, about to go out. But as she is already in the street this reconstruction is excluded. Ussher correctly observes that in some papyri tau and upsilon can be confused because only half of the horizontal stroke of tau was written before the vertical and it was then completed carelessly.

22–3 Ussher and Sommerstein adopt Dover's transposition of these lines because otherwise δεῖ is too far away from the words it governs, and the joke about Phyromachus can be enjoyed at greater length if it comes nearer the end of the sentence. On balance I agree. The position of ἅς is now such that it does not refer to ἕδρας, and so we must reject the scholiast's notion that an actor, whom he calls Cleomachus, produced this word by an amusing slip of the tongue. So the mistake concerns ἑταίρας in some way. If the context was political one is surprised that the person named is not a prominent figure, since the political history of the time is reasonably well documented. (I am indebted to Mr N. D. Worswick for comments on this passage).

The intrusion of πως in all the MSS is odd. The best explanation I can suggest is that it was caused by πώγωνας in 25.

186 *Ecclesiazusae*

51, 54 The particles here are difficult. In 51, if the transmitted text is retained, the meaning seems to be 'Even the wives of Ph. and Ch. ...', with the implication that they were lazy or unpunctual. Perhaps it is better to follow Meineke with γε: 'And what's more ...'. In 54 the addition of γ' by AΓ might well be right; it is easy to imagine that some speakers have larded their conversation with particles more copiously than was strictly necessary.

78 Unless a papyrus comes to our aid it is unlikely that the puzzle of this line will be solved. The scholiast cites from Crates, *Lamia* (fr. 20) cκυτάλην ἔχουc' ἐπέρδετο. This suggest that attempts to emend should retain the transmitted πέρδεται, as they mostly do. Holzinger (p. 48 n. 1 of his *Plutus* commentary) made the much bolder proposal τοῦτ' ἔcτ' ἐκεῖν' ᾧ περδόμενοc ἐρείδεται, which presumes the loss of the bracketed letters in περ(δόμενοc ἐρεί)δεται and the insertion of τῶν cκυτάλων as a gloss. This makes sense and is palaeographically acceptable.

95 ff. seem better as a scornful question. Denniston, *GP* 129, did not contemplate alteration, nor did he include this passage in his list on p. 423 of οὔκουν ... γε, because here the context is not one of 'dialogue, introducing an emphatic negative answer'. He noted on pp. 430 and 433–4 the difficulty of distinguishing between the interrogative and affirmative uses of the particle.

105 The oath is a trifle odd, despite the parallels cited by Sommerstein. It seems just worth mentioning Blaydes's tentative suggestion, since γέ τοι δή is a known combination (cf. Denniston, *GP* 551).

142 One cannot absolutely rule out the compound found in RΓ ἐκπίνειν, which would mean that the men have drained a cup before the assembly.

146 I cannot see why the neuter form δύψοc should be banished from the text, given the evidence of LSJ and *DGE*, who cite inter alia Thuc. 7. 87, where it is the reading of the *veteres* according to Alberti, Xen. *Cyr.* 8. 1. 36, Plat. *Phaed.* 94 B, and post-classical occurrences.

151 The opening formula ἐβουλόμην was often used without ἄν; see Dover on *Frogs* 866. Here editors are probably right in the text they print, but one could imagine that ἄν was inserted in an attempt to regularize the construction, in which case one might take a hint from the variant in AΓ and conjecture that the original text was τιν' ἕτερον.

153 κατά γε τὴν ἐμὴν is clear enough, but the addition of μίαν needs a better parallel than any adduced so far and I would not rule out either Dindorf's μιᾶς, even though that would constitute a lapse on the part of the speaker not picked up by Praxagora, or Meineke's hypothetical tavern-keeper Μίκαν.

167 I agree with Sommerstein against Ussher that ἐπιβλέπειν implies a deliberate glance, which is not what we want here. So Elmsley's emendation is justified.

199 The singular of the personal pronoun has caused editors surprisingly little diffculty. Even Blaydes contents himself with the remark 'populum alloquitur'. For cύ as an individual in a group being addressed the nearest analogies I can find are in pseudo-Xenophon, *Ath. Pol.* 1. 8–9, Dem. 22. 11, 26.

218–20 In this difficult passage Dobree made a good suggestion. Although Sommerstein defends the transmitted text, in my opinion τοῦτο has no satisfactory point of reference in the context and πού τι is an easy change. But Dobree's paraphrase is very free; he says 'If anything had happened to be in the best possible order (or trim), the Athenians would think the *country could never be saved* till that was altered'. I italicize the clause which fails to satisfy me. The middle ἐcῴζετο can be taken to reflect the self-interest the Athenians could be displaying; but it is easier to imagine that the speaker intended to say 'would no longer preserve it', with active verb and ἔτι. What I think the speaker said next is 'they instead/merely introduced some other novelty' and the sense 'instead, merely' can be achieved by restoring the usage εἰ μή . . . γε discussed by Denniston, *GP* 121, with the omission, however, of one passage where the expression has been plausibly restored in a clause with a verb, *Birds* 1681. This second emendation was originally proposed in CR^2 26 (1976), 13, and I was pleased to find it adopted by Sommerstein.

253 Van Leeuwen, followed by Sommerstein, accepts the scholiast's view that κεραμεύειν is a metaphor for mishandling the city's affairs.

This is possible, but so far unparalleled as a usage, and somehow a bit odd in a city renowned for the high quality of its pottery. It may in any case be no more than a typical scholiast's inference from the context, unsupported by any real knowledge. Praxagora's third attempt ought ideally to be a statement that is decisive because everyone knows it and will take it for granted, but I do not see how to extract that from any of the current interpretations. Richards had a complex proposal: to alter κακῶc to καλῶc and then at the end of the line read κακὸν κακῶc. He noted that R omitted εὖ καί. Though this is tempting, I have chosen to obelize.

264 As Sommerstein says, Ussher's ποτε for the transmitted τότε is tempting. I have hesitated to adopt it because it is separated by several words from the conjunction that it is meant to intensify, and the resulting word-order might have been unidiomatic.

273 ff. The articulation of the sentence is complex. (i) We may follow Denniston, *CR* 47 (1933), 215, in reading ἐπαναβάληcθε parallel to ἀκριβώcητε. Denniston's basic point is that 'the apodosis, the climax, ought to come at 'march', not before'. Then the particles καί ... γε in 275 are a common combination, as indicated at *GP* 157, and one can accept the reading of A, as was also proposed by Toup. κᾆτα then has the apodotic καί (*GP* 308). Perhaps this is too formal for Praxagora. (ii) Alternatively one could accept the reading of B and the *Suda* ε 1593 ἐπαναβάλεcθε. Then καὶ in 275 has its other meaning, and καί ... γε is less common (*GP* 158). That invites consideration of Elmsley's transposition ἅπερ γ'. Sommerstein follows Coulon, *REG* 50 (1937) 31, who defended καί ... γε by reference to *Thesm.* 819–20 and *Plutus* 838.

280 'And let's go ahead of them' is Sommerstein's translation. Who is referred to? Praxagora must be talking to herself, not to the First and Second Woman, as indicated in his stage-direction. If this seems unsatisfactory, αὐτῶν should be replaced by οὕτωc or εὐθύc, as Richards saw.

285–7 The position of ἡμᾶc, if it is taken to be dependent on χρή in the main clause, probably confers too much emphasis on it, as Richards claimed. But those who take it with ἐξολίcθῃ create a dubious construction. There must be a possibility that Blaydes or Meineke

Ecclesiazusae 189

was right with τὸ ῥῆμ᾽ or ὁρμᾶcθ᾽ respectively (the latter requiring heavy punctuation at the end of 286). A simpler solution is to suppose that the accusative is an error induced by μεμνημένας above—yet another example of assimilation— and that ἐξολίcθη was constructed with a dative of the person concerned.

In 286 Dobree changed ὡc μήποτ᾽ to μὴ καί ποτ᾽. He has been followed among recent editors by Sommerstein. In similar vein Elmsley in *Museum criticum*, 1 (1826), 483 observed that 'Aristophanes seldom, if ever, prefixes ὡc to the subjunctive, in the sense of ἵνα, without adding ἄν. Read καὶ μήποτ᾽ ἐξολιcθῇ (i.e. ἐξολιcθέτω) ἡμᾶc.' A decision on this point of syntax does not affect the other problem.

298–9 Recent editors note the incompleteness of the syntax, and perhaps they are right to assume that a sudden realization of the linguistic lapse explains the abruptness. But it is far from clear how the sentence would have been completed, and Blaydes's proposal δοκῇ ταῖc ἡμετέραιc φίλαιc has some chance of being right.

306–8 The iterative ἄν at the end of the sentence is very far away from its verb. I think Blaydes was right to introduce the particle in its natural position, after which it can be duplicated, even if the second occurrence looks rather like a metrical stopgap.

307 Sommerstein objects to Reiske's αὖον on the ground that dry bread would have been bad and potentially unhealthy food. But I am quite sure that the poor often had nothing better, and so do not think that Reiske's simple correction should be rejected There is a contrast between the meagre lunch and the three obols now expected.

330 *Pace* Ussher, R has πόθεν with an accent, as does Γ, which I inspected *in situ* in June 2003.

350 ὅ τι κἄμ᾽ εἰδέναι is recognized by K–G ii. 511 (A.3) as equal to ὅcον/ὅcα with infinitive, but they do not cite other examples, and I wonder if Blaydes was right to suggest alternatives such as ὅcα γ᾽ ἔμ᾽. *Thesm.* 34 would hint at ὥcτ᾽ ἔμ᾽, which is palaeographically a little closer.

351 Despite what Ussher says in his apparatus, the particle δ᾽ is not a supplement by an unknown scholar. In R it is written by the main scribe, but at the beginning of l. 352, and that is where it also figures in Γ (another detail which I verified *in situ* in 2003). See above on *Birds* 1717.

365 The transmitted text can be translated, but Meineke's ἀλλ' οἶδ' is worth considering. Sommerstein translates this as 'Ah, I know . . .', which might suggest instead ἐγῷδ'.

397 LSJ took καθεῖναι to be comic adaptation of language appropriate to entering a race, while Ussher adduced Dem. 29. 46, where καθεῖκεν seems to mean 'entered a plea/produced an argument for consideration'. On balance I prefer to think that a corruption was caused by the occurrence of κᾆτ' later in the line.

448 The particle γ' is transmitted by all witnesses. It is not essential to the meaning. Though it makes sense, it may be a mistake anticipation of 451, where it is entirely suitable.

494–5 The chorus once again express their anxiety about being detected. The repeated personal pronoun seems unnecessary and Hermann's frequently accepted transposition does not wholly remove that difficulty. T. L. Agar, *CQ* 13 (1919), 15, perhaps made some improvement by transposing μὴ καί τις ἡμᾶς ὄψεται and πώγωνας ἐξηρτημένας. A. von Blumenthal, *Hermes*, 71 (1936), 455–6, proposed ἡμέρας 'in daylight'. To this one may object that the chorus have failed to mention the semi-nocturnal timing of their recently concluded operation. If it is reasonable to think that the women might have been tempted to sit down while waiting, then ἡμένας would be a possibility: 'in case someone sees us sitting here'.

502–3 are difficult. I share the unease of Jackson, *MS* 160–2, about μίσει, whereas recent editors accept it without comment. Palmer's proposal to replace this word with παῦσαι has no palaeographical plausibility, whereas Nairn's μὴ θεῖ is an example of a conjecture made with no thought for anything except palaeography. Jackson's μἀμισθί presumably means 'not unrewarded'. If dislike or discomfort is the notion to be retained, perhaps μισητὸν for καὶ μίσει is worth considering. In 503 Palmer's emendation is slightly easier than Agar's, which yields very much the same sense.

514 Dobree's supplement καὶ is popular with editors and the

Ecclesiazusae 191

omission is easy to understand. But Bentley's <δ' ἤ>δη is also ingenious and seems worth a mention as an equally plausible cure for a mistake of haplography.

560–1 Since ἔcται τὸ λοιπόν continues the sense of the preceding line adequately, I think Sommerstein's attractive suggestion of a lacuna should be modified, so as to assume that the loss occurred in the middle of 560b.

573–4 Ussher noted that the phrase ἐπ' εὐτυχίαιcιν occurs with different meanings at *Knights* 1318 and *Clouds* 1205, but he did not say what they are. The former passage in fact reads ἐπὶ καιναῖcιν δ' εὐτυχίαιcιν, rendered by Sommerstein 'in honour of the good fortune newly come to us'; in the latter we have ἐπ' εὐτυχίαιcιν ᾀcτέον μοὐγκώμιον 'I ought to sing a song of praise over this good fortune'. In both of those passages there appears to be reference to something that has already happened; here one is probably dealing with something good that is in prospect. Blaydes's suggestions, though not essential, deserve a mention.

577 Musurus may have been right with γάρ τι. But I confess to a feeling that τι is something of a stopgap. Besides, the sense is better if the speaker says 'the city is in real need', as opposed to 'in some need'; one would prefer a forceful statement: δεῖται νῦν γε would be suitable, but has no palaeographical plausibility. Though γέ τοι is common, τοί γε would be odd.

581 There is nothing wrong with ἅπτεcθαι, but if a construction with the dative (διανοίαιc) is to be retained, perhaps ἐγχειρεῖν is worth considering, on the assumption that the correct word was replaced by a synonym.

587 While accepting Bergk's emendation on the ground that ἀρχῆc could easily have been induced by the proximity of ἀρχαίων, I note that Sommerstein translates 'takes the place of *every* other virtue' (my italics), and wonder if ἄλληc can bear that meaning. So it seems to me that van Leeuwen had a point with his proposal αὑτῆc ἀρχῆc if it could mean 'as good as empire itself'. He also cited ἀρχῆc μεγάληc by von Velsen, who compared *Wasps* 575.

603 I agree with Sommerstein that it is better not to assign the word ψευδορκήcει to Praxagora. Can one then accept the MSS reading καί, which is confirmed by P60? We really need a question, introduced by a conditional. Hence Rogers proposed κἄν and adjusted the verb to an aorist subjunctive. It is even easier to follow Wecklein and read κεἰ, leaving the verb in the future indicative.

612 Sommerstein translates 'he'll be able to take some of his money and give it to her', while Thiercy has 'il pourra prendre de quoi lui faire un cadeau'. They are on the right track, but I confess to finding τούτων difficult; what are the objects and what relation do they bear to τῶν ἐκ κοινοῦ? Blaydes regretted that τῶν ὧν cannot be proposed; H.-S.'s tentative suggestion may well be right.

629 At 630 R has the scholium cιμὸc καὶ αἰcχρὸc ὁ Λυcικράτηc. What inference does this permit? Van Lennep and others have thought it safe to infer that the scholiast had cιμοῖc in his text. Though that is possible, the presence of ῥίc in the following line would have been enough to induce a typical scholiast to word the note as he did. It may be worth recording that Willems iii. 234–5 detected in 627–8 a case of *Binneninterpolation* and deleted καὶ τηρήcουc'... οἱ φαυλότεροι, accepting van Lennep's cιμοῖc in 629 ('correction tellement réclamée par le contexte que je ne comprends pas qu'on ait pu songer à la contester'). Ussher and Sommerstein easily dispose of Willems's claim that stature had nothing to do with physical attractiveness.

633 In my view T. L. Agar, *CQ* 13 (1919), 16, was probably right to insert the article; one ought also to consider the possibility that a rare name lurks here. While Daniel Heinsius hit on one that seems not to be attested, an alternative, not much further from the paradosis, is revealed by *LGPN* ii.

650 In R the last syllable of the verb ἐπεπόνθειν is written with a compendium that usually signifies ην but occasionally—and perhaps only because of confusion in the mind of the scribe—signifies ειν. See plates II and V in G. F. Tsereteli, *Sokrashcheniya v grecheskikh rukopisyakh*, 2nd edn. (St Petersburg, 1904).

656 There are various ways of making this line yield good sense. Though Ussher accepts τῶν κοινῶν, understanding the genitive as dependent on πόθεν without the need of ἐκ, this is not the general view of editors, and I agree with them that the omitted preposition would be an oddity in conversational Greek such as we have here. Once we admit the need for ἐκ possible solutions include: (i) Changing ταύτην to ταῦτ' (Jackson, MS 154, followed by Sommerstein), with οὐ γὰρ δὴ 'κ to follow, as originally suggested by Cobet. Though this is possible, ἐκτίνειν δίκην is a perfectly well attested expression, despite Jackson's description of ταύτην as having a useless suffix. (ii) Retaining ταύτην but deleting ἐcτί, with Cobet. (ii) Retaining ταύτην but deleting τῶν.

657 Hansing's ingenious emendation (*Philologus*, 7 (1852), 196–7) amounts to a combination of the variants in the MSS, and assumes that R wrote a single instead of a double sigma, while the ancestor of ΓΛ lost a syllable. But it has to be said that Bentley's γε πόcουc is ingenious also and makes explicit the point that many people stand to lose a great deal through the new dispensation.

663 Though the general sense is clear, what is the syntax of τῆc ἀκείαc? Ussher understands δίκην. This would be much clearer with Dobree's τὴν, which I have adopted; Dawes' τὰc is also worth considering (he also recommended ἀκείαc as the correct spelling of this noun (*Miscellanea critica* (Oxford, 1781), 310–11). Agar's clever substitution of φεύγοντες for τύπτοντες depends on a parallel expression in *Ach.* 1129 and the assumption of a gloss displacing the original word.

682 After πάντας Blaydes's change to ὅπως is welcome, because the duration of the process, as indicated by ἕως, is irrelevant unless a plural or 'all' is stated in the subordinate clause; here 'all' is in the main clause.

688 'Everyone (who has been allotted a place) will chase them away' makes sense, but as Sommerstein notes, the Aldine reading ἅπαντας has its attractions: 'they will chase them all away'. This could be a slip, as he says, because early editions were by no means free from misprints; but one should bear in mind that the editor of the Aldine was none other than Musurus, an extremely able scholar.

719b–720 Sommerstein is probably right in seeing the cynicism and type of humour in this remark as evidence that it belongs to one of the men. Most previous editors assigned it to Praxagora and raised doubts about the text. But αὗται can presumably refer to the chorus, in which case all is well. Invernizi, however, perhaps bothered by the absence of a deictic pronoun, thought the reference should be to the prostitutes and therefore proposed <μὴ> ἔχωςιν. According to Ussher Scaliger proposed αὐταί; what the 1670 Amsterdam edition reveals (p. 927) is that he recommended ἔχωμεν, which in turn implies the emphatic pronoun. Given the uncertainty of attributions to speakers, and the fact that we cannot always be sure of absolute consistency in the portrayal of characters (note the case of Lysistrata), I have with some hesitation burdened the apparatus with these details.

735 Jackson's emendation, *MS* 193–4, produces rather staccato Greek and yet is very close to the paradosis. I adopt it with some hesitation. Another way of preserving most of the paradosis is Blaydes's rejected alternative μέλαιν', ὡς οὐδ' ἂν εἰ. Sommerstein's belief that there is deeper corruption may well be right.

756 Sommerstein accepts Ussher's palaeographically easy οὔτι μήν. As the only close analogy seems to be Plat. *Legg.* 906 E, which is not a question, it is arguable that one should not punctuate in that way here either: 'You surely can't be …'. A question is introduced by Dobree's οὔτι που. The corruption could be explained by supposing that a scribe having just written one negative added the other by association of ideas.

795 Heindorf's emendation is so easy that I have accepted it; but one cannot entirely rule out the possibility that the verb lost by ellipse was in the past tense, which would justify an optative (so Ussher, following van Daele).

799 is improved if the verb in the response matches precisely the verb used by the Neighbour; I think Elmsley was right to treat κομίςωςι as an erroneous anticipation of its occurrence in 800.

807 αὔτ' is vague, and the point would be made more clearly by πάντ'.

810 αὐταῖςιν was proposed by Lenting, but is probably over-precise, since the conversation turns on communism rather than government by women.

Blaydes printed τι as an interrogative, whereas more recent editors tend to prefer an enclitic. As Blaydes saw, if the latter is right, it would be good to have something equivalent to 'Yes' in the Greek, which he was easily able to supply in the form of πλέον γε.

848 I accept Dindorf's κονίποδε, which assumes the change of one letter, reversing the common process of assimilation. Sommerstein infers that the *Suda* knew a different form κονίποδα, which it gives as a γράφεται variant. However, the *Suda* entry κ 2035 deals initially with the lemma κονιόπους, and the variant in question is the alternative spelling κονι-.

881 With the transmitted ὅπως one has to query the syntax of ἄν with the optative dependent on παίζουσα. Such optatives are dealt with by Cooper–Krüger i. 715–16 (§54. 8. 3). Dobree's adjustment to indicate a wish is very good idiom, and on balance I prefer his text. His further adjustment of the verb seems unnecessary.

897–8 Metre and sense are both difficult. Von Velsen's sequence τοι ... τις ... φίλον <ἄν> has the drawback of not placing ἄν as either second word in the clause or next to its verb. The absence of an expressed subject in the text as Sommerstein prints it seems to me awkward; his tentative proposal has the great advantage of providing a subject and putting ἄν where it belongs.

917 Recent editors tend to accept the insertion of ἄν, which Hermann placed after σαυτῆς and Wilamowitz after ὅπως. The syntax that results is very dubious. Ussher compared 881, but see my note there. Wilamowitz, *GV* 478, cited *Birds* 1338, not knowing that Shilleto had emended that passage with good grounds. Excellent sense is obtained with Faber's οὕτως for ὅπως. This can be accommodated metrically by adopting Jackson's σεαυτῆς οὕτως.

937 For what it is worth I report that the Ravennas has coῦ with the accent. Hall–Geldart and Ussher printed the enclitic form, and Vetta says that this is the reading of the other MSS.

950 The paradosis gives us a present infinitive. The required sense is more precisely conveyed by Dindorf's change to the future, which might have been lost here owing to the influence of *vitium Byzantinum*. Confusion of the tenses of this verb is not unknown elsewhere, as I have found by collating the text of Archimedes, *On Floating Bodies*, in the palimpsest.

972 The oddity of the metre could perhaps be removed by transposition to give a common colon; but as Dr Parker points out to me (private communication) the transmitted text is not peculiar enough to demand emendation.

985 Sommerstein prefers Γ's πρότερον to προτέρας as given by RΛ; he probably took the genitive termination to be an error of assimilation, which it could well be (Ussher fails to mention this variant). I have not followed his lead, because it seems equally possible that the adverb arose from the occurrence of πρῶτον in the line below.

998 The alternative reading provided by the lemma to the scholium in Γ is attractive, and may be still further improved by Elmsley's notion. In either case one is tempted to think that the sentence is incomplete, interrupted by the old hag. (The scholium in Γ is misplaced; it is on f. 94^r at l. 937, but such displacements are by no means unknown.)

1002 Cobet replaced the optative with ἄν by the indicative ὠνούμεθα. He was followed by many editors, but not Sommerstein. Though the reason for the alleged corruption is not immediately obvious, I do find the indicative more forceful.

1018 The line could well be dispensed with, especially if we follow van Herwerden is adjusting πρῶτον to πρότερον in 1017. If the text is sound, it is perhaps intended to make fun of the pedantic style of legal documents.

1037 Since the young woman asks 'Where are you dragging him off to?', it may be best to restore the old hag's response in such a way that she replies accurately to the question and says where she is taking her victim. Other emendations, closer to the transmitted text, imply that she disregards the specific point of the question. But one cannot be quite sure that this would be appropriate for her. Hall–Geldart assumed the loss of one syllable, and their idea is attractive.

1063 At first sight the καί in κἀγώ seems out of place (as the scholiast appears to have thought, but his conjectural explanation is no help). I suspect the line should be translated 'I too am afraid I'll shit—indeed more than I want', with a slight pause in the middle.

1067 ἀτάρ ... γε with one intervening word is cited by Denniston, *GP* 119, from Xen. *Oec.* 21. 1 and several passages in our author. He includes the present one in his list; but is it made different by having as the intervening notion a subordinate clause? I wonder if the emphasis provided by γε is appropriate. Perhaps Cobet was right with cύ. He could point to the preceding ἔγωγε and γέ(νοιτο) later in the line as factors inducing corruption.

1117 W. Kraus, *Testimonia Aristophanea* (Vienna, 1931), 50, preferred to retain the form of the verb given here by the MSS for two reasons: it is supported by the noun at the end of the line and it is attested in Pollux 7. 177 (and occasionally elsewhere, he could have added). But Athenaeus 15. 691 B cites this verse to illustrate the use of μυρίζω. Eustathius 1295. 20 says that μύρωμα, not μύρισμα, is the correct form. Though he is aware of the Athenaeus passage he does not justify his assertion; but from van der Valk's note ad loc. I infer that he is repeating a notion stated earlier at 974. 61.

1155 Sommerstein's apparatus reports that R omits the termination of κρίνειν. I doubt if this is so; the scribe seems to have written it with a standard abbreviation, but the ink is very faint.

1156 Porson's τὸ γελᾶν is attractive, so as to create more regular metre and avoid what appears to have been a form of the noun confined to elevated poetry. Because of this second consideration I am not convinced by Dunbar on *Birds* 373, who defends the tradition. G. P. Goold, *Phoenix*, 13 (1959), 153, took the view that substitution of two shorts for one was incompatible with the musical accompaniment.

1159 The speaker has addressed various categories of people and asked them to do one thing; so ἅπαντας should be preferred to πάντα, as Dobree saw.

Plutus

12 Blaydes's report that V reads μοι is refuted by the facsimile. It is worth remarking, in confirmation of the general opinion, that his reports of V are incorrect elsewhere.

17 Bentley's proposal of a participle in the nominative receives support from 23–4, where the slave says 'I shan't stop until you tell me...', as if he had been importuning his master for some time and expecting an answer. The one drawback that I see to his visualization of the scene is that in 26 Chremylus responds without appearing to admit that hitherto he has not been willing to do so. It is worth noting from Carolus Girardus' edition of the play (Paris, 1549) the comment 'erit itaque genitivus absolutus loco nominativi positus'.

Holzinger's long note is principally concerned with the apparent inconsistency of 13 and 19 with 54; one may now refer to Sommerstein's discussion at 54.

22 Holzinger argues in favour of R's reading γε as opposed to τόν, supposing the article to be an intrusive gloss and claiming that γε is as necessary for l. 22 as it is for 21. This seems to me manifestly false, even if the particle would be welcome enough. Holzinger has not allowed for the obvious possibility that the scribe of R mistakenly repeated the particle that he had copied in the preceding line. Blaydes accepted γε and wrote τοῦτον for cτέφανον, but the repetition of the noun in the generally accepted text hardly merits his criticism 'minus venuste'. If one is to make a change, a slightly less drastic alteration is his later suggestion γέ c' αὐτόν (p. 388 of his edition).

26 Holzinger suggested that in view of the phrasing of the question in 24, if Chremylus had replied 'I won't hide (it) from you', we should expect the name to be revealed at once. But instead he begins a rigmarole, 'I won't indulge in any concealment', which is a good way to begin a full account leading eventually to the naming of the mysterious figure. This usage of οὔ τι is shown to be not rare in Plato by Cooper–Krüger ii. 1418–19 (§69. 54. 1).

27 As the slave makes brief interjections at the end of ll. 29 and 31, it is not out of the question that he made one here as well. Is the joke better coming from the clever slave than from the master? A matter of taste perhaps.

32 Holzinger claimed that πρός was the right reading because it occurs in this phrase later in the play no less than five times; so here it must have been displaced by the gloss ὡς. The inference is highly dubious; no-one needed a gloss on πρός and ὡς was a rarer usage, though admittedly well known to Atticists. As to the other passages in this play, in all of them πρός happens to be more convenient metrically.

50 V's reading ἔτει is odd, but Holzinger is wrong to say that it cannot have arisen as a gloss on χρόνῳ or γένει. At least the former word already in late antiquity could mean 'year', as LSJ s.v. I. 3c indicates, and it has this meaning in Modern Greek. It is perhaps best to accept γένει as the *difficilior lectio* and to treat the other readings as trivializations or glosses. But I would not rule out the possibility that γένει is an attempt by an educated reader to improve the text.

52 Thiercy, having accepted R's reading at 17, marks a change of speaker before ἦν δ' and thereby alters a good deal of the subsequent dialogue. But does his rearrangement suit the characters any better? He sees that Chremylus must have asked some questions of Plutus, who did not deign to reply. Is it not better that in 56 Carion should now do the questioning, to see if he can get an answer?

61 Sommerstein rightly notes that εὐόρκου does not seem to be the obvious word to describe the speaker in the present context, but fails to mention Schaefer's ingenious suggestion εὐόργου, a very rare word now attested in Soph. fr. 33a Radt and P.Oxy. 3317. 14. It suitably emphasizes the difference in mood between master and servant.

66 Rutherford, *CR* 10 (1896), 98–100, having divided 65 between master and servant, which seems sensible, then gave ὦ τᾶν to the master, whereas generally it is given to Plutus. He thought this arrangement of the dialogue more in accordance with the characterization implied elsewhere.

67 R's comparative βέλτιον makes sense and is likely to have been adjusted to the superlative.

Does Carion address his master with the word ὦ? The omission would be lively and perhaps none too courteous, which suits the slave's mood here; R and V have ὦ here, and I suspect that it was an addition by some scribe.

75 Is the verb used by Plutus active or middle? Either is possible in Attic usage; but the active in Chremylus' reply is likely to have matched what Plutus said. In *Wasps* 434 and 437 the middle of this verb is followed by an active, but there the interval between the two occurrences makes some difference.

78 ff. Holzinger, arguing largely on the basis of attributions of lines in the MSS (which we now know to be an unsound approach), rejects as unnatural the idea of giving only 80 to Carion, as Blaydes had done. 78b–79 seem to suit this slave.

I am surprised that editors see no attraction in Blaydes's ὦ for καί in 82, which makes for a more forceful outburst and could well be right.

98 Modern editors tend to adopt R's πω, but I have doubts. Holzinger's parallels from Soph. *Aj.* 663 and *El.* 513 are sentences with a different structure: 'since *x* happened, up to the present time ...'. Here πω sits uneasily with πολλοῦ χρόνου. VΘW9 are reported to have που, which gives the sense 'I haven't seen them anywhere in a long time', which is odd given that the reference is to the period of the speaker's blindness. Meineke's ἐγώ gives excellent sense, especially in view of the wording of 99. The omission of the word by most MSS may not be unconnected with the fact that Byzantine scribes were happy to accept or create verses of twelve syllables in accordance with contemporary practice (in these verses the classical rules of prosody did not apply).

Plutus   201

111 As usually printed this line begins with Plutus contradicting Chremylus' assertion that not all men are bad, followed by the slave saying as an aside 'You'll suffer for that remark.' The slave is aggressive and presumably is thinking still of his boast in 106; hence this threatening retort. There is another way of distributing the parts: the first words are a jocular contradiction by the slave of his master, who then loses patience with his slave and says οἰμώξει μακρά. So (tentatively) V. Tammaro, *Museum criticum*, 18 (1983), 134.

115 Blindness would not normally be called ὀφθαλμία. Sommerstein accepts the alternative line quoted in the scholia (τῆc cυμφορᾶc ταύτηc ce παύcειν ἧc ἔχειc) as coming from the other version of the play; he reckons it was an authorial improvement made soon after the original performance. Holzinger thought it pure prose, concocted out of glosses on the line that is transmitted in the MSS. A better way of stating this objection would be to say that it looks like a paraphrase; *Plutus* was a school text, and school texts were often treated in this way. The difficulty of ὀφθαλμίαc can perhaps be met by saying that it is a deliberate euphemism or that in the conditions of the ancient world any complaint that could initially be so described led in most cases to blindness.

128–9 There may be a case for preferring the emphatic form cέ in 128, even if it is not strictly necessary to match the following ἐμέ.
  Holzinger argues in favour of R's μείζω and cites as a parallel Xen. *Ages.* 4. 2; that could be right, but it is quite likely that the scribe allowed his eye to be distracted by the termination of ἐγώ immediately above.

135–6 Here I follow R in essentials, accepting Dindorf's adjustment of ὅτι to ὁτιή. Sommerstein and others accept παύcειεν with ἄν separated from its verb and postponed to the last position in the sentence; this word-order seems to me less likely.

145 LSJ s.v. χαρίειc report the doctrine of ancient grammarians (Herodian i. 350, Apollonius Dyscolus, *Adv.* 160. 22) that when adverbial the neuter was accented proparoxytone and say that no example was cited. Hence I think it worth noting that this is the accentuation found in RKL and the Suda entry χ 103, which quotes a general rule and this line. The scholia here make a different point about Attic usage.

166 Threatte i 560 says that the spelling γν- begins to appear c.400 in inscriptions; so one can accept it here. But since RVL have the older spelling in κν-, it may be prudent to note simple emendations that would accommodate it.

168 Sommerstein's ingenious interpretation of παρατίλλειν may well be right. Badham's attribution of διὰ cὲ κτλ. to Carion is attractive as a continuation of what happened in the previous lines, and is not excluded.

197 The MSS have an unmetrical text. It looks as if either the pronoun αὐτῷ or the infinitive εἶναι must be deleted, unless one is willing to adopt the transposition suggested by Bamberg and Hall–Geldart. Blaydes claimed that the pronoun was harder to omit than the verb, but in his text he accepted Bentley's proposal, and in this context the pronoun is so easily understood that this cannot be an argument of any weight.

ἀβίωτον appears to be in A only; can this be a trace of the truth, despite the agreement of the other early MSS? Does its recurrence in an extremely similar context in 969 point in favour of restoring it here, or is it to be supposed that A's reading is due to a scribe who already knew the full text of the play and allowed his memory of the later passage to influence him here? That is the explanation I incline to favour myself, while not excluding the possibility that it is a gloss. Holzinger 72 notes that Q (MS Paris gr. 2821, = Par 8), representing the early recension of Triclinius, has the line without εἶναι; but Triclinius evidently changed his mind, as is indicated by Koster, *Autour d'un manuscrit*, 68–9 and confirmed by autopsy of L.

205 If the transmitted reading εἰc τὴν οἰκίαν is to be defended, it seems to me necessary to assume that εἰcδύc refers to penetration of the exterior or courtyard wall, after which the burglar would still have to make his way into individual rooms. This, as Holzinger points out, accords with the layout of many Athenian houses. Even so, there is a brachylogy, with which I do not feel entirely comfortable, despite the approval of Wilamowitz, *Aristophanes: Lysistrate* (Berlin, 1927), 39. But Holzinger's scornful dismissal of van

Herwerden's deletion of the line is harsh; to me it reads like prose that happens to scan.

209 αὐτός is rendered 'whole-heartedly' by Sommerstein, 'en ce qui te concerne' by Thiercy, and Holzinger has the phrase 'sein Schicksal kräftig in die eigene Hand zu nehmen' as a description of what is being requested of Plutus. These are not convincing justifications of the pronoun on which Blaydes cast doubt; curiously he did not see here the possibility of an alteration he had tried elsewhere, εὐθύς (see his notes on *Wasps* 255 and 715, *Peace* 1176, and compare also *Birds* 781 and *Eccl.* 280). αὐτός was perhaps induced by its occurrence below in 213.

216 Neobari in Sommerstein's apparatus perhaps deserves a word of explanation. The minor emendation in question appears in an exceedingly rare edition of the Byzantine triad plays, printed in Paris 'per Conradum Neobarium regium in graecis typographum M.D.X.L.' This information is given on the title page; there is no preface or colophon. I have examined the copy that once belonged to Rogers; he acquired it (and some other editions) from the Duke of Marlborough's sale of his Sunderland Library, and it now belongs to Wadham College, Oxford, to which he bequeathed it. There happens to be no other copy in Oxford or the British Library, and it seems that the Bibliothèque nationale de France has only a defective copy. Neobar was a naturalised German appointed by the king in 1539 with a salary of 100 gold écus; he died the following year from overwork and was succeeded by Robert Estienne (see P. Renouard, *Répertoire des imprimeurs parisiens*, rev. edn. (Paris, 1965), 322). This book is not to be confused with the full edition published in Paris in 1540 by Wechel, in whose shop Neobar had served as a corrector (see A. Charon-Parent, in *Histoire de l'édition française*, i (1982, no place stated, published by Promodis), 247.

261 Denniston, *GP* 267, lists this example of δήπου in what appears to be a small category of questions (his (2)); but I would suggest that it really belongs in his category (3), 'surprised or incredulous questions' introduced by οὐ δήπου.

268–9 Despite Sommerstein's thoughtful note I still have some difficulty with 269 as the 'immensely excited' (his stage-direction) response to Carion's description of the decrepit elderly stranger; it seems rather far-fetched to assume the chorus have instantly inferred the great wealth of the stranger as the only reason for his welcome by Chremylus. Richards 57–8 proposed transposition of 268–70 to follow 263. There is a slight difficulty: in 269 αὐτόν refers to Chremylus, and 270 with Carion's deflation of enthusiasm has ἔχοντα 'with a heap of the miseries of old age', which might look as if it applied to him rather than to the stranger. Presumably there is a reference to the troubles that Chremylus is bringing on himself by welcoming such a stranger.

A variant of Richards's proposal would be to transpose 268 only, exchanging its position with 264. The single line with an exclamation and a request for information is answered by 265–7. The chorus then in 264 ask another question and add 269, which is just as good after 264 as it is after 268. 269 then receives a sarcastic response; 'a heap of the miseries of old age' can then refer to the battered appearance of Plutus. Should 269 then be a question?

343 If the oath is part of the preceding sentence, μά is required with the negative οὐδέν. Is the whole of the line an aside, as Sommerstein takes it? The alternative is to suppose that though Blepsidemus was talking to himself in 335 ff., as he got nearer to Chremylus the latter was able to hear what he said and therefore responds at once in such a way as to allay suspicions about his odd behaviour. If that is what happened on the stage, νή as found in RV can be made part of Chremylus' second sentence.

353–4 Sommerstein accepts τό τε ... τό τ' αὖ, essentially the reading of the MSS. Denniston, *GP* 504–5, deals with τε ... τε in parallel clauses. He does not cite any example of the double use of the particle from our author, but *Lys.* 40–1 and *Frogs* 818–19 for the triple use. However, in both of those passages what we have is a series of three less complex expressions governing one verb. I feel Holzinger was right to accept Meineke's proposal, which incorporates R's variant in 354 and gives a stronger contrast, which I find desirable.

397 'If there's any other Poseidon, then I mean the other too' is the translation of Sommerstein; Thiercy concurs. But the Greek does not have 'too'. As Holzinger 153 says 'Unrichtig ist es auch, τὸν ἕτερον so zu erklären als stünde καὶ τὸν ἕτερον im Texte und als handelte es sich um verschiedene Beinamen des Poseidon.' I think Chremylus is offended by Blepsidemus' scepticism and sarcastically replies 'If there is another Poseidon, that's the one.'

401 The dative form of the pronoun in R and V may well be right; see Cooper–Krüger i. 289 (§48. 7. 3, 4), for the dative with δεῖ and χρή, a rare construction but sufficiently well attested.

422 Sommerstein retains ὠχρά, but I think Jackson, *MS* 78–9, offers a superior text. He notes that 'the Furies were dark as the raven's wing', so that Blepsidemus' suggestion in 423 fits less well with the adjective as transmitted in 422.

431 In VAL coι precedes τὸ βάραθρον. It is tempting to accept the word-order which brings the unstressed pronoun nearer to the beginning of the sentence. Blaydes's note suggests that he inclined to this view, but his reason is not stated in his apparatus; from his supplementary note on p. 399 it may be inferred that βάραθρον tends to be found occupying a position overlapping the junction of the second and third metron (cf. Holzinger's note 'die Silben βαρα- fast regelmäßig in der Arsis stehen').

445 Sommerstein follows Rogers in accepting δειλότατον, the variant found in late MSS, on the ground that for an action to be described as δεινότατον it must be audacious. I remain unconvinced: to fail in one's duty to a divinity deserves the epithet 'shocking'.

493 The scholia distinguish between βούλευμα and βούλημα. But if one reads the wording attentively, it gives no support or proof that they knew of MSS with both words; the author of the note is simply making a pedantic distinction, which has no place in the apparatus criticus.

499, 511 The unmetrical text of l. 499 as given by all important MSS was discussed by Fraenkel, *BzA* 147–50. He raised a linguistic objection to the simple transposition made by Hall–Geldart and followed by Coulon, noting that in this anapaestic metre a dactyl normally results in a trochaic word being followed by one which is a bacchius, i.e. – ⌣ / ⌣ – –. A few exceptions to this rule remained to be accounted for, and Fraenkel felt that Hall–Geldart's text was inferior

206   *Plutus*

to τούτου coι μάρτυc ἐγώ, which gives coι second position in the sentence and provides good contrast between ἐγώ and the imperative in the next sentence.

Fraenkel's point about the position of coι is partially valid; he should have printed it as an enclitic (his failure to do so is perhaps no more than an oversight), and then it would occupy its typical position within the clause. But his treatment of the passage is open to two objections. (i) His transposition is more complex and presupposes greater confusion in the archetype. (ii) His concern about the metrical shape of ἐγώ coι seems to me misguided. The enclitic may well have been felt by the Greeks to be almost part of the preceding word, and Fraenkel's own explanation of other prima facie exceptions to his suggested rule at *Wasps* 350 and *Knights* 533 in fact relies on a similar principle, since he quite reasonably claims that in those lines two or more words (ἔcτιν ὀπὴ δῆθ' and γέρων ὤν) constitute a single concept. He was also in difficulty when dealing with a third case, at 511 below. There in the end he opted to leave the text unaltered, although the simple transposition of τέχνην ἄν to ἄν τέχνην would have removed the alleged anomaly and had the additional advantage of letting ἄν occupy second position, which it commonly does. This is in fact the reading of V, rejected by Fraenkel on metrical grounds (p. 148 n. 1); but it is not certain that he was right. White, *Verse*, 365 (§792), gives instances of lengthening with mute and liquid in anapaests; although some of these have to be discounted, a few remain which defy easy emendation; see Dover's note on *Clouds* 320, referring to B. Sachtschal, *De comicorum graecorum sermone metro accommodato* (Diss. Breslau 1908), 13.

The matter is further complicated by the word-order in the badly preserved P. Ant. 3. 180 (P21). It lends support to Hall–Geldart. Rather hesitantly I follow them, despite being aware that the relative antiquity of papyri does not guarantee that they offer better texts.

502 Commentators seem not to be bothered by the word-order (at ὄντεc Triclinius noted ἐνταῦθα cύναπτε τὸ πονηροί). It seems to me abnormal and I wonder if ὄντεc intruded from the following line. πλούτῳ θάλλουcι (or χαίρουcι) is the wording one might expect; H.-S. thought of πλουτοῦc', εἰcὶν δὲ πονηροί. There is no obvious solution.

505 Sommerstein's note on this line seems to me important for its

Plutus 207

arguments against seeing in this line a reference to Penia in the third person. I would add one further point. Though the scholia here, as so often, are a mixed bag, it is worth remarking that some of them have ταῦτα rather than ταύτην in their paraphrase, which perhaps affords a modest degree of support for Meineke's undoubtedly necessary conjecture.

521 Though editors have been exercised by a problem in 521, there is also a difficulty in 522 which they have failed to address. In 521 πλείςτων is unexpected; one would prefer a descriptive word. Holzinger took it to mean 'the majority', but that requires the definite article, which his paraphrase includes. Thiercy and Sommerstein are constrained to supply 'pays' and 'home' to deal with the preposition παρά. F. Allègre, *REG* 10 (1897), 10–13, emphasized the need for a word that has point in the context. Hemsterhuys's ἀπλήςτων has some attraction: the slave-dealers have an insatiable desire for profit and the word picks up ἀργύριον κἀκεῖνος ἔχῃ. (Sch. V has αἰςχροκερδεῖς, but that may be guesswork.) Holzinger confessed that he would have accepted this reading if it were the paradosis. Hemsterhuys also tried ἀπίςτων, which gets support from the scholium διαβάλλονται οἱ Θετταλοὶ ὡς ἀνδραποδιςταὶ καὶ ἄπιςτοι, since scholia often repeat words from the text. It perhaps gets further support from the scholium on Eur. *Phoen.* 1408, where 521 is quoted with πλείςτων but is sandwiched between Eur. fr. 422 and Dem. 1. 22, which both focus on the word ἄπιςτος and are therefore a hint that this was originally in the text of 521 as cited in the ancient commentary from which this note derives. But the fact is that ἄπιςτοι has little point in 521 unless it was already a standard insult directed at Thessalians, in other words proverbial, and though Kannicht on Eur. fr. 422 cites Strömberg to this effect I am not convinced. A similar claim in Triclinius' scholium is equally dubious; it could be an inference from the scholium on the *Phoen.* passage, which he will have known well, since that play was part of the school curriculum.

Another suggestion which is no less attractive palaeographically is Bergk's λῃςτῶν. It is improved by Kappeyne van de Koppello's addition of καί to ἀνδραποδιςτῶν. The reason for preferring this approach is that it can help us with the hitherto undiagnosed problem of οὐδεὶc οὐδ' in 522. If οὐδ' is to be read here it should introduce the second concept of a pair. But οὐδείc and ἀνδραποδιcτήc are no such pair. I think, as H.-S. has suggested to me, that we need to find a means of creating a pair of nouns in this line. λῃcτήc is the word required. It could replace ἁπάντων, but one would have some difficulty in explaining how the corruption came about, and πρῶτον ἁπάντων is attested below at 716 and at *Peace* 754. It seems better to propose that it replace οὐδείc; on this view the corruption was facilitated by the adjacent word οὐδ'.

544 Sommerstein says that the correct reading φυλλεῖ' is given by the lemma to the scholium in R. The recent edition by M. Chantry (Groningen, 1994) agrees. Rutherford's antiquated (and illconceived) edition (London 1896), i. 58 prints φυλλεῖ' with a line underneath the letters epsilon and iota, which means (p. xxviii) 'When letters have become so dim that they cannot be read with certainty, a thick black line is drawn beneath them in the transcript'. However, examination of the facsimile leaves me in little doubt that R has φύλλ'.

566 Blepsidemus has precious little to say in this scene, but Sommerstein follows Bentley and others in allowing him to intervene at 580, and another such intervention at 566 is not to be ruled out. I would not myself accept Sommerstein's view that all attempts at emendation include 'at least one particle that is worse than redundant'. The line is not exactly a paraphrase that ought to be deleted. It seems to me that the right way to approach the problem is to ask whether the metrical difficulty created by λαθεῖν can be solved; in other words, can a suitable short syllable be found to precede it? I accept, admittedly with some hesitation, Reisig's solution.

573 If the main verb is not in the future tense, I am rather hesitant about accepting a dependent infinitive in the future; so I should not regard Soph. *Phil.* 1394 πείcειν δυνηθηcόμεθα as a secure parallel. There are a number of difficult cases of this type; K-G i. 185 listed them with the remark that they are few enough to permit the hypothesis of textual corruption. Cooper–Krüger i. 658–61 (§53. 7. 11), has a nuanced discussion and accumulates a larger number of examples than might have been inferred from the earlier discussion.

Many are very easy to emend, and have been emended. Here too it is easy, given the similarity of theta and sigma in ancient scripts.

578 'It is so difficult to recognize what is good for one' is the sense required, and δίκαιον will not do, as the meaning is wrong and the definite article is needed. Holzinger suggested τό γ' ὀρθόν, which is picked up by ὀρθῶc in the next line; but the important concept in the next line is τὸ κράτιcτον, and Sommerstein not unreasonably thinks well of Dindorf's τὸ κρεῖττον. I have a slight preference for Blaydes's τὸ χρηcτόν. The corruption could have been caused by the occurrence of δίκαιοι at the end of l. 568.

586 (592) Can κότινοc be an adjective? Holzinger thought so; most editors deny this and follow V. I suppose they are right. The reading of the other MSS may be just another instance of assimilation.

632 Sommerstein suggests that the scholia may have known the variant ἥκων, which would give a more confident—and indeed more appropriate—statement. The paraphrase in M and Vat. Reginensis gr. 147 (= Vs¹) (p. 174 in Chantry's edition) does not seem to me to be strong support for this hypothesis. But perhaps one should emend anyway.

681 ἥγιζεν used humorously may be right. The muddle in R and V has led some scholars to wonder if the truth has yet to be found. Reiske's suggestion ἥλιζεν and Blaydes's ἤθροιζεν do not convince, not does Holzinger's defence of ἥτιζεν in the sense of 'collect'. Perhaps one should assume that as the first stage of corruption an uncial gamma was misread as tau; this would account for the reading in R.

689 Fraenkel, *BzA* 154–60, inferred from the scholium in V that a form of the verb εἴρω was in the original text and proposed ἐνείρει, 'she slips her hand in', admitting that from a palaeographical point of view the change is not easily explained. J. C. B. Lowe in his review of Fraenkel, *JHS* 84 (1964), 167, preferred ὑπείρει, 'she slips her hand underneath (me)', and said this 'would fit the situation in which Carion is bending over the pot beside the recumbent woman'. Sommerstein translates 'stuck out her hand from under her cover'. I think the nuance of the preposition in the compound verb may be to convey an implication of surreptitious or furtive action.

696 It is tempting with Holzinger to attach importance to R's reading, but does the verb deserve to be emphasized? And did γ' intrude in R from 701?

725 Girardus in his 1549 edition prints the verb in his text on p. 134 as ἐπομνύμενον, but in his note on p. 136 makes the emendation ὑπ- and remarks 'significat hoc verbum aliquo praetextu, puta peregrinationis vel morbi, causam in aliud tempus rejicere, qui mos est calumniatorum et subterfugientium'.
Sommerstein in his apparatus says that P82 reads τα[, but the editor's diplomatic transcript is τ.[.

736 I note that editors print the emphatic form ἐμοί, although their translations do not seem to reflect it. R has μοι. But I suppose the implication is 'I think this is what happened, though you might take a different view'. There does not seem to be any need to change the verb into an imperfect, as Dindorf proposed, followed by some others.

815 Sommerstein's note invites a supplement. If the Greek is taken literally, a kitchen of ivory is meant, whereas he refers to a kitchen decorated with ivory, i.e. not completely covered from floor to ceiling. Perhaps it is hair-splitting to insist on the difference, but one ought to mention Bentley's view of this line. He cited Pollux 10. 155, which says that Aristophanes in the *Plutus* used the word ἶποc 'mousetrap'. If this, the earliest evidence for the text of this line, is to be rejected, we have to say either that Pollux referred to the other version of the play or that he had a text which was already faulty. Either of these inferences is legitimate, and it is also true that Athenaeus, not much later than Pollux, had a text with ἰπνός. Yet the humour of ending the list with an ivory mousetrap would not be unsatisfactory. I quote Bentley's words: 'legendum inquam ὁ δ' ἶποc; cum auctoritate Pollucis; tum ipsius sententiae causa; quae hoc pacto plus salis Comici et plus ridiculi in se habet'.

839 If ὦν τῶν is right, 'a drought in my stores ...' is the meaning. The participle ὤν is not entirely easy; perhaps it is an example of the 'imperfect' participle. Van Herwerden suggested that αὐχμὸc γὰρ ὤν could be equal to τὸ αὐχμὸν εἶναι. Fritzsche's ὄντωc is worth considering, as is Reiske's ὦ τᾶν. It is tempting to write γὰρ οὖν, which

Blaydes also considered, although this is rare in comedy according to Denniston, *GP* 446. The speaker's addiction to the formula μὲν οὖν invites the thought that he enjoyed using other odd combinations of particles.

840 As Sommerstein remarks, if the words ἀλλ' οὐχὶ νῦν are given to Carion, the Just Man's continuation might be expected to acknowledge them in some way, for example by the particle γε. That could easily be inserted by reading ἀνθ' ὧν <γ'> ἐγώ.

865 οὗτος is open to doubt. Though Blaydes printed it in his text, he expressed a preference for the alternatives αὐτός or θεός or ὄντως, of which the first seems best.

885 Thiercy 1321 proposes δήγματα without comment. Presumably he takes δήγματος to be an error of assimilation, whereas Fritzsche and Rogers explained the genitive by assuming that medicine boxes were marked in a way that presupposed the word φάρμακον.

949–50 Hall–Geldart contemplated transposing βουλὴν πιθών and ἐκκλησίαν, which is attractive, because the Boule is not commonly described as consisting of citizens. They cited a scholium, but not in very clear fashion, and the scholia set out in Chantry's now standard edition give no support to their proposal. That is not, however, a decisive objection.

973–4 The difference between (κατα-)κνάω and (κατα-)κνίζω or their nominal derivatives is not made very clear by LSJ. Without much confidence I have followed the majority of the MSS; the confusion of iota and eta is of course found on almost every page of any Byzantine MS.

1010 Holzinger and Sommerstein prefer to follow R by omitting γ'; the former asserts that this yields a clause 'ohne glossematischen Aufputz', which invites the reply that γ' is not a gloss. What incentive was there to add the particle to a line which originally did not have it? The *Suda*, which normally agrees with R, here preserves the particle, suggesting that the omission in this case is a minor slip by the copyist of R.

1012 Holzinger 33, on l. 136, states that here, *pace* von Velsen, U has ᾔτει c' ἄν.

1081 The transmitted verb ἐπιτρέψω is defended by some on the ground that it appears in the sense 'order' at Xen. *Anab.* 6. 5. 11, which is accepted as such by LSJ. But I suspect the meaning there is 'he left it to them to . . . /assigned the task of . . .', which only in later Greek developed semantically to 'order' (this passage may be taken as evidence that the semantic shift was beginning). For this reason, given also the proximity of the verb used in its normal sense at 1078, I have adopted van Leeuwen's proposal.

1098 Blaydes punctuated with a question mark after κλαυcιᾷ, and Denniston, *GP* 274, was inclined to favour this.

1110 Sommerstein takes the view that 'the tongue is cut out' = 'the tongue ought to be cut out'. I have my doubts, and am inclined to follow Holzinger's interpretation. The sentence was perhaps originally one commonly uttered at a sacrifice; γίγνεται is then natural enough, and τέμνεται is a variant or an explanation of it. If τέμνεται was original, it is hard to see why γίγνεται should have been added. I realize, however, that not all variants of this kind are necessarily to be treated as evidence of glossators' activity.

Addenda

***Knights* 539.** Bonanno sees the adjective as an allusion to the supposed power of the vegetable to deal with a hangover, but the witticism seems rather complex and the formation of the adjective raises doubts.

***Clouds* 1170.** Similar aspirated forms are found in the Herculaneum papyri, in which they are regarded as erroneous; see D. Obbink, *Philodemus On Piety I* (Oxford 1996), 342.

***Wasps* 570.** Bergk and Wiliamowitz, *Kleine Schriften* i.327, favoured ἀμβληχᾶται. Holzinger had a point when he observed (*SB Wien* 208(5) (1928), 27) that this compound was unattested. But the position is now complicated by *DGE* revealing an instance of it in Cyril of Alexandria, *Glaphyra in Genesim* (Migne *PG* 69.33D) applied to bleating lambs. Wilamowitz scornfully dismissed ἅμα as if it suited only the description of a concert; but "all together" seems acceptable. The question of prosody remains difficult; a similar difficulty arises at *Lysistrata* 384.

***Wasps* 943.** Might it also be possible to punctuate more heavily after φεύγουσιν and continue with exclamatory ὡς?

***Peace* 345.** R follows this convention in the text here but not at 317, whereas V in both passages has an oxytone accent. Schwyzer ii. 600–601 appears to have had doubts about the distinction, and I have taken the same view, but without much conviction.

***Peace* 536.** The discussion by W.J. Slater in J.N. Grant (rd.), *Editing Greek and Latin texts* (New York 1989), 54, is incomplete. He omits the point that ἱπνόν is a γράφεται variant and cites the Triclinian instead of the old scholia.

***Plutus* 689.** For the aspiration of the verb see the evidence in H. Frisk, *Griechisches etymologisches Wörterbuch* (Heidelberg 1961–72), s.v εἴρω.

Index

abbreviations in MSS 40, 105, 151,
 161(bis), 192
 for numerals 55
 see also nomina sacra
accentuation
 aorist middle imperatives 169, 180
 εἶναι 80
 μοχθηρος, πονηρος 20, 55, 56, 66
 other words 21, 22, 35, 36, 41, 43, 64,
  70, 89, 145, 153, 165, 201, 213
 see also enclitics
action on stage 23, 34, 35, 39, 43, 47, 78,
 86, 109(bis), 111, 118, 126,
 160, 168, 185, 188, 190, 198,
 204, 208
actors' interpolations 117
address, forms of *see also* vocative 78,
 91, 200
adjective/adverb as variants 101
adjective, two-termination 102
Aldine edition *see also* Musurus 34, 65,
 78, 90, 104, 182, 103
anacolouthon 136–7
anapaest, split 20, 23, 116, 167
Andronicus Callistus 12
aorist 19, 23, 33, 41, 70, 80, 889, 101,
 118, 140(bis), 154, 182
apocope 139
Aristarchus 83
article, definite and indefinite 24, 38, 55,
 56, 78, 82, 01, 100, 121, 123,
 164, 169, 181, 182, 192, 207,
 208
asyndeton 67, 141, 163
attribution of parts to speakers 20, 24,
 25, 43, 100, 101, 115, 121, 126,
 179, 180, 182–3, 191–2,
 193–4, 199(bis), 200(ter),
 201, 202, 211
augment 59, 100, 148

author's variants or alternative drafts
 108, 110, 136, 149, 201

brevis in longo 109

Callistratus 89
Casaubon 52
coinage of new words (in comedy) 64,
 67
colloquialisms 16, 46, 57, 63, 161, 167,
 181(bis), 193
conditional sentences 80, 86
conscience 42
correption 67, 160
corruption in MSS *see* error, types of
curriculum, Byzantine school 201, 207

dative, forms of 124
 instrumental 36
 of person affected 28, 45, 182
deictic forms 19, 25, 40, 41, 67, 79, 90,
 108, 142, 144, 155, 194
Demetrius Triclinius 8–9, 13, 22, 26, 38,
 60, 62, 63, 65(quater), 66, 69,
 91, 97(bis), 102, 104, 105, 109,
 110, 119, 207
diaeresis 121
Didymus 109
difficilior lectio 106, 142, 164, 166,
 199
Divus, Andreas 13, 81, 150, 159(bis)
dochmiac 156
Doric forms 128, 168
dramatic illusion 78
dual forms 27, 31, 73, 109, 172, 179

ellipse 105, 124, 151, 194
enclitics 26, 28, 54, 67, 80, 87, 120, 133,
 166, 195(bis)
epexegetic infinitive 21

216 Index

epigraphic evidence 3, 144
Eratosthenes 88
errors of the poet, possible 32(bis), 46,
  74, 123, 134
errors in MSS, types of
  additions in margin 27, 110, 116
  assimilation 27, 43, 57, 65, 76, 129,
    137, 147, 171, 189, 195, 196,
    211
  Binneninterpolation 192
  Christian ideas, intrusion of 3, 41–2
  confusion of majuscule/uncial letters
    56, 99, 107, 114, 150, 158, 209
  minuscule letters 45, 121
  words αὐτόc/εὐθύc 118, 188, 203
    πάντα/αὐτά/ταῦτα 48, 49, 72, 93,
    172
    μέγαc/μέλαc 81
  deictic forms 19
  dictation interne 143
  dittography 87
  glosses 26, 39, 40, 49, 57, 66, 73, 77,
    77, 78, 86, 91, 95, 97, 107, 110,
    143, 153, 155, 163, 167, 174,
    181, 185, 191, 193, 198, 199,
    201, 212
  haplography 99, 191
  inversion of inflections 175
  iotacism 131, 211
  numerals 55, 97, 102
  transposition 22, 58, 73
  trivialisation 70
  vitium Byzantinum 114, 180(bis), 195
  word-division 102
euphony 138
Euphorion 88
Eupolis 152
Euripides 24, 101

Florens Christianus 83
future perfect 103

Gelenius 116
genitive 112
gestures 16, 63, 67, 110
Girardus, Petrus 13, 198, 210
glosses *see* errors in MSS

haplography *see* errors in MSS
Heliodorus 102
hiatus 156, 159
hyperbaton *see* word-order

imperfect 33, 69, 92, 94, 112, 116, 140
imperatives 66
inconsistency on the part of characters
  84, 187, 194
indirect questions 15
indirect tradition 19, 71, 107, 133, 153,
  154, 166, 169, 184, 196, 210
infinitive 92(bis), 101, 208
interpolation *see* errors in MSS
iota adscript/subscript 64–5, 82, 124

John Tzetzes 64, 72

kenning 129, 151

literary criticism 49

MSS and papyri 3–13
MSS (principal)
  R 5, *passim*
  V 6, 36, 55, 57, 59, 64, 67, 70, 72, 77,
    82(bis), 87, 89(bis), 100, 101,
    102, 105, 106, 109(bis), 110,
    111, 127, 139, 164, 165, 169,
    170, 171(bis), 172, 173, 174,
    175, 180, 181, 198, 199,
    200(bis), 202, 204, 205(bis),
    206, 209(ter)
  A 9, 20, 28, 57, 67, 111, 127, 175, 181,
    185, 187, 188, 202, 205
  B 12, 34, 52, 53, 888, 92, 97(bis), 103,
    104, 109, 139, 140, 145, 178,
    188
  E 9, 22, 26, 57, 63(bis), 74, 75, 78, 80,
    127, 135, 139, 166, 171, 173,
    175, 180
  K 7, 63, 72, 111, 175, 181, 182, 201
  L 8, 22(bis), 55, 62, 63, 65(bis), 72, 89,
    109, 175, 178(bis), 182, 201,
    202(bis), 205
  M 9, 55, 59, 64, 75, 127, 164, 175, 178,
    109

Md1 6, 171
U 9, 55, 63, 72, 135, 166, 171, 173, 175, 180, 211
Γ 9, 20, 22, 26, 53, 55, 89(bis), 109, 136, 139, 146, 186(bis), 187, 189, 190, 193, 196bis)
Θ 9, 57, 63, 73, 77, 78, 164, 181, 200
(others)
C 52, 84, 88, 99
Ct1 169
Ct2 66, 169
Elbingensis 62
G 62, 88, 163, 170, 178
H 20
Ln5 70
Mu2 149, 155, 161
N 63, 72, 80
Np1 164, 175
O8 65(bis)
O10 134
Par8 66, 202
Par9 72
Par19 62
Par20 166, 176, 180
V2 62
Vb3 64, 171(bis)
Vc1 66
Vp2 (=P) 20, 99
Vp3 89
Vs1 135, 171, 173, 209
Vv4 65
Vv5 66
W9 200
Δ 170, 178
Λ 193, 196
X 52, 65, 70
metre 20(bis), 23, 37, 45, 46, 48, 56, 67, 70, 72, 73, 76, 83–4, 91, 86, 97(bis), 100, 101(bis), 102(bis), 109, 110, 116, 117–18, 122, 124, 136, 138, 140, 146, 151, 156, 160, 195, 196, 197, 202, 205
metrical responsion 73, 76, 90
rules in Byzantine 72, 200
middle voice 17, 103

minuscule script 121
Musurus, Marcus *see also* Aldine edition 12, 78, 90, 193

names, personal 17, 83, 84, 87, 95(bis)
Neobar 203
nomina sacra see also abbreviations 38, 160
nu ephelkustikon 67
numerology 51, 102

obscenity 59, 61
omission of ἄν 85
omission of personal pronoun 87
optative, forms of 184
orthography 23, 125

palaeography
  displacement of scholia 75
  position of δέ 130
  see also minuscule, uncial
papyri 3–4, 22, 58, 79, 82, 135–6, 152, 174, 192, 206, 210
parody, paratragedy 24, 52, 57, 82, 90, 101(bis), 127
participle
  as noun 119
  imperfect 210
particles
  ἀλλά 45, 141
  ἀλλ' οὖν 94
  ἄρα 46, 71, 158
  ἆρα 85, 93, 101
  ἀτάρ ... γε 197
  γάρ 46, 129, 150
  γάρ οὖν 106, 210
  γε 15, 20(bis), 22, 35, 38, 42, 63, 72, 73, 85, 88(bis), 92, 94, 96, 97, 99, 109, 115, 116, 117, 122, 139, 140, 144, 149(bis), 170, 179, 181, 185, 1998, 210, 211(bis)
  γ' ἄρα 158
  γέ που 111
  γέ τοι 111, 191
  γέ τοι δή 186
  γοῦν 19

218   Index

δαί 100, 114
δέ 71, 78, 112, 130, 152, 182
δέ... γε 21, 128
δ'οὖν 121, 164
δή 15, 40, 110, 122, 127, 150, 154, 157
δήπου 203
δῆτα 80, 117
εἰ μή... γε 187
εἶτα δέ 16
ἤ 35(bis), 36, 57, 65, 99, 101
καί 104, 124, 196
καί... γε 188
καί... δή 174
καί μήν 140
καίτοι 78
μέν 181
μὲν οὖν 125
μέντοι 117
μῶν 99
οὔκουν 82, 136, 164
οὖν 151, 164
οὔτι μήν 194
οὗτοι 149
περ 120, 172
που 19, 111, 120, 157, 170, 200
τε 20, 55, 66, 106, 111, 122, 152, 169, 177, 182, 204
τοι 120, 127, 154
Porson's Law 146
proceleusmatic 91
prodelision 103(bis)
pronouns, especially stressed/unstressed 28, 30, 52(bis), 53, 54, 57, 67, 78, 87, 93, 103, 134, 139, 141, 146, 171, 173, 195, 201, 206, 210
prosody 45, 84, 90, 113, 114, 134–5, 135, 139, 140, 213
proverbs, proverbial expressions 23, 41, 112–13, 116, 140
punctuation 47, 54, 62, 63, 212

repetition of lines 24
of words 22, 35, 89, 96, 98, 106, 111, 118, 140, 149, 157, 168

sarcasm 28, 42, 71
Scaliger 33, 52, 182, 184
scholia(sts) 16, 18, 28, 35, 59, 63, 64, 66, 69, 72, 74, 75, 83, 88–9, 89, 91, 101, 102, 108, 109, 110, 116, 120, 123–4, 127, 133, 134, 136, 140(bis), 142, 150, 152, 154, 156, 175, 176, 179, 185, 187, 192, 196(bis), 202, 205, 207(bis), 208, 209(bis), 211, 213
scriptio plena 102
subjunctive 21, 54
Suda (Suidas) 20, 23, 33, 36, 40, 446, 65, 74, 79, 90, 118, 133, 134, 151(bis), 156, 161, 179, 188, 195, 201, 211
syntax 74(bis), 83, 123(bis), 124, 127, 131, 142
of ἄν 80, 139, 174, 181, 186, 189(bis), 195(bis)

theatres at Eleusis 68
Piraeus 68
Priene 50
Thomas Magister 7–8, 63, 666, 69, 71, 76
tmesis 178
transposition of lines 2–3, 47, 52, 85–6, 155, 185, 204
of words 60, 121, 123, 156, 211

utrum in alterum 63, 72, 103, 133, 148, 153–4

variant readings 73, 74
vocative 18(bis), 44, 53, 77, 91

Wackernagel's Law see also enclitics 42, 122, 147, 178
word-order 27, 31, 40, 42, 47, 87(bis), 100, 119–20, 123, 133, 135, 141, 156(bis), 171, 174, 175, 177(bis), 178, 188, 201, 205–6(bis)

Zanetti 13, 159(bis)